CW00919337

# Ernest Mandel

NLB

# From Stalinism to Eurocommunism

The Bitter Fruits
of 'Socialism in One Country'

*Translated by Jon Rothschild*

First published as *Critique de l'Eurocommunisme*,
by François Maspero, 1978

© François Maspero, Paris 1978

This edition first published 1978

© NLB, 1978

NLB, 7 Carlisle Street, London W1

Designed by Ruth Prentice

Filmset by Servis Filmsetting Ltd, Manchester

Printed in Great Britain by
Lowe and Brydone Printers Limited, Thetford, Norfolk

Bound by Kemp Hall Bindery, Oxford

Cloth ISBN 86091 005 9
Paper ISBN 86091 010 5

# Contents

# Foreword

The present work consists of eleven essays on Eurocommunism, five of which were drafted at varying times and published in the magazine *Inprecor* (namely Chapters 2, 3, 5, 7, and 10). They have been slightly revised so as to constitute a whole with the six other essays, written specially for this book. In spite of the various dates at which they were written, we think these essays represent a coherent analysis of Eurocommunism, covering its distant historic roots, its present role within the deep crisis now shaking capitalist society in West Europe, its connection with the disintegration of Stalinism, and its repercussions within the USSR and the People's Democracies.

E.M.

# 1
# The Bitter Fruits of 'Socialism in One Country'

On the eve of the First World War, the Second International represented a vast and impressive political force. It had millions of members in Europe. It possessed hundreds of deputies in the various parliaments. It mobilized enormous crowds in public meetings and demonstrations, particularly against militarism and the threat of war. Socially, politically, and morally, it appeared to embody resistance to the cataclysm taking shape on the horizon.

At the Stuttgart Congress of 1907, the Second International, after heated debate, adopted a crystal clear formula: 'Should war break out despite everything, it is the duty of Socialists to act for its rapid conclusion and to work with all their strength to utilize the economic and political crisis provoked by the war to rouse the peoples and thus accelerate the abolition of the rule of the capitalist class.' Similar formulas were voted by the congresses of Copenhagen (1910) and Basel (1912).[1] Indeed, up to 27 July 1914, the major Social Democratic Parties continued to swear that they would oppose the war by any means necessary. Then, on 1 August 1914, a sudden volte-face was made in all the major European powers (with the exception of Italy, which remained neutral). Under the pretext of 'national defence', Social Democracy in each country plunged into virtually unqualified support of the enterprise of plunder by its own imperialist bourgeoisie – for that is what the war objectively represented for each of the capitalist powers that unleashed it.

---

[1] Jaurès, who was neither a leftist nor a revolutionary socialist, proclaimed at Basel: 'We will not go to war against our brothers! We will not open fire on them! If the conflagration breaks out despite everything, then there will be war on another front, there will be revolution'.

The traumatic shock of this sudden turn for the revolutionary left of the workers' movement was profound and lasting. It took the form not merely of a more thorough settling of accounts with the opportunist, reformist, and revisionist currents within Social Democracy, which had for many years objectively paved the way for class collaboration and 'sacred union'. It also took the form of a profound internationalist reaction.

Of course, neither at the time nor subsequently were Marxists unaware that the open passage of Social Democracy into the camp of the imperialist bourgeoisie had many social roots. The change could not be explained solely as an ideological and political degeneration. For this degeneration was itself the product of a mounting integration of the bureaucratized apparatuses of the mass parties and trade unions into bourgeois society.

The multiplication of benefits the officials of the Social Democratic parties enjoyed within the bourgeois-democratic state eventually created a community of interest between these officials and the bourgeoisie. The considerable rise in the living standard of the privileged layers of the working class fostered a political atmosphere in which the minimum programme (the immediate demands) of these parties was increasingly separated from the maximum programme (the overthrow of the capitalist system). Other political and theoretical weaknesses also undoubtedly paved the way for the August 1914 catastrophe: absence of any overall understanding of the nature of the era of imperialism; refusal to orient to great mass mobilizations outside parliament (the position advocated without success by Rosa Luxemburg as of 1910); lack of revolutionary perspectives and inability to modify gradualist tactics when violent shocks later became inevitable.

But while they cannot be considered decisive, the absence of international discipline and the lack of any tradition of actually applying the resolutions adopted by majority vote at the congresses of the Second International must be counted among the major factors that contributed to the spectacular reversal of the principal socialist parties at the end of July 1914.

Lenin was not alone in proclaiming that the Second International was dead and that a Third International would now have to be built, on a much firmer doctrinal and organizational basis. Rosa Luxemburg and a good part of the 'centrist' majority of the Zimmerwald Conference also accepted the idea that 'the International is our only fatherland' and that international discipline should be imposed within the revolutionary workers' movement, at least on major international questions.[2] This concept was not the product of the October Revolution, the predominance acquired by the Bolsheviks with the founding of the Comintern, or of any inclination of Lenin's to extend 'Russian organizational conceptions' throughout the entire world. It was the common patrimony of all internationalists, whether Bolsheviks or not, from 1915 onwards. It was the nearly unanimous reaction to the catastrophe that struck the European workers' movement in August 1914.

But it was also more than that. It was a conviction which conformed to a more correct theoretical view of the trend towards the internationalization of the class struggle in the imperialist epoch. The notion of world revolution, which before 1914 had floated vaguely in the background of 'orthodox Marxism' like a memory of what had happened in 1848, or at most was viewed as a tendency for revolutions to spread from one to several countries,[3] now acquired a burning actuality as the organic and contradictory unity of the world economy forged by imperialism became patent.

Nearly all revolutionary Marxists correctly rejected the utopian notion that revolutions would break out simultaneously in all the major countries of the world. (Behind its radical appearance, this idea merely supplied an excuse for the reformist and centrist refusal to struggle for the conquest of

---

[2] In the 'Theses on the Tasks of the International Social Democracy' drafted by Rosa Luxemburg and adopted by the first conference of the *Internationale* group (later the Spartacist group) in the spring of 1915, we read: 'The centre of gravity of the class organization of the proletariat lies in the International. In time of peace the International decides the tactics of the national sections on the subjects of militarism, colonial policy, commercial policy, Mayday festivals; even more does it decide the tactics to adopt in time of war. The duty to apply the decisions of the International takes precedence over all other duties of the organization. National sections which contravene these decisions exclude themselves from the International'. And further on: 'The fatherland of the proletarians the defence of which stands above all else is the Socialist International'.

[3] Thus, Kautsky correctly foresaw that the Russian revolution of 1905 would open a revolutionary cycle in the countries of the East.

power by the proletariat in each country, whenever the relationship of political and social forces permitted.) But they understood the inevitable interlacing of various processes: revolutions conquering power in one or several countries and then facing the international intervention of the bourgeoisie, including military intervention; temporarily victorious counter-revolutions in other countries, which would significantly sharpen the contradictions confronting a temporarily isolated victorious proletariat; the international radicalization and exacerbation of the class struggle in the wake of victorious revolutions and counter-revolutions; the economic effects of such class struggle on the medium- and long-term development of the cycle of the world capitalist economy and the repercussions of this cycle on the class struggle itself. Further, they understood that the conflicts between imperialism and oppressed nations (primarily, but not exclusively, those of the colonial and semicolonial countries) would be integrated into this entire complex.

It was to master the specific strategic and tactical problems that flowed from this complex reality of the international class struggle – that is, the *reality of the world revolution* – that the Communist International was founded on the basis of a commonly accepted international discipline. The idea of a democratically centralized International is an essentially *political* concept, a comprehensive theory of world social reality in the imperialist epoch; it is not the by-product of an 'international extrapolation of the organizational conceptions of Lenin'. Nothing that has happened in the sixty years since the October Revolution challenges the fundamental validity of this theory. It was the granite foundation on which the Communist movement was based after 1917. Trotsky simply had the merit of enunciating it more systematically, in the second portion of his theory of permanent revolution.[4] It remains the foundation of revolutionary Marxism today.

---

[4] 'The completion of the socialist revolution within national limits is unthinkable. One of the basic reasons for the crisis in bourgeois society is the fact that the productive forces created by it can no longer be reconciled with the framework of the national state. . . . The socialist revolution begins on the national arena, it unfolds on the international arena, and is completed on the world arena. Thus, the socialist revolution becomes a permanent revolution in

Stalin and his majority faction in the Central Committee and among the leading cadres of the Communist Party of the Soviet Union (CPSU) planted a tremendous explosive charge under this foundation in 1924, when they suddenly expounded their theory that it was possible to complete the construction of socialism in a single country.[5] Once again, the origin of the turn was obviously not ideological. It should not be sought in a breakdown of the theoretical capacities of one individual or the political perspicacity of a group of party cadres. The turn had social origins and was linked to specific material interests. In the final analysis, this sharp theoretical rupture resulted from the ascent and self-assertion within Soviet society of a new social layer with material privileges, the Soviet bureaucracy, and from the growing symbiosis between this layer of society and the apparatus of the party. The Stalinist theory of 'socialism in one country' expressed primarily the petty-bourgeois conservatism of this bureaucracy, as well as the mounting appetite of the party apparatus for the privileges of power. The idea advanced by innumerable commentators that the theory was accepted because it offered 'a concrete perspective for the economic development of the country' in the wake of the real failure of the world revolution is profoundly anachronistic.[6] In no way does it explain the real interpenetration of the vicissitudes of the international class struggle, of the economic policy of the USSR, of the social struggles in the Soviet Union, of the political conflicts and theoretical debates within the CPSU, and of the evolution of the Comintern.

---

a newer and broader sense of the word: it attains completion only in the final victory of the new society on our entire planet'. 'Insofar as capitalism has created a world market, a world division of labour and world productive forces, it has also prepared a world economy as a whole for socialist transformation'. (*The Permanent Revolution and Results and Prospects*, New York, 1970, p. 279.)

   [5] Up to the beginning of 1924, that is, through the first edition of *Fundamental Problems of Leninism*, Stalin himself wrote: 'To overthrow the bourgeoisie the efforts of a single country suffice; the history of our own revolution attests to this. For the definitive victory of socialism, for the organization of socialist production, the efforts of a single country, especially a peasant country like Russia, are no longer sufficient; the efforts of the proletarians of several advanced countries are required. . . . Such are in general the characteristic features of the Leninist theory of the proletarian revolution'. This passage was modified in subsequent editions of the same work.

   [6] See, among others, Jean Elleinstein, *Histoire du phénomène stalinien*, Paris, 1975, pp. 64–65.

## The Transformation of the Comintern

But although theoretical revisions are in the final resort to be *explained* by socio-economic changes (any other interpretation breaks with historical materialism, which is founded on the thesis that social existence determines consciousness), this does not at all mean that such revision, once initiated, does not have its own relatively autonomous dynamic. Indeed, the adoption of the theory that it was possible to complete the construction of 'socialism in one country' had deep repercussions which shook the entire international communist movement. That the immense majority of convinced and sincere communist cadres were unaware of this in 1924, 1928, or 1934, is proof of the difficulty for any system of thought, even an analytic instrument such as the Marxist method, immediately to grasp a really radical upheaval in the coordinates of its social field. This further augments the merits of the communist minority grouped around Leon Trotsky, which understood nearly at once what the disastrous long-term effects would be.

The adoption of the theory of 'socialism in one country' led to five transformations that were to convulse the theory, strategy and organization of the Communist parties and the Third International, radically modifying their objective function in the contemporary world:

§ It implied a revision of the very concept of world revolution and of its relevance in the imperialist epoch, which in turn entailed a revision of the whole theory of the imperialist epoch.

§ From this flowed a no less fundamental modification of the relationship between the defence of the isolated proletarian state in Russia (and of the *beginning* of socialist construction within this state) and the international revolution. Defence of the 'bastion' was proclaimed the number one task of the communist movement and the world proletariat, which gradually dictated a subordination of the interests of the international revolution to the (supposed) interests of the defence of the 'bastion'.

§ This subordination led to the transformation of the Communist parties from forces acting for the revolutionary overthrow of capitalism in their respective countries (and of the Communist International from an instrument for the revolutionary overthrow of the imperialist system and capitalism on a world scale) into instruments primarily for the defence of the Soviet fortress which increasingly entailed the automatic adaptation of the tactics of these parties and of the Communist International to the zigzags of Kremlin diplomacy.

§ Such an adaptation inevitably led to Soviet 'national messianism' (in reality, the petty-bourgeois nationalist messianism of the Soviet bureaucracy),[7] for this systematic subordination could be justified only on the basis of the decisive importance attributed to the USSR, the Soviet proletariat, and the Communist Party of the Soviet Union for humanity as a whole. The concepts of the guiding state and the guiding party, which played such a central role during the Stalin era and which Khrushchev and Brezhnev tried to salvage from the wreckage of Stalinism, originate in this petty-bourgeois messianism. Their inevitable organizational corollary was monolithism within the Communist International and the Communist parties, the suppression of any debate or critical reflection that threatened to upset the tranquillity and interests of the leaders of the 'guiding state', and the bureaucratization of the Communist International as a by-product of the bureaucratization of the CPSU and the Soviet state.

§ Precisely because this theoretical, political and organizational degeneration undermined the bases upon which the programme and existence of the Comintern had been founded, it inevitably acted to decompose the Third International in the long run. The bureaucracies of the Communist parties submitted blindly to the orders of the Kremlin – which ever more obviously corresponded neither to the interests of the proletariats of their respective countries nor even to the interests of their own apparatuses – only to the extent that they saw no alternative, either because of their material dependence on Moscow or because of their view of medium-term national and international political perspectives.[8]

Once this situation changed, it was only a matter of time

[7] The formula was used by Trotsky in *The Permanent Revolution* (op. cit. p. 280).
[8] Hitler's seizure of power and the inevitability of war between Nazi Germany and the Soviet Union played a decisive role in this regard for many cadres of the Communist parties in the 1930s.

before Stalin's 'iron monolithism' collapsed like a house of cards. The 'national messianism' of the CPSU was to produce as many 'messianisms' as there were powerful Communist parties materially independent of the Kremlin. The 'single centre' was to give way to polycentrism. 'Proletarian internationalism' identified with the 'defence of the Soviet bastion' was to lead to a proliferation of 'national communisms'. *In this sense, the threads of Eurocommunism were woven into the future of the world communist movement from the very moment the theory of 'socialism in one country' was adopted.* Trotsky, with his prophetic genius, understood this and proclaimed it from the outset:

'Marxism has always taught the workers that even their struggle for higher wages and shorter hours cannot be successful unless waged as an international struggle. And now it suddenly appears that the ideal of the socialist society may be achieved with the national forces alone. This is a mortal blow to the International. The invincible conviction that the fundamental class aim, even more so than the partial objectives, cannot be realized by national means or within national boundaries, constitutes the very heart of revolutionary internationalism. If, however, the ultimate aim is realizable within national boundaries through the efforts of a national proletariat, then the backbone of internationalism has been broken. The theory of the possibility of realizing socialism in one country destroys the inner connection between the patriotism of the victorious proletariat and the defeatism of the proletariat of the bourgeois countries. The proletariat of the advanced capitalist countries is still travelling on the road to power. How and in what manner it marches towards it depends entirely on whether it considers the task of building the socialist society a national or an international task. If it is at all possible to realize socialism in one country, then one can believe in that theory not only *after* but also *before* the conquest of power. If socialism can be realized within the national boundaries of backward Russia, then there is all the more reason to believe that it can be realized in advanced Germany. Tomorrow the leaders of the Communist Party of Germany will undertake to propound this theory. The draft program empowers them to do so. The day after tomorrow the French party will have its turn. It will be the beginning of the disintegration of the Comintern along the lines of social patriotism. The communist party of any capitalist country, which will have become imbued with the idea that its particular country possesses the "necessary and sufficient" prerequisites for the independent construction of a "complete socialist society," will not differ in any substantial manner from the revolutionary social democracy which also did not begin with a Noske but which stumbled decisively on August 4, 1914, over this same question' (*The Third International After Lenin*, New York 1970, pp. 71–73).

## The Turn of the Seventh Congress of the Comintern

The transformation of the Communist International from an instrument of socialist revolution into an instrument of the diplomacy of the Soviet bureaucracy contained the germs of the possibility of its periodic transformation into an instrument of bourgeois counter-revolution, for the defence of private property. The conservative character of the bureaucracy, its fear of the international repercussions of any advance of the revolution elsewhere in the world, its awareness that the passivity and depoliticization of the Soviet proletariat constituted the foundation of its power and privileges, and the risk that this passivity and depoliticization could be placed in question by any major progress of the world revolution – all these factors inclined the bureaucracy towards a policy of peaceful co-existence with imperialism, attempts to divide the world into spheres of influence, and determined defence of the status quo.[9]

The switch to a defence of the bourgeois state and the social status quo in the 'democratic' imperialist countries – which implied the defence of private property in the event of severe social crisis and national defence in the event of imperialist war – was made officially at the Seventh congress of the Comintern. It had been preceded by an initial turn in this direction by

---

[9] Those Maoists who date the policy of peaceful coexistence back to Khrushchev are in ignorance or bad faith. Must we remind them of Stalin's famous interview with the American journalist Howard in 1936, in the course of which the 'father of peoples' called the idea that the Soviet Union was striving to serve the cause of world revolution a 'tragi-comic misunderstanding'?

the French Communist Party (PCF) when the Stalin–Laval military pact was signed. The clearest reflection of this turn was the Popular Front policy; its most radical effects came with the application of this policy during the Spanish Civil War. In Spain, the Communist Party made itself the most determined, consistent, and bloody defender of the reestablishment of the bourgeois order against the collectivizations spontaneously effected by the workers and poor peasants of the Republic and against the organs of power created by the proletariat, particularly the committees and militias, which had inflicted a decisive defeat on the militaro-fascist insurgents in nearly all the large cities of the country in July 1936.

It is of course true that the Communist Party did this not as the agent of the bourgeoisie but as the agent of the Kremlin, which was obsessed by the fear that a victorious socialist revolution in Spain or France would lead to a 'grand alliance' of all the imperialist powers against the Soviet Union. It remained a tactical turn. Once Soviet diplomacy shifted gears and concluded the Hitler–Stalin pact, the European Communist Parties began calling the 'Anglo-French imperialists' warmongers, became 'defeatists' in the 'democratic' imperialist countries again, and even went so far as to support the Nazi peace offensive in autumn 1939, demanding a halt to hostilities without the reestablishment of the independence of Poland and Czechoslovakia.

These two considerations are important in understanding how it is that on occasion, within narrow limits, the Soviet bureaucracy, the material bases of whose privileges rest on a mode of production that grows out of the abolition of private property and capitalism, can seek to extend its power by broadening the zone in which this new mode of production holds sway. This was done in 1939–40 in Eastern Poland, the Baltic countries, and Bessarabia. It was done on a grander scale in 1947–48 in the countries of East Europe that were liberated at the end of the Second World War. But on both occasions the Russian bureaucracy did this by military fiat, without leading a genuine mass popular revolution, under conditions such that no enthusiastic repoliticization of the Soviet proletariat could result, and after prior agreement had been reached with imperialism on a division of the world into spheres of influence. It is out of the question that this could occur again in Europe or Asia in the foreseeable future. Thus, these few exceptions actually confirm the overall assessment of the foreign policy of the bureaucracy as counter-revolutionary, once this bureaucracy had been transformed into an ossified social layer in the USSR that could not be removed except through a political revolution.

The Communist Parties made the turn of 1935 out of fidelity to the Soviet Union as they understood it – in other words, loyalty to the Soviet bureaucracy, on which they increasingly depended both materially and politically. But the turn of the Seventh Congress of the Comintern and all it implied touched off another autonomous mechanism over which the Kremlin was later to lose control. Increasingly integrating themselves into the bourgeois state and amassing the material advantages to be won within bourgeois-parliamentary democracy as a result of their electoral and trade-union successes, the apparatuses of the Communist parties in the 'democratic' imperialist countries began to come under material pressure independent of and to some extent antagonistic to the pressure of the Kremlin. If 'Socialism in One Country' led to national-communism, the theory and practice of the Popular Front led to a political line which fuelled a gradual process of Social Democratization. Such are two of the principal historical roots of Eurocommunism.

The majority of the most lucid Eurocommunist leaders are perfectly conscious of this. They constantly refer to the 'great historical precedents' of the policy of the Popular Front and the 'Antifascist Union of the Resistance' during and immediately after the Second World War as preparatory stages of Eurocommunism. They thus make no mistake when in their own way, they remind sometimes ignorant and sometimes dishonest Maoists that the real ideological progenitor of Eurocommunism is Joseph Stalin himself. One has only to examine the documents of the French, Italian, Spanish, and many other Communist parties during the periods 1935–38 and 1941–47 to find – under the signatures of their leaders of the time, the most faithful lieutenants of Stalin both inside and outside the Soviet Union, and even of Stalin himself – the same revisionist formulas about the bourgeois state, 'new democracy', and 'advanced democracy' over which today's Maoists or Stalinists feign such indignation, forgetting that Mao himself faithfully repeated them in 1941.[10]

The Kremlin's disagreeable surprise arises from the fact that it had believed it would be able to control all the motions of this mechanism: 'right-face, left-face, about-face'. Its bureaucratic complacency was actually in danger as long ago as the Hitler–Stalin pact. Subsequent events have effaced the memory of the grave crisis that racked the French Communist Party, in particular, at that time. Up to 40% of the PCF's parliament members, including several members of the Political Bureau, objected to Moscow's line; some of them passed into the camp of their own bourgeoisie.[11] Nevertheless, the bulk of the apparatus remained loyal to the Kremlin.

The same process occurred after the beginning of the 'Cold War', which succeeded the 'Great Antifascist Alliance'. All the Communist parties of capitalist Europe obediently made a 180 degree turn. To a man they asserted that if 'in pursuing the imperialist aggressor' the Red Army arrived at the borders of their country, it would be greeted with open arms as a liberating force. This was certainly not the language of a Social Democratic party.

At various times during the 1960s (and in some cases even during the 1950s), certain Communist parties of capitalist Europe again made a turn towards adaptation to the Social Democracy, more or less simultaneous with a parallel turn by the Kremlin: end of the Cold War; reaffirmation of 'peaceful coexistence'; Khrushchev's trip to the United States; the 'spirit of Camp David'; the Kennedy–Khrushchev meeting in Vienna, and so on. This time, however, the machinery was not merely more difficult to control than it had been in 1935–38 or 1941–47; it was fairly well thrown out of gear.

The principal reasons for this lay in the cumulative effects of the successive turns, the duration of the new reformist line, the modified composition of the apparatuses of the Communist parties, and the alteration in the recruitment to the Communist parties due to a now long-standing neo-reformist policy. The

[10] See, for example, 'On New Democracy'.
[11] A. Rossi, *Physiologie du PCF*, Paris, 1948; *Les Communistes Français pendant la 'Drôle-de-Guerre'*, Paris, 1951.

pre-war series of turns at something like three-year intervals, which gave the bureaucrats and cadres of the Communist parties great flexibility and varied experiences, was replaced from the later 1950s onwards by a reformist practice applied without interruption for nearly twenty years or more. An entire generation of Eurocommunist cadres has learned nothing except how to prepare for routine elections and immediate wage struggles. The progressive disappearance of the whole Communist generation trained during the years prior to 1935, during the Resistance, and even during the years of the 'Cold War', whose practical experience was quite different from that of the current generation, has played a very important role in this regard.

There is another, no less significant, cumulative process, too: the virtually permanent installation of the apparatuses of the Communist parties within the machinery of the bourgeois-democratic state. In this regard a process of degeneration is occurring which is very closely analogous to that experienced by classical Social Democracy between 1900 and 1914. This is especially true of the Italian and French parties. So far, long years of clandestinity have protected the Portuguese and Spanish Communist parties from the direct effects of this corruption (but this can change rapidly); for the moment, the rightist line of these parties is determined by ideological factors and their strategic orientation. But even some smaller Communist parties, like those of Sweden, Belgium, Switzerland, the Netherlands, Finland, and Britain, are partially affected by the same development, either at the municipal level or in the trade unions. Sometimes ideology, aided by the example of a neighbour, outstrips reality. The desire to gain access to the machinery precedes the access itself, thus dictating the political line.

But the change in the international arena has been the most important determinant of all. The joint crisis of imperialism and Stalinism has undermined the concepts on which Stalinist ideology was founded. The Chinese revolution broke the encirclement of the USSR. Along with the Yugoslav, Vietnamese, and Cuban revolutions, it destroyed the myth of the Soviet Union as the sole bastion of world revolution. The Sino-Soviet conflict allowed Togliatti to adopt a Pontius Pilate attitude ('both are somewhat guilty') and further undermined the concept that there was a 'central bastion' that had at all costs to be defended. Furthermore, it is less and less credible to identify the advance of the world revolution solely with the defence of the 'socialist camp', especially when first Yugoslavia and then China were ejected from this 'camp' and whqn the latter permitted the bombing of socialist Hanoi virtually without reaction. Paradoxically, the military and industrial growth of the USSR itself has weakened one of the principal mainsprings that drove the Stalinist machine during the 1930s and 1940s. Nobody seriously believes that the Soviet Union today is mortally threatened with annihilation, which is something many Communists obviously did believe – and correctly so – at the time of Hitler. (Whether or not they opted for the correct response to this threat is another question.) Officially, a new myth has now been substituted by the CPSU for the old: the idea of 'peaceful competition between the two camps', which the 'socialist camp' must win before socialism can triumph in the West. But its power of persuasion is much reduced.

Under these conditions, no implacable necessity for subordination to the orders of the Kremlin is any longer evident, even according to the crippled logic of 'Socialism in One Country'. The interests of the apparatuses of the 'national' Communist parties are becoming increasingly autonomous of those of the Soviet bureaucracy. This autonomy has its own logic and its own consequences. To win votes in elections, gain posts in municipal councils and parliaments, and maintain or conquer control of trade unions and mass cooperatives progressively takes precedence over the exigencies of the 'defence of the Soviet Union' and even of the 'socialist camp'. Any Communist party bureaucrat in capitalist Europe capable of keeping his eyes and ears open can see that the two exigencies can come into conflict; he need only look at the reactions of rank-and-file Communist militants, the working class, and the toiling masses in capitalist Europe to the crushing of the Hungarian revolution in 1956 and the invasion of the Czechoslovak Socialist Republic in 1968.

**The Stages in the Crisis of Stalinism**

In this sense, the gradual emergence of the phenomenon of

Eurocommunism – for we are dealing here precisely with a gradual development and not a radical overnight transformation, as many observers pretend to believe – is inextricably linked to the progressive crisis of Stalinism, which is little by little becoming a crisis of decomposition.[12]

As we have already pointed out, the crisis of decomposition of Stalinism results inevitably from the conquest by some Communist parties of material and political bases independent of the Kremlin, once all these parties had universally accepted the doctrine of 'Socialism in One Country'. The clearest cases are obviously those of the Yugoslav and Chinese Communist parties. Both took power at the head of great popular revolutions[13] mobilizing millions of workers and peasant producers (tens of millions in the case of China), even though in both cases the revolution was bureaucratized from the outset and the mobilization was bureaucratically controlled and manipulated to a large extent. Hence, these parties and their leaderships enjoyed enormous prestige among the toiling masses of their countries and acquired an autonomous material and political base from which successfully to resist the *ukases* of the Kremlin, which no Communist leadership desiring to remain within the framework of the Comintern in the thirties had been able to do.

The case of the Czechoslovak Communist Party points in the same direction. This party was handed power by the Kremlin in February 1948, military-bureaucratic pressure playing a more decisive role at the time than the mobilization of a sector of the working class controlled by the Communist Party. Because of its imitation of Stalinist methods and its fealty to the Soviet bureaucracy, the Czechoslovak CP suffered a precipitous decline in its social support between 1949 and 1967. But

[12] Trotsky defined the Seventh Congress of the Comintern as the congress of its liquidation. (See the article dated 23 August 1935 in *Writings of Leon Trotsky 1935–36*, New York, 1977, pp. 84 and following.) This assessment was confirmed formally in 1943. There never was an Eighth Congress. The formula was proved substantively correct after the Second World War, during the progressive crisis of Stalinism.

[13] The term is used here not in the sense of a revolution with a specific class content different from that of a bourgeois revolution or a proletarian revolution, but in the descriptive sense of a revolution in which the majority of the popular masses participate actively.

the decision of a 'centrist' faction to open the process that was to lead to the Prague Spring in 1968, the popular enthusiasm for this new orientation, and the rapid politicization of the working class created wide support for the party among the toiling masses when it defended these initial gains (which objectively represented something like a prologue to a political revolution) against the rising pressure of the Kremlin. This support made the Fourteenth Congress of the Czechoslovak Communist Party possible, a clandestine assembly of resistance to the Kremlin's *diktat*. But the *diktat* was backed up by tanks, and the 'centrist' faction was soon swept away by the 'normalizers' under the effects of these tanks and of the hesitations of the 'centrist' faction itself.

The case of the Fidelista team in Cuba confirms the same rule, but from a negative direction. This grouping took power at the head of a formidable mass mobilization of workers and peasants, much less bureaucratized and manipulated than that of Yugoslavia or China. It swept aside the reservations and resistance of the Cuban Stalinists and completed a process of permanent revolution by the destruction of the bourgeois order and the creation of a workers' state, thus acquiring almost complete political independence of the Kremlin at the outset. But the isolation of the Cuban Revolution in the Western hemisphere, the blockade and aggression of American imperialism, the fragility of Cuba's military and economic situation throughout the 1960s, and the defeats suffered by the cause of socialism in Latin America resulted in a nearly total material dependence on the Soviet bureaucracy. Hence the political regression of the Fidelista team.

In the case of Yugoslavia, the Soviet bureaucracy, accustomed to dealing only with flunkeys to whom orders are given or 'Trotskyist enemies of the people' who are exterminated, was baffled by the unexpected resistance it suddenly faced in its own orbit. Its initial reaction was violence raised to the level of state relations: the excommunication of Tito, the blockade of Yugoslavia, the mobilization of the Soviet army on the Yugoslav border, calls to insurrection and even to assassination.

This brutal method failed. Khrushchev then bent the stick towards conciliation. Overnight the 'Fascist-Trotskyite bandits of the Tito–Rankovic clique' were transformed into 'very dear Yugoslav comrades'.[14] The arrival of Khrushchev himself at Belgrade airport to embrace these same 'comrades' dealt as severe a blow to the myth of the infallibility of the CPSU and to the subordination of all the Communist parties to Kremlin orders as had been dealt by the excommunication of Tito seven years previously.

Then the very same Khrushchev, followed by Brezhnev, dealt with the Chinese leadership in the same brutal manner when the latter refused to back down: economic blockade, rejection of military aid, mobilization and concentration of the army on the Chinese frontier, occasional skirmishes which sometimes degenerated into more extensive armed clashes, as over the Ussuri River. Once again the failure was complete. The Chinese leadership, far from bowing to pressure and excommunication, increasingly asserted its political and organizational independence.

The effects of the 20th Congress of the CPSU and the beginning of de-Stalinization must of course be added to the Yugoslav and Chinese shocks. Not only was the myth of infallibility destroyed by this Congress, definitively; in addition, a series of other factors deprived the 'Soviet model' of credibility as the 'model for the construction of socialism' and hence irremediably undermined the principle of the 'guiding state' and 'guiding party': the manifest inability of the bureaucracy to explain the deeper reasons for the Stalinist degeneration; the flagrant inadequacy of the formula 'cult of the personality'; the incapacity of the Soviet apparatus to implement any institutional reform that could afford the slightest guarantee against a return to such monstrous crimes and errors. Togliatti was the first to understand this and to argue, in his Yalta Testament,

---

[14] The Chinese CP scarcely acts any better. After dragging the Yugoslav Communists through the mud for a decade, calling them the worst 'revisionists' and even 'fascists' who had allegedly 'restored capitalism', it suddenly halted all public criticism of the League of Communists of Yugoslavia as of August 1968. Nor have the Maoists ever explained how the relations of production and socio-economic structure of Romania differ from those of Bulgaria or the USSR. But *for the simple reason* that Ceausescu has never attacked the Chinese Communist Party publicly, they continue to refer to Romania as 'socialist', while the USSR is 'social-imperialist' and capitalism has supposedly been restored in Bulgaria.

that there were causal links between the inadequacy of the theory of the 'personality cult', the 'imperfections' of the 'Soviet model of socialism', and the inevitable ascendancy of 'polycentrism' within the international Communist movement.[15] The Kremlin was in the process of losing control over everything it could no longer dominate by the most direct military and economic means.

The invasion of the Czechoslovak Socialist Republic was the straw that broke the camel's back. A long road had been travelled between the crushing of the Hungarian revolution by Soviet tanks in 1956 without a single Communist party leadership, except the Yugoslav, expressing the slightest public criticism and the many protests from European Communist parties which followed the invasion of Czechoslovakia. The transformation was not solely due to the real enthusiasm the Prague spring had generated among the ranks of the European Communist parties, if not among the entire European proletariat. The many links the Dubcek leadership had forged with the Eurocommunists clearly had some effect. The manifest unpopularity of the invasion among the toiling masses of Europe and the fear of a new wave of anti-communism and of serious electoral losses also played a role.

Most of all, however, the leaders of the European Communist parties felt an ominous political-historical anxiety: 'If tomorrow', they wondered, 'we Italian, French, or British Communists were in power and if our policy was displeasing to the Kremlin, what would prevent it from treating "our" country like Czechoslovakia; what would prevent it from roughing us up or worse, the way "they" roughed up Frantisek Kriegel and his comrades, who were kidnapped when the tanks rolled into Prague?' The capacity to imagine the unthinkable, which had not yet been acquired in 1936 or 1949, was fully operative in 1968. Time had done its work. The experience of Stalinism, or at least of its worst aspects, had been assimilated. There was a unanimous *cri de coeur*: 'Can it happen here? Never!'

The Stalinist International was no more. Or at least it was increasingly reduced to skeletal organizations directly depen-

---

[15] On this famous 'Yalta Testament' of Togliatti, as well as its antecedents, see Giorgio Napolitano, *La Politique du Parti Communiste Italien*, Paris, 1976.

dent on Kremlin subsidies. There was no longer any room within it for mass parties with roots in their own working class, to the very extent that the international working class had now learnt the lesson of the nature of Stalinism.

## Eurocommunism and Peaceful Coexistence

The turn of the Seventh Congress of the Comintern had been essentially justified by the USSR's need to 'manoeuvre among the imperialist powers'. This necessity was an objective fact. The Russia of Lenin and Trotsky also had to conclude the treaties of Brest-Litovsk and of Rappallo. On the other hand, it is not a necessity but an abandonment of the elementary principles of Marxism for the workers' parties to modify their irreconcilable opposition to the imperialist bourgeoisie as a function of such treaties and to determine their tactics on the basis of necessarily conjunctural and transient manoeuvres of the diplomacy of the workers' state.

The 'division among the imperialist powers' opened a field of manoeuvre both before and after the Second World War. It was not aimed exclusively at setting the imperialist powers against one another, but was increasingly intended (temporarily) to support this or that faction of the imperialist bourgeoisie of a single country against this or that opposing faction. Any Communist party that allows itself to drift onto this road compounds the abandonment of the class independence of the proletariat and of the elementary principles of communism by the growing risk of abandonment even of the defence of the most immediate material interests of the working class. Must we recall the French Communist Party's support for De Gaulle's 'defence of national independence' against the 'Atlanticists' who supported the CED? The result is well known. De Gaulle came to power in 1958 through a military coup and established a 'strong state' which threw the French working class back for more than a decade. The ground lost was not made up until May 1968.

But here again, we are dealing with a mechanism the Kremlin finds more and more uncontrollable. Who will decide, and on the basis of what criteria, which *imperialist* faction, which variant of *bourgeois* policy, is more favourable to 'peace'? In the old days the choice was simple. Stalin was always right, even in 1940, when he suddenly informed the German workers that their main enemy was no longer Hitler but rather the 'pro-war faction of Fritz Thyssen', which wanted to abrogate the German-Soviet non-aggression pact. Since the rehabilitation of Tito and the Twentieth Congress of the CPSU have eliminated infallibility forever, the betting windows are now open to pick which horse to back for the 'peace prize'.

Are the 'Atlanticists' the number one enemy of peace and détente? That is what Georges Marchais seems to believe. (As for the Kremlin, it does not fully approve of this assessment. Moscow was hardly unhappy with the 'Atlanticists' Nixon and Kissinger; on the contrary.) Does the danger of independent German (or German-British, or Franco-German-British) nuclear weaponry tend to make NATO a lesser evil? Sergio Segre's preferences seem to lean in this direction (and we would not be surprised if he had received the discreet blessings of Gromyko.) Can NATO be rendered less noxious if a Socialist finger is on the trigger? Marchais and Berlinguer cautiously lean towards this 'intermediary' solution. Would it perhaps be better to proclaim a position of 'positive neutralism'? This seems to be the position of Santiago Carrillo. As for Cunhal, who still sticks to yesterday's vociferous denunciations of NATO, to the great pleasure of the Communist Party of the United States, he notes uneasily that *Pravda* reprints his ardent professions of faith less and less frequently. It is only the West German Communist Party that has no problem: like a parrot, it repeats whatever is said in East Berlin.

As for the Maoists the contortions they are compelled to execute to fit complex reality into their simplistic system when they draw up indictments of the foreign policy of the Eurocommunists are positively grotesque: the Eurocommunists, these 'modern anticommunists', demonstrate their servitude to Soviet social imperialism by refusing resolutely to oppose American imperialism and by sacrificing national independence, which can be safeguarded only through a fierce struggle against the two superpowers, which have agreed among themselves to enslave Europe and whose mutual accord implies a ferocious and implacable struggle for hegemony which will someday lead to an inevitable third world war; that is why a tactical alliance with American imperialism, which is less aggressive because it has been weakened, is not excluded *a priori!*[16] Does Eurocommunism foster 'détente' or does it increase 'tensions'? Does it favour the hegemony of American imperialism or on the contrary does it accentuate the affirmation of imperialist Europe against the United States? Posed in this vulgar form, these questions render any reasonable response impossible.

Eurocommunism marks a political and ideological regression by a section of the European workers' movement, in conditions of the exacerbated social tension and class struggle. It is this exacerbation and not the increasingly reformist policy of the Eurocommunist leaders which has caused the successive flights of capital from Portugal, Italy, France, and Spain. Likewise, if some sections of the European bourgeoisie are frightened by the prospect of the participation of European Communist parties in governments, it is not because of the blows these good ministers are preparing to deal private property. Everyone understands that their intentions are more moderate than those of the Executive of the Labour Party in 1945 or 1977. Moreover, as this example demonstrates, there is a big difference between plans and government policy. What the imperialists fear is the prospect of a *revolutionary upsurge of the masses that will be difficult for the Communist parties to control*, stimulated by the accession of 'left' governments to power despite the intentions of those governments.

It would be absurd to suppose that the Eurocommunist leaders have become direct agents of American imperialism, even though some of their manoeuvres may serve this or that operation of the Carter administration. There is no materialist evidence to support such a preposterous proposition. At the most, their increasing integration into the bourgeois state apparatus would make them agents *of their own bourgeoisie*, which is the *European* bourgeoisie, allied to American imperialism, of course, but also its competitor (and an increasingly fierce and

---

[16] Are we exaggerating perhaps? One has only to read the article by José Sanroma Aldea, secretary-general of the Revolutionary Workers Organization (ORT) in Spain, published in the daily *El País*, 6 August 1977. It is eloquently titled, 'Eurocommunism, a Form of Modern Anticommunism'.

30

self-assured competitor at that). Does Eurocommunism impede
the European bourgeoisie's manoeuvres relative to Washing-
ton? The answer is yes, if one assigns to Eurocommunism
responsibility for flights of capital, investment strikes, and
virtual economic stagnation, which is absolutely unjustified.
The answer is no, if one sees Eurocommunism as an additional
element of restabilization of the bourgeois order in *capitalist
Europe*, as the last impediment the socialist revolution will
have to sweep away in order to triumph.

For two decades the entire militant section of the working
class of South-West Europe has been fiercely hostile to 'its'
bourgeois state, along with 'its' army and police. If the 'historic
compromise' has any meaning, it is precisely to eliminate this
hostility.[17] Once again, the parallel with Social Democracy
during the period 1914 to 1929 is striking. Should this manoeuvre be successful, which is unlikely in our view, then the
European bourgeoisie would emerge strengthened and not
weakened relative to American imperialism. Paradoxically, the
most convinced partisans of the Maoist theory of the two
'superpowers' ought to assess the Eurocommunist strategy
favourably, for it moves in the direction of reinforcing the
'independence' and strength of imperialist Europe against the
United States. How also is it possible to overlook the fact that
the transformation of the great workers' parties from an agency
of the Soviet bureaucracy into independent political forces
which lean towards a 'historic' alliance with a section of their
own imperialist bourgeoisie, also strengthens imperialist
Europe against the USSR?

There is no doubt that the Eurocommunist parties are sincere
advocates of détente. They are convinced that their reformist
projects of participation in coalition governments, have not
the slightest possibility of success in the event of a return to the
Cold War, not to mention a shooting war. It would be absurd to
accuse them of warmongering. If there is a reproach to make,
it is that they are spreading the dangerous pacifist illusion that
peace can be preserved in the long run merely through exerting

---

[17] See the interesting recent discussion between the Italian Communist
Party and certain 'left intellectuals', in which the former explicitly proclaimed
that its task is to preserve and defend the 'democratic state'. (*Le Monde
Diplomatique* of August 1977 contains an account of this discussion.)

'pressure' on capitalism, without abolishing it. But this pacifist illusion has been inherited from Stalinist orthodoxy, an integral part of which it was and remains. It is another ·logical corollary of 'Socialism in One Country'.

Some bourgeois circles have expressed the fear that regardless of the 'good faith' with which the Eurocommunist leaders are taking their distance from Moscow, their increased weight in political life and their possible presence in the governments of capitalist Europe 'objectively' pose the danger of the 'Finlandization' or 'neutralization' of Europe. Such fear is doubly unfounded. First, the leaders of the French and Italian Communist parties have already clearly affirmed that they no longer demand the breakup of the Atlantic alliance as a precondition for participation in government (it is important to note that the Portuguese Communist Party, which nonetheless remains a faithful 'follower' of the Kremlin, served in various provisional governments in 1974 and 1975 without Portugal's withdrawal from NATO). Secondly, the Eurocommunist leaders have stated that they favour the strengthening and not weakening of the national defence of 'their' bourgeoisie, contrary to the situation in Finland. These bourgeoisies are anything but 'neutral'.

Hence, the only realistic element in these fears of the most ossified sectors of the bourgeoisie is that the very *transformation of the relationship of socio-political forces* which could lead to the entry of the Eurocommunists into governments could also result in ruptures in the Atlantic alliance. This is incontestably true. But if we are to avoid sinking into sophism, then we must immediately add that the political objective of the Eurocommunist leaders is precisely to limit these transformations, to channel them into paths compatible with the maintenance of the bourgeois order (and if need be with the maintenance of the Atlantic alliance too). If this or that country of western Europe ever breaks with NATO, it will be in spite of, and not because of, the political efforts of the Eurocommunists.

It remains to be seen whether the Soviet bureaucracy considers NATO and the present situation preferable to the new alignment that would result from an autonomous strengthening of European imperialism, to which Eurocommunism would have contributed in its own way. This is quite possible, just as it is possible that the Kremlin's winks of complicity at Giscard, which were repeated just before the last elections to the protests of Marchais (who even spoke of 'a lack of proletarian internationalism'), indicate a sombre disquiet at the prospect of a 'tripolar' Europe accompanied by independent German-French-Italian-British rearmament (not to mention a 'quadripolar' Europe with a victorious socialist revolution in one or several countries of Southwest Europe).

For the international workers' movement and the European proletariat these are generally useless games, and excessively dangerous at that. The working class has no business choosing among different variants of *bourgeois* international policy. For that is what is involved in all these speculations. The working class must fight for a *proletarian* international policy, which means an independent class policy opposed to any alliance with one faction of imperialism against another. Today this can be expressed in two formulas: Against armament (especially nuclear armament) and against the war preparations of *any* imperialist bourgeoisie! For the Socialist United States of Europe!

### Is there any Room for 'Genuine Reformism' in Capitalist Europe Today?

When we speak of a process of Social Democratization of the Communist parties of Western Europe, the representatives of Eurocommunism bristle: we have nothing in common with Social Democracy today, they affirm. But we have never said that the Communist parties are in the process of being transformed into the miserable Social Democracy of Helmut Schmidt, Wilson-Healey-Callaghan, or Mario Soares. What we have underscored are the evident parallels with the evolution of classical Social Democracy of 1910–30, which should not be confused with contemporary Social Democracy. The Eurocommunist leaders have never seriously responded to that parallel.

What we are speaking of here is a *process*. Today's Social Democracy is the product of the Social Democracy of the 1920s, but it is at the same time substantially different from it. Likewise, the Social Democracy of the 1920s was the product of the capitulation of 1914, but the capitulation itself had caused important transformations compared to the period before August 1914; while the capitulation of August 1914 was in turn the product of the changes that had occurred within classical Social Democracy prior to the First World War.

By way of analogy, Eurocommunism, which has not yet transformed the Communist parties into Social Democratic ones but has merely accelerated their evolution in that direction, is the product of an increasingly systematic and lasting option which dates from the end of the Cold War, an option which itself resulted from the transformations introduced in the Comintern by the Seventh Congress, the Popular Front, and the policy of 'Anti-fascist Union' during the period 1941–47. These transformations in turn would have been inconceivable without the turn to 'Socialism in One Country' in the USSR and in the Comintern in 1924.

Describing the origins of the social-patriotic betrayal of international Social Democracy in 1914, Trotsky stressed the following feature: 'The patriotism of the German social democrats began as a legitimate patriotism of their own party, the most powerful party of the Second International. On the basis of the highly developed German technology and the superior organizational qualities of the German people, German social democracy prepared to build its "own" socialist society. If we leave aside the hardened bureaucrats, careerists, parliamentary sharpers, and political crooks in general, the social-patriotism of the rank and file social democrats was derived precisely from the belief in building German socialism. It is impossible to think that hundreds of thousands of rank and file social democrats (let alone the millions of rank and file workers) wanted to defend the Hohenzollerns or the bourgeoisie. No. They wanted to protect German industry, the German railways and highways, German technology and culture, and especially the organizations of the German working class, as the "necessary and sufficient" national prerequisites for socialism' (*Third International After Lenin*, Pathfinder Press, New York, 1970, p. 70).

The analogy with the evolution of the French, and particularly Italian, Communist Parties is striking. A *leitmotiv* that crops up again and again in the writings of the Eurocommunists is that any 'catastrophic' crisis of the 'democratic state' would endanger the 'gains of the working class'. This is the deeper reason why the Communist parties are turning themselves into 'forces of order'.[18] They hope to win acceptance by the 'middle layers' through their self-denial, their 'sense of the state', and their refusal 'to take advantage of difficulties for partisan ends'. In this way they intend to consolidate the gains already won and then extend them, little by little.

Further on we will return to the manifest contradictions inherent in the strategy founded on such reasoning.[19] What is incontestable is that Eurocommunism today is repeating the reasoning of Social Democracy yesterday word for word. The third historic root of Eurocommunism is then the 'attrition strategy' of Karl Kautsky. This strategy is condemned to lead to the same defeats as those suffered by classical Social Democracy.

For this entire project ignores the decisive factor in politics in bourgeois society: the elementary class struggle. The successive mediations which have been introduced by the Communist Party between socio-economic analysis and political analysis, have finally detached the latter from its base. Politics is now regarded as a thoroughly independent procedure in which tricks, tactics, manoeuvres, compromise, and psychology are everything and material class interest no longer counts at all. But the entire history of the 20th century belies such bureaucratic, manoeuvrist, and manipulative conceptions of politics, which are not Stalinist *in essence*, inasmuch as they are common to both the Social Democratic and Stalinist bureaucracies. The European bourgeoisie is far too well-schooled and experienced to be paralyzed by 'tricks'. As for the working class, which is less experienced politically, it can certainly be fooled by clever manoeuvres at times. But trickery results in demoralization, which leads to the weakening of the working class – which in turn tips the balance of forces in a direction inimical to all reformist (and Eurocommunist) designs.

[18] See, for example, the Italian Communist Party's acceptance of measures aimed at 'reinforcing law and order' proposed by the Andreotti government during the summer of 1977.

[19] See chapter 10 of the present book, 'The Strategy of Eurocommunism'.

Two essential features of the current situation render the 'gradual transformation of capitalism' sought by the Euro-communists even less realistic than the similar projects of Kautsky and company before the First World War. First, capitalist Europe is now moving through a long-term economic and social crisis which drastically narrows the room for manoeuvre of the imperialist bourgeoisie, as well as its ability to grant reforms. Today, what is on the agenda every-where is not reform but austerity. Most of the Eurocommunist projects (beginning with the French Common Programme) were drawn up under the assumption of a medium- and long-term annual economic growth of 5 per cent. This has now become largely utopian for the coming years under the capitalist sys-tem, even an 'improved' one. Any reformist orientation is a policy designed to *administer the crisis* and not to make 'profound transformations'. This will remain true in capitalist Europe during the 1970s and 1980s. It is only by breaking with the bourgeoisie, by abolishing the capitalist system, that a road to accelerated growth can be opened.

Second, the internationalization of productive forces, capital, and class struggle is vastly more advanced today than it was in 1914, 1936, or 1945. The international interpenetration of capital within the Common Market countries is a fact, even though it continues to develop in an uneven and contradictory manner. Under these conditions, any scheme for the 'gradual transformation of capitalism' on a national basis, any project that maintains the basic structures of the capitalist economy, is thoroughly utopian, if not reactionary. For it will inevitably force a rending choice between two evils which the working class must avoid like the plague: either successive capitula-tions to the dictates of international finance capital (like Wilson-Healey-Callaghan), or a mounting resort to protection-ism. Both options eventually result in declines in the living standard of the working class. Both plunge the working class into a political impasse.

Indeed, the leaders of the Italian Communist Party sense this, although in a confused way. They insist that they do not want a return to protectionism. They even wind up hailing the Common Market, the Europe of capital. But this makes the Eurocommunist political project all the more unrealistic. Who can possibly believe that socialism could be 'gradually' introduced in Italy and France while these countries remain associated with West German and British big capital?

'Socialism in one country' translated into a 'national communism' to be achieved gradually and separately in each country of Europe leads to a total impasse. Like any class policy or project of the proletariat, communism must be international or it cannot be. There is no substitute for an orientation towards the Socialist United States of Europe, the only historically valid and superior response to the capitalist integration of Europe. No overthrow of capitalism is conceivable in Europe unless it is based on this goal.

## The 'Single Centre', Proletarian Internationalism, and the Future of Eurocommunism

Proletarian internationalism is founded on the community of class interests of the proletariat of all countries; it stands opposed to capitalist competition structured in states and markets separated from one another by the logic of private property in the means of production. It implies indispensable solidarity with all workers' struggles compatible with the class interest of the proletariat.[20] A denial of the community of interests of the world working-class means a rejection of the principal premises of the Marxist theory that the socialist emancipation of humanity is indeed possible. In the best of cases such a negation would imply a regression to utopia, to a socialism born of indoctrination and propaganda rather than of a consciousness of common material and social interests. In the worst of cases it would imply the abandonment of any socialist perspective, and a lapse into pessimism or indifference about the future of the human race.

But proletarian internationalism, like all facets of the class consciousness of the proletariat, can be acquired by the mass of wage-earners only gradually, on the basis of the experience of struggle and actual solidarity. To believe that it will result

---

[20] Obviously, some struggles by workers are reactionary, strikes against the employment of workers of another race or nationality, for example. But a moment of reflection indicates that these are conflicts setting workers against other workers and not conflicts between workers and capitalists.

automatically from orders handed down from on high or from the distribution of speeches, articles, pamphlets, and books, however important this sort of education may be, is to understand nothing of the concrete formation of class consciousness among the broad masses. It is to fall into historical idealism.

Now, the only sort of practice that can lead to an ever broader spread of proletarian internationalism is a practice of *reciprocal solidarity*. By turning the Communist International away from its initial objectives and watering it down into a docile instrument of Soviet diplomatic manoeuvres and particularist privileges, the Stalinist bureaucracy dealt a death blow to proletarian internationalism in the ranks of the movement it controlled on a world scale.

The German, Spanish, and French workers; the Polish and Yugoslav Communist parties (both dissolved); the German and Austrian Communists who took refuge in the USSR and were then delivered to Hitler by Stalin; the Tartar people, 'wiped off the map'; these are some of those who have been force-fed the bitter fruits of 'socialism in one country'. The Stalin–Tito conflict, the Sino–Soviet conflict, the conflict with the leadership of the Czechoslovak Communist Party in 1968, and the quarrels over Eurocommunism are the successive boomerangs that have struck the Soviet bureaucracy as consequences of its chauvinism.

When the representatives of the CPSU and their parrots in the Bulgarian, 'normalized' Czechoslovak, German, Austrian, and North American Communist parties now accuse the Eurocommunist leaders of 'betraying proletarian internationalism', their cynicism is equalled only by their naive clumsiness. By what right can those who have betrayed and continue to betray innumerable revolutions, strikes, and economic and political mobilizations of workers in a hundred different countries throughout the world invoke this principle, which has no conceivable value unless it is based on strict reciprocity and universality? Do the Spanish miners of Asturias, who saw several of their mobilizations under the Franco regime weakened by the import of coal from the 'socialist countries', need lessons in 'proletarian internationalism' from those who acted as vulgar strike-breakers? Can the militants of the British Labour party, who remember that the Kremlin, concerned not to upset the 'grand antifascist alliance', advised them in 1945 to leave intact an alliance with their Tory exploiters Churchill and Eden, have any faith in appeals to proletarian internationalism coming from this suspect source? Can militant Indian workers, who know that the Kremlin compelled the leadership of the Indian Communist Party to combat the movement for national independence in that colonial country in August 1942, have any faith in the references to proletarian internationalism uttered by Brezhnev and Dange?[21]

Implied in this whole campaign is the famous formula of Maurice Thorez: 'Proletarian internationalism is solidarity with the Soviet Union'.[22] No, proletarian internationalism is the *common* defence of the interests of the proletarians of *all* countries (among them, of course, those of the Soviet Union, which means defence of what remains of the conquests of October). Anyone who fails to understand that the formula of Thorez is now unacceptable to the immense majority of the militants of the Communist parties and to virtually all the world proletariat has understood nothing of what has changed in the world during the past thirty years.

The Eurocommunist leaders believe that in rejecting a 'single centre' that directs the international communist movement they are rejecting subjection to instructions from the Kremlin, the subordination of their parties to interests which are not their own. (We do not say which are not those of their own proletariat, for they themselves have long since ceased to defend these interests consistently.) Communist militants believe they are rediscovering a long-coveted 'autonomy' and

[21] There is one recent and particularly striking example. The Japanese Communist Party has called for the return of the Kurile Islands, which were annexed by the USSR in 1945, to Japan. The Soviet Communist Party has accused the Japanese party of chauvinism, which is correct. But what about the chauvinist position of Stalin, who cynically identified with Tsarist imperialism when he wrote, at the end of the Second World War: 'The defeat of the Russian troops in 1904 left bitter memories in the minds of the people(!). It was like a black stain for our country(!). Our people believed and hoped that the day would come when Japan would be crushed and this stain eliminated. We(!), the people of the old generation, have waited forty years for that day.'

[22] The formula was invented by Stalin himself. According to him, a communist is defined as 'one who unevasively, unconditionally, openly, and honestly' regards the cause of the world revolution as synonymous with the interests and defence of the USSR. (*Works*, Volume X, p. 61. 1949 edition.)

'independence'. But the dialectic of the class struggle is implacable. While escaping the tutelage of the Soviet bureaucracy, they will fatally fall under the tutelage of their own bourgeoisie, so long as they do not rediscover the line of intransigent anticapitalist struggle.

No such struggle is at all possible in the imperialist epoch unless it is international. No consistent international struggle is possible without an international organization. The idea of a 'single centre' was profoundly discredited by Stalin when he converted it into a system of bureaucratic command by the CPSU. Yet its undistorted form remains the only alternative for communist militants who really want to rediscover class independence from the bourgeoisie and the Soviet bureaucracy.

Any 'national communism' in a capitalist country is condemned to become a 'communism' integrated into the bourgeois state. Any rejection of integration into the bourgeois state can be coherent and credible in the long run only if it is based on an international project of class struggle and proletarian organization. One cannot oppose one's own bourgeoisie in internal policy and stand neutral or even support it in international and military policy. Indifference to or betrayal of international class struggles sooner or later becomes indifference to and betrayal of the national class struggle itself. Such is the objective dialectic of bourgeois society, confirmed by innumerable historical precedents.

Of course, when a handful of revolutionary Marxists around Leon Trotsky set to work to reconstruct the International, they knew very well that their enterprise merely anticipated what would be the new, mass Communist International of the future. They constituted only the initial nucleus of that International. Although today they are already ten, twenty times as strong as they were at the time of their founding conference or just after the Second World War, they still remain only that: a nucleus which assures the continuity and enrichment of the communist programme and which educates thousands of cadres on that basis. The rest, the fusion of these cadres and this programme with the broad masses, will be the combined product of their political abilities and the developments of the class struggle (which stimulates leaps forward in class consciousness, but not automatically).

Resolutely swimming against the stream, revolutionary Marxists must reaffirm forcefully today: 'No to "national communisms"! Yes to the "single centre"!' Not a bureaucratic 'centre' that commands by administrative measures. Not a 'centre' that appoints or ousts national leaderships independent of the maturation and comprehension of the majority of the members of the national parties. Certainly not a centre which dictates obligatory 'tactics', failing to take account of the uneven development of the relationship of class forces in various countries (which the Eurocommunists coyly call 'not taking account of the historical peculiarities of each nation'). Above all not a 'centre' that issues orders subordinating the interests of the class struggle of the proletariat of any country to the interests of a section of the proletariat of another country or to the diplomatic manoeuvres of any state.

Rather a 'single centre' that permits the centralization of the experience, practice, and consequent lessons of the proletariats of all countries. A 'centre' which, on this basis and through open discussion and persuasion, elaborates a common orientation for all communists on the great international problems. A 'centre' which thus allows the stage of verbal 'solidarity' and insipid 'exchanges of experiences' to be transcended for a growing number of *common actions* of the proletariat on a world scale. A 'centre' which thus opposes the international centralization of bourgeois counter-revolution with a progressive centralization of international revolutionary initiative.

In the epoch of the 'multinationals', of the increasingly complex internationalization of capital, the growing internationalization of the class struggle is an *objective* and irreversible tendency. Only internationally coordinated class action can effectively respond to the international manoeuvres of capital. To reject international centralization of class politics and organization is to lag behind the objective and spontaneous tendencies of the class struggle rather than stand in advance of them. How could effective action have been taken against imperialism's support of Pinochet's militaro-fascist putsch in Chile if not through a response on an international scale? How can the colonial slaves in revolt against imperialist aggression be aided if not through a response on an international scale? How could the blockade of Portugal during the revolutionary process which unfolded there in 1975 have been neutralized if not through an internationally coordinated response by the workers? Meanwhile Eurocommunism produces the tragicomedy of the French Communist Party defending 'French wine' against the 'Italian wine' supported by the Italian Communist Party.

In an epoch of wars, revolutions, and counter-revolutions, the alternative 'permanent revolution or socialism in one country', 'proletarian internationalism or national communism', 'single centre' (that is, international *organization*) or social-patriotic fragmentation has a terrible logic to which Lenin, Trotsky, Luxemburg and their companions were sensitive as early as 1914, but which many communists seem to have forgotten today. Because of the multiplication of armed conflicts in the world, any rejection of international discipline on international questions threatens to lead sooner or later to the situation Rosa Luxemburg invoked in the acid formula with which she refuted centrist sophisms against international discipline: 'Proletarians of all countries, unite in time of peace but cut each other's throats in time of war'.

The only alternative to such catastrophes is a genuine, democratically centralized International that deals with all parties on an equal basis, accepts the 'national messianism' of no country, national proletariat, or party, and constantly, patiently, and obstinately strives to disengage the common class interest from the entanglement of partial and local interests and the fragmentary consciousness which reflects them.

Constructing such a world organization is probably the most difficult task humanity has ever set itself. The proof of this is that Marx, Engels, Lenin, and Trotsky were all unable to accomplish it completely in their lifetimes. We do not know how long it will take to do so. But we do know that humanity never sets itself tasks it cannot fulfill. We are convinced that none of the vital problems with which humanity is confronted today – problems of survival in the literal sense of the word – will be resolved without the creation of this mass communist International and without the extension of proletarian internationalist consciousness among the broad masses of the world which it requires.

# 2
# Three Facets of Eurocommunism

## I. Eurocommunism and the imperialist bourgeoisie

More than anything else Eurocommunism represents a codification of the rightward evolution of the West European Communist parties since the Seventh Congress of the Comintern. With the exceptions of the period September 1939 to spring 1941 and the period of the Korean war, this evolution has led them to apply a policy of ever closer collaboration with their own bourgeoisies.

Viewed from this angle, the latest congress of the French Communist Party (PCF), like the abandonment of the dictatorship of the proletariat by the Italian, Spanish, British, Swedish, and Belgian Communist parties, may be regarded as the counterpart to the Görlitz congress of the German Social Democracy. After a long period during which day to day reformist practice came into ever sharper contradiction with formal (literary) programmatic orthodoxy (the Erfurt Programme for the Social Democracy in the past, the supposed 'principles of Marxism–Leninism' for the Stalinist Communist parties today), the programme was finally adjusted to the daily practice. Revisionism has thus been officially codified in theory.

Does this mean that the official codification of the neo-reformist practice of the West European Communist parties will not alter their practice very much? It is clear that these parties have already been practising class collaboration for decades. At the end of the Second World War they literally saved the capitalist system in France and Italy by participating in governments, disarming the partisans, and actively aiding the reconstruction of the bourgeois state, the bourgeois apparatus of repression (even under conditions of colonial war), and the capitalist economy, just as the Social Democracy in central Europe saved capitalism after the First World War. The counter-revolutionary role of the Communist party leaderships had already been prefigured in republican Spain in 1936–38. At that time this policy was still being applied in the name of 'defence of the Soviet Union'. Today they are openly renouncing the Marxist–Leninist theory of the state. But does this change anything in practice?

To answer this question correctly, it must be understood that the reformist degeneration of the mass organizations of the working class constitutes a *process* and not an event. Day to day practice, official theory (as the basis on which cadres are educated), the manner in which members are recruited, the objective effects of the class struggle, and the very way the leadership, cadres, and militants of the party see themselves all come into play in this process as interlocking factors which cannot be considered either as independent elements or as forming a homogeneous whole.

After the turn towards the policy of the Popular Front during the 1930s and 1940s, the average militant of a West European Communist party joined this party, in spite of its reformist practice, because he or she identified it with the October Revolution and with the Soviet Union as the incarnation of the revolution. This is less and less true today. In the past, the cadres of these parties were prepared for tactical zigzags in Comintern policy (the tactics changed every three or four years). The present cadres of the Communist parties of West Europe, with a few rare exceptions, have been engaged in purely reformist tactics for twenty or twenty-five years now. *In this context*, the codification of neo-reformism marks a new and significant stage in the rightist evolution of these parties.

The imperialist bourgeoisie is quite conscious of these changes. It is not enchanted by the prospect of Eurocommunist participation in governments, at least so long as it is not facing an explosive revolutionary crisis. The bourgeoisie is still qualitatively more suspicious of these Communist parties than of the Social Democracy. But it understands that something has changed. One of the leading ideologues of the cold war, George Kennan, expressed this clearly in a television interview the text of which was published in the 20 January 1977 issue of the *New York Review of Books*: 'Today, when questions are being raised on the subject of the Italian and French Communist parties, we are not dealing with the same parties we had to deal with in 1947'.

For several years we have used the concept of the *gradual social democratization* of the Communist parties of West Europe. Recent developments fully confirm this diagnosis. Nevertheless, as we have said, what is involved here is a process. Even if the Communist parties of West Europe no longer support merely bourgeois parliamentary democracy but also the bourgeois police (in the image of the classical Social Democracy), they still maintain specific links to the Soviet Union and the 'socialist camp'. In spite of all the mounting criticisms of the domestic policy of the Soviet bureaucracy, their relationship to this bureaucracy remains different from that of the Social Democratic parties. Their relations with international imperialism (American, European, and Japanese) are in no way identical to those the Social Democracy maintains with imperialism.

From the other side, both the Soviet bureaucracy and international capital continue to act differently toward the Communist and Social Democratic parties.

The so far uncrossed limit of the process of gradual social democratization of the West European Communist parties is accounted for primarily by the political and material self-interest of the enormous bureaucratic apparatuses of these parties. The existence of this bureaucracy is based on its own particular identity, and this identity is still closely linked to 'special relations' with the 'socialist camp'. Indeed, the leadership of the French Communist Party launched its spectacular offensive against Social Democracy in autumn 1977 precisely in order to defend this specific identity, as well as its hegemonic weight within the organized working class in the factories.

Should the process of social democratization continue to the bitter end, the basis for the separate existence of these Communist parties from Social Democracy would disappear. Most leaders of Communist parties today do not (yet) want to take this risk, nor are they able to. Many other factors – such as tradition, continued material links, advantages the Communist parties maintain against the Socialist parties through clinging to their historical identity in the eyes of the combative sections of the working class, the danger that many members and sympathizers might join organizations to the left of the Communist parties – also come into play in accounting for the present limits to the process of social democratization.

From the historical standpoint, however, Eurocommunism is not simply a confirmation of the (further) rightward turn of most of the West European Communist parties. It also represents a right turn under particular conditions, new in and of themselves. First, it is occurring during a period of rising and sometimes stormy upsurge of mass struggles in Southern Europe, which has bordered on pre-revolutionary and revolutionary situations. Under *these* conditions the shift to full adherence to bourgeois parliamentary democracy and class collaboration, even with big capital (as in Italy), marks a sharper and more open turn to class betrayal than in the past. The events in Italy during spring 1977 illustrate this. The Eurocommunists, like the Social Democrats after 1914, are compelled to sacrifice not only the revolutionary class struggle but also the day-to-day interests of the wage earners on the altar of class reconciliation with the bourgeoisie ('in order to avoid a test of strength at any price').

It is indispensable to destroy the state and repressive apparatus of the bourgeoisie if one is to prevent these apparatuses from being used to protect private property, even against the democratically expressed will of the majority of the population, with the bloodiest violence if need be. That is a lesson the Eurocommunists did not draw from the Chilean experience. On the contrary, the old 'wisdom' of Social Democracy was affirmed: avoid a comprehensive test of strength with the bourgeoisie. When the exacerbation of class contradictions and the polariz-action of political forces in the context of a pre-revolutionary or revolutionary situation leads to such a test of strength, then the political conclusion drawn from this 'wisdom' is simple: curb the mobilization of the workers, even if this divides the toilers and demobilizes entire layers of the proletariat. The successful application of such a line can lead only to the victory of counter-revolution.

On the other hand, the *decisive* motive in the right turn of the

Eurocommunists is no longer unconditional adaptation to the exigencies of Soviet diplomacy (that is, to the interests of the Soviet bureaucracy), as was the case in 1935 or after Nazi imperialism's attack on the Soviet Union. This time the decisive factor is the attempt to break out of domestic political ghettos, to overcome parliamentary isolation, and to link up with Social Democracy and the 'liberal' bourgeoisie. Thus, in no way does the turn of Eurocommunism represent the response to a command from Moscow issued at more or less the same time in various countries. The turn was made years apart in countries like Italy, Sweden, France, Spain, and Britain, which clearly shows that national and not international factors have been decisive.

In and of itself, of course, the right turn of the West European Communist parties does not disturb the Kremlin. It falls within the policy of 'peaceful coexistence' and 'détente', that is, the freezing of the European spheres of influence of world capital and the Soviet bureaucracy as they were established at Yalta and Potsdam. Nevertheless, this turn is regarded uneasily, if not with overt hostility, by the Soviet bureaucracy and its satellite bureaucracies in East Europe. There are various reasons for this, none of which have anything to do with the 'loyalty' of Brezhnev and his friends to the 'dictatorship of the proletariat'.

One of these reasons is that the implementation of class collaboration with the bourgeoisie by the Eurocommunists, not in order to cover for some diplomatic manoeuvre by the Kremlin but ever more exclusively out of electoral and parliamentary opportunism – that is, growing integration into bourgeois society and the bourgeois state apparatus, raises the prospect that in the event of a conflict between the Soviet Union and the West European imperialists the Eurocommunists might stand on the side of their own bourgeoisies against the Soviet Union.

For the time being, one can only hypothesize about whether this would happen. Developments have not yet gone far enough for this question to be answered yes or no. But the loss of any real political instruments in West European internal politics would be a serious setback for Moscow. The Kremlin now clearly imagines that such a danger exists, at least potentially.

Trotsky foresaw this back in 1938, although he was wrong about the timing of developments. In an article entitled 'Munich, the Last Warning,' he wrote the following commentary on the evolution of the West European Communist parties, which should serve as the basic point of departure for an understanding of Eurocommunism:
'As regards the ex-Comintern, its social base, properly speaking, is of a two-fold nature. On the one hand, it lives on the subsidies of the Kremlin, submits to the latter's commands, and in this respect every ex-Communist bureaucrat is the younger brother and subordinate of the Soviet bureaucrat. On the other hand, the various machines of the ex-Comintern feed from the same sources as the Social Democracy, that is the superprofits of imperialism. The growth of the Communist Parties in recent years, their infiltration into the ranks of the petty bourgeoisie, their installation in the state machinery, trade unions, parliaments, municipalities, etc., have strengthened in their extreme their dependence on national imperialism at the expense of their traditional dependence on the Kremlin.

'Ten years ago it was predicted that the theory of socialism in one country must inevitably lead to the growth of nationalist tendencies in the sections of the Comintern. . . . Today we can predict with assurance the inception of a new stage. The growth of imperialist antagonisms, the obvious proximity of the war danger, and the equally obvious isolation of the USSR must unavoidably strengthen the centrifugal nationalist tendencies within the Comintern. Each one of its sections will begin to evolve a patriotic policy on its own account. Stalin has reconciled the Communist Parties of the imperialist democracies with their national bourgeoisies. This stage has now been passed. The Bonapartist procurer has played his role. Henceforth, the communo-chauvinists will have to worry about their own hides, whose interests by no means always coincide with the "defense of the USSR"' (*Writings of Leon Trotsky, 1938–39*, New York, pp. 70–71).

## 2. Eurocommunism and the Soviet bureaucracy

But much more important than this uneasiness on the part of the Soviet bureaucracy about the future relations of the

Eurocommunists with the Soviet Union and the 'socialist camp' is the fear and hostility of the Kremlin with regard to the timid criticisms the Eurocommunists have made of the worst excesses of bureaucratic repression: condemnation of the invasion of Czechoslovakia in 1968; condemnation of the internment of political dissidents in 'psychiatric clinics' in the USSR; condemnation of attacks on democratic freedoms and civil rights; support for Charter 77 in Czechoslovakia; more discreet protest against the repression of strikes in Poland; mild reproof of the expulsion of Wolf Biermann from East Germany and the lifting of his citizenship.

We are dealing here with a phenomenon that revolutionary Marxists have increasingly stressed in their analysis of the crisis of Stalinism since 1948, one which other tendencies critical of the Soviet leadership have not understood (or not fully understood): the fact that the Soviet bureaucracy has not cut the umbilical cord to the international workers' movement and therefore to the international working class. Consequently, everything that happens in the Communist parties outside the Soviet Union (or the People's Democracies) has repercussions on internal relations in the Soviet Union and the People's Democracies. Under certain conditions these effects can be damaging, and even downright threatening, to the stability of the rule of the Soviet bureaucracy.

In East Europe and the USSR the statements of the Euro-communists in favour of political pluralism and democratic freedoms are avidly received *not* because they strengthen capitalism and the bourgeois state, but because they are seen as an alternative to the present form of political rule in *East Europe and the USSR* (alternative models of the workers' state). Therein lies the great objective explosive potential of Eurocommunism from the standpoint of the Kremlin.

When Carter calls for civil rights in the USSR or when Solzhenitsyn drags the October Revolution through the mud, the domestic policy of the bureaucracy can only benefit. Such actions enable the bureaucracy to paralyze its own working class with the alternative: either the massive unemployment of the capitalist system or bureaucratic monopoly of power. But when Berlinguer, Carrillo, and Marchais plead for 'political pluralism in the building of socialism', that turns against the

Kremlin. Either the latter must explain that the largest Communist parties in the capitalist world have crossed over to the camp of imperialism, or it must acknowledge that there are working-class alternatives to the Stalinist and post-Stalinist form of rule. Either option would undermine the Kremlin's political authority and clearly broaden the room for manoeuvre of the opposition in the USSR and the People's Democracies. From this standpoint it may be asserted that Eurocommunism has opened a deep breach in the international Stalinist apparatus and has aggravated the crisis of this apparatus, particularly in its relations with the masses in the USSR and the People's Democracies. It therefore accelerates development toward a political revolution in Eastern Europe.

Isn't it a contradiction, then, to assert that Eurocommunism represents primarily a right-wing turn, an adaptation to West European Social Democracy, to the petty bourgeoisie, and in part to big capital? To resolve the apparent contradiction it is sufficient to formulate the question differently: *Why* are the West European Communist parties now criticizing the internal repression of the Soviet bureaucracy in growing (although still quite insufficient) measure? Is it mainly an attempt to win the favours of the Western bourgeoisie, to break into bourgeois 'salon society'? This would be a simplistic interpretation.

As we have already shown, the main reasons for the tactical turns of the Eurocommunists during past years have related to electoral policy: the aim is to overcome a specific obstacle to reaching voters (and trade-union sympathizers to some extent). From this standpoint, the Eurocommunists' criticism of the repressive policies of the Soviet bureaucracy can in no way be designed to win bourgeois or 'upper middle class' votes. Their opportunist electoralist policy is aimed at the working class and some lower petty-bourgeois layers. It is among these circles that the strongest Communist parties (especially the Italian, French, and Spanish) can hope for the greatest success with their Eurocommunism. In other words: the growing criticism of the Soviet bureaucracy is a concession primarily to the West European working class itself and not to the bourgeoisie.

One may try to undercut this analysis by stressing reformist and Social Democratic influences within the working class, that is, the weight of bourgeois or petty-bourgeois ideology within the working class. There is undoubtedly a kernel of truth in this contention, but only a kernel. In Italy it is the Communist Party and not Social Democracy that has held hegemony over the working class and the workers' movement for years. It is difficult to claim that the combative working class in Spain during recent years has been completely dominated by reformism. On the contrary, insofar as there is an upswing of workers' struggles in Southern Europe, and to some extent in other European countries, this upsurge is accompanied by the growth of anticapitalist and not class collaborationist trends among broad layers of workers. Under these conditions, the Eurocommunists' criticism of the Kremlin is in large part not a concession to bourgeois ideology and influence within the working class, but *a concession to the anti-bureaucratic components of the average consciousness of the combative layers of workers*, which is now undoubtedly much stronger than it was in the past.

It follows that we must regard *this* aspect of Eurocommunism positively and not negatively. It would be paradoxical to say the least if revolutionary Marxists, who for years have denounced the crimes of the Soviet bureaucracy against its own working class and that of East Europe, should suddenly become uneasy when a small echo of this criticism is heard from the leaders of many official Communist parties in the West. What we condemn in the Eurocommunists' attitude *on this point* is not 'capitulation to imperialism', but inconsistency and lack of courage in carrying their own thought through to the end. An 'objective' critique of Stalinism in the style of Elleinstein, who seeks to explain everything by 'historical conditions'; a vague call for 'political pluralism' which does not clearly demand the right to form as many different soviet parties as the working people of the Soviet Union and the People's Democracies desire, including opposition parties and an opposition press; a fleeting reference to 'socialist democracy' without clearly and openly calling for a democratic regime of workers' councils, that is, for freely and democratically elected councils as the political backbone of workers' self-administration – all these things make the current Eurocommunist criticism of the political relations which prevail in East Europe incoherent and scarcely credible. Only a Marxist explanation of the nature of the Soviet bureaucracy as a privileged social layer; only an explanation of Stalinism as based on the material interests of this bureaucracy; only an understanding of the interaction of this political problem with the problems of any society midway between capitalism and socialism, with its specific relations of production and its own contradictions and dynamic, can clarify the structural and superstructural reality of Soviet society. They alone can scientifically define the perspectives of a struggle to break the bureaucracy's monopoly of power, by a political revolution in Eastern Europe. All this is lacking in Eurocommunism. That is why we criticize the Eurocommunist theses on Soviet society. But the dialogue with Eurocommunist cadres and members on this question is qualitatively easier today than it was in the past. This is progress and not retrogression.

Die-hard sectarians who would seek to deny this assert that Eurocommunism represents either a cynical Kremlin trick aimed at facilitating 'international détente' or outright abandonment of 'defence of the Soviet Union'. The first argument is ridiculous. Does anyone believe in all seriousness that the Kremlin ordered Carrillo, Marchais, and Berlinguer to criticize the Kremlin? The second argument leads to dangerous conclusions, for in reality neither in Czechoslovakia nor in Poland, not to mention the USSR itself, is there a conflict today between imperialism and Soviet society that poses the restoration of capitalism as an immediate possibility. Instead there are conflicts between the Soviet bureaucracy and layers (or the majority) of the oppressed, muzzled, and atomized working people, which in no way involve attempts to restore private property. (Only the most hopeless idiots fall for the crude slanders spread by the bureaucracy on this score.) In a conflict between the working class and the bureaucracy we stand 100% on the side of the workers, whatever their ideological level may be (and if it is low and confused, this is a result of the bureaucratic dictatorship; it will be raised only through a struggle to overthrow this dictatorship). Those who equate a conflict between the bureaucracy and the toiling population with a conflict between Soviet society and international capital are capitulating to Stalinism. For it is a surrender to Stalinism to regard the timid support the Eurocommunists have accorded the struggle for human rights, for democratic liberties in the USSR and the People's Democracies, as a 'concession to imperialism' under the pretext that Carter is also making noises about human rights. By the same logic, the unreserved support revolutionary Marxists accorded the Hungarian revolution in 1956 or their opposition to the invasion of Czechoslovakia in 1968 could be called 'support to imperialism', since the imperialists made even more noise on these issues.

We judge these conflicts according to the social forces in motion and not according to imperialist propaganda. A just strike does not cease to deserve support from the entire union movement simply because some employer in competition with the capitalist whose factory is struck decides to use the strike to score some public points against him. The political conflict in the USSR and the People's Democracies pits the bureaucracy against the toiling masses and not against the imperialist bourgeoisie. When the Eurocommunist leaders commit themselves (insufficiently) against the bureaucracy in this struggle, they place themselves on the side of the masses and not on the side of imperialism.

### 3. Eurocommunism and the West European Working Class

The fact that the programmatic and political right turn of the Eurocommunists coincides with an upsurge of mass struggles and a sharpening of the social crisis, at least in the countries of southern Europe, where the strongest Eurocommunist parties exist, accounts for an important contradiction: the Eurocommunists are compelled to make concessions simultaneously to reformist petty-bourgeois pressure from the right and anti-bureaucratic pressure from the left. An understanding of this specific aspect of Eurocommunism is important in grasping its internal contradictions, especially the contradictions in its dynamic, which cannot be fully explained solely by considering Eurocommunism's relations with the Soviet bureaucracy.

Classical Stalinism was an internally sealed system expressing a particular social logic (albeit a logic which led to totalitarian madness). It may be summarized this way: the Soviet Union is the homeland of the toiling people of the entire world and the capital of world revolution. The interests of all sectors of the international workers' movement must absolutely be subordinated to the interests of the defence of the Soviet Union. These interests are represented by the 'Leninist Central Committee of the CPSU', headed by the omniscient general secretary. Any criticism of the Central Committee or the general secretary is thus automatically an expression of the political pressure (or influence) of enemy social classes and in the final analysis an expression of betrayal of the working class. Whoever does not stand behind Stalin unconditionally is 'objectively' against socialism and for imperialism.

At least since the Twentieth Congress of the CPSU, if not since the rehabilitation of Tito or even since Moscow's break with Tito, this closed system has been springing more and more leaks. With the Eurocommunists there is scarcely anything left to salvage. Today it is openly or implicitly accepted that one can remain 'in the camp of the international workers' movement' while also making merciless criticisms of the policy of the Soviet leadership on many questions. At the same time, it is being openly or implicitly acknowledged that Soviet society, far from being a 'workers' paradise', has many features that *no* Eurocommunist party would introduce in the event of the overthrow of capitalism in their own countries. In place of a series of solidified dogmas, we now increasingly find critical questions and timid demands for open discussion (in which our movement – the Fourth International – must take as active a part as possible; it has worked far longer on these questions and has reached much more serious Marxist conclusions than any other current of the international workers' movement).

But there is no Chinese wall between the 'infallibility' of the 'great Stalin' and the 'infallibility' of the 'little' Stalins on the national, regional, and local levels. If the leadership of the CPSU can make a mistake, so can the leadership of the Italian, French, or Spanish Communist parties. The demand for critical reflexion on the current policy of the Soviet bureaucracy (beginning with critical reflexion on the history of Soviet society) inevitably leads to a demand for critical reflexion on the current policy of the Eurocommunists themselves (beginning with their understanding of their own history).

In other words, the dynamic of Eurocommunism undoubtedly

widens the *field of workers' democracy*, for free internal and public discussion in the West European workers' movement, in the West European Communist parties, and in the mass organizations controlled or influenced by them, particularly the unions. You cannot eternally call for 'pluralism' in the state and society (including in a future workers' state) and simultaneously cling to the dogma of the 'monolithic' party, and still less the 'monolithic' trade union.

But the greater space for workers' democracy objectively opened by Eurocommunism clashes with the objective and especially subjective consequences of the right turn of the Eurocommunists. You cannot preach 'tolerance' and 'democracy' and simultaneously expect that an austerity policy (in      or pressure politics (Spain) can be forced down the throats of combative workers with impunity. Eurocommunism thus inevitably leads, at least in the phase of rising mass struggle, to growing differentiation within the Communist-led trade unions, growing differentiation within the mass Communist parties themselves (above all among the youth and working-class members), a growing instability of bureaucratic control over significant sections of vanguard workers, and growing demands for the right of tendencies in Communist parties, trade unions, and mass organizations. The difference may be easily seen by comparing the results of Berlinguer's course in 1974–77 with those of Togliatti's policy in the big factories of Northern Italy from 1943 to 1947.

Apart from the revolt of the working-class and trade-union rank and file against the course followed by Berlinguer, the Central Committee of the Communist Party itself has begun to divide into three tendencies: a 'right wing' around Amendola, a 'centre' around Berlinguer, and a 'hard-line' wing around Cossuta and old Stalinists like Luigi Longo. A similar phenomenon has arisen in the Spanish Communist Party, where a 'left wing' around Camacho opposed a 'right wing' which favoured the dissolution of the Workers Commissions, while the 'centre' around Santiago Carrillo finally lined up with Camacho on this question, after first negotiating with the right.

We have no illusion in the possibility of a 'self-reform' of the Stalinist bureaucracy, whether in the USSR or in the Eurocommunist mass parties of the imperialist countries. These parties cannot be transformed into revolutionary or centrist parties 'under the pressure of the masses'. But we are fully convinced that the slackening of bureaucratic control caused by the effects of the dynamic of Eurocommunism will introduce a new and higher stage in the crisis of these parties. How will this crisis evolve? What portion of militant Communist workers and youth will be able to break from the bureaucratic apparatus? To what extent will the growing oppositions in these parties set some limits on the leadership's ability to manoeuvre? These are questions which will be answered only by the relationship of forces. In the final analysis, the activity of the masses and the role played by revolutionary Marxists both in mass struggles and in programmatic and political debate will be of decisive importance in determining this relationship of forces.

The big trump card the Eurocommunists have been able to play up to now in countries like Italy, France, and Spain has been the fact that in the eyes of the masses they seem to present a *credible comprehensive political strategy.* The reformist content of this strategy is less noticed (and taken less seriously: the anti-communist campaigns of the big bourgeoisie play an important role in concealing this aspect from the view of the broad masses). What has attracted the workers, and still attracts them in part, is the fact that for the first time since 1948 they see a possible way out of a political stalemate which has lasted for years and which the masses instinctively or semiconsciously identify with the deepening social crisis of late capitalism. 'The "Unions of the Left" will win more and more votes. After two or three attempts they will win majorities in parliament. Then when it comes to a test of strength, they will have a better starting point.' This is how the broad masses understand Eurocommunism; it is also how the German toilers understood Kautsky's 'attrition strategy' (the historical precursor of the strategy of Eurocommunism).

But the sharper the economic difficulties of the era of late capitalism become, the stronger the employers' attacks on the gains the working class has already won, and the more social crises and class conflicts intensify, the faster this strategy will approach its moment of truth. Collaboration with the bourgeoisie, not to mention a 'historic compromise', is no longer possible on the basis of new reforms. It requires new sacrifices, which are imposed on the working class in order to raise the rate of profit. No matter how positive and credible the broad masses may find the 'left alternative', they are less and less prepared to accept sacrifices in their living standards and democratic freedoms in order to bring it about. They will inevitably clash with the Communist party apparatus on this point. This collision will precipitate a severe crisis for Eurocommunism, precisely as a consequence of its own ideological-political dynamic.

A negative outcome of this crisis – that is, a defeat of the workers in a struggle against the employers and the bourgeois state as a consequence of the diversion of the struggle by the Communist party bureaucracy and the lack of a political alternative – would involve a shift in the relationship of forces to the advantage of big capital, which could have weighty consequences. A victory of the working class in this crisis (unthinkable without the qualitative strengthening of a new revolutionary leadership) would require the involvement of broad layers of workers in anti-capitalist self-organization and mass political strikes *against* the will of the Eurocommunists. This would open the way to socialist revolution in West Europe. One way or the other, the Eurocommunist strategy is doomed to failure.

Many sincere Communist workers, youth, and intellectuals who have been encouraged in their critical attitude toward Stalinism by Eurocommunism will in the future fight in the front ranks for the interests of their class, for the socialist revolution. A firm and principled policy of unity in action for immediate and transitional demands which correspond to the burning needs of the masses, combined with a patient and pedagogical explanation of the essence of Stalinism, of workers' councils, and of our strategic alternative, is the decisive weapon in opening their road to our own ranks. Eurocommunism is but a way station. For real communists there is no other road than Leninism, the road of the Fourth International.

# 3
# The Conference in East Berlin

A conference of twenty-nine Communist parties of Europe was finally held in East Berlin in June 1977. The Communist press in some countries, beginning with *Pravda* itself, hailed its convocation as a great victory. It was known that Brezhnev had staked his personal prestige on the conference. In fact, the differences of a number of Communist party leaderships – notably in Yugoslavia, Italy, Spain, France, and to some extent Romania – with the leadership of the Soviet Communist Party over some key passages of the common declaration were so deep that for a long time it seemed that the conference might not even be able to meet.

If it was eventually held, this was essentially because the Kremlin yielded on practically all the points on which its adversaries had insisted. Probably the most costly concession for the Kremlin was the elimination of any condemnation of the Chinese Communist Party or Maoism from the text of the common declaration, and the abandonment of the dogma of the 'leading role of the CPSU'. But even these concessions did not prevent the most determined advocates of polycentrism – beginning with Berlinguer of Italy and Carrillo of Spain, but also including Tito – from clearly asserting that such conferences were in fact useless, that common documents should no longer be drafted in the future, and that the strategy and tactics for achieving socialism were the exclusive province of each national party.

## Some False Interpretations and a Correct One

How should this conference be situated in the history of the

Stalinist movement? There are a number of interpretations that can be rejected straightaway. One, which is shared by the most conservative sectors of the bourgeoisie (of the Kissinger–Fanfani variety) and certain so-called far left dogmatists, blithely asserts that this conference was nothing but a charade aimed at deceiving the gullible and that in reality Brezhnev, Berlinguer, Tito, and Santiago Carrillo are in complete agreement on all points.

Were this the case, it would be difficult to understand the interminable discussions and the many conflicts and flare-ups that nearly prevented the conference from being held, not to mention such events as the acid diatribes of the Suslovs, Ponamarevs, and Bilaks against Eurocommunism, the public attacks of *Rude Pravo*, organ of the Czechoslovak Communist Party, against the French and Italian Communist parties, Moscow's attempts to create a Communist party of Spain (Lister) to counter the Communist party of Spain (Carrillo), the letter of the CPSU to all 'fraternal' parties denouncing 'the absence of a critical attitude on the part of our (French) Communist comrades towards the anti-communist inventions of the bourgeoisie'.

The second thesis, diametrically opposed to the first but equally false, claims that Eurocommunism means the end of special relations between the French, Italian, Spanish, British, or Swedish Communist parties and Moscow. According to some variants of this thesis, there are even signs of the dawn of the 'reunification of the western workers' movement'. If the French Communist Party abandons the dictatorship of the proletariat, certain people in France have asserted, then the historic scission of Tours becomes pointless. Moreover, it appears that Ceaucescu posed the question in similar terms during the East Berlin conference itself.

As against these theses, any correct interpretation of the East Berlin conference must begin from a phenomenon which has been developing since 1948 and which revolutionary Marxists call the crisis of Stalinism. This crisis has been advancing, now at an accelerated pace, now more slowly and hesitantly, under the impact of a series of contradictions, partially independent, partially linked together by a system of interconnected compartments. The crisis of Stalinism may be described as an ensemble of five crises:

*The crisis of Russian control over those Communist parties
that themselves hold state power, beginning with those parties
that seized power in a manner independent of the Soviet
bureaucracy, at the head of a genuine mass socialist revolution,
even if it was bureaucratically deformed from the outset (the
Yugoslav, Chinese, Vietnamese Communist parties).

*The crisis of Communist party control over the toiling
masses (especially the working class) in the capitalist countries. These masses are exhibiting rising combativity, anti-
capitalist consciousness, and clear distrust of bureaucratic
manipulation; they are now exposed to the still limited but
nonetheless expanding influence of a vanguard which is more
influential, effective, and strongly implanted in the class than at
any time during the past thirty years.

*The crisis of control of the Communist parties in power in
Eastern Europe and in China over the masses, whose political
combativity and activity are in the process of awakening. This
crisis can advance to the brink of genuine political revolution
(October–November 1956 in Hungary, the 1968 Prague spring
in Czechoslovakia, and, partially, the workers' uprisings in
Poland in 1956, 1970, and 1976).

*The crisis of control of the Soviet bureaucracy over Russian
society. This society is not yet characterized by an awakening
of activity and politicization among broad masses, but the
dialectic of de-Stalinization and the development of the *objective* conditions for political revolution have triggered an initial
confrontation between the bureaucracy and political dissidents, which adds a new dimension to the crisis of Stalinism.

*The crisis of relations between the Communist parties of
capitalist Europe and the Kremlin, which results from the
manner in which these parties have been compelled to assimilate de-Stalinization, the manner in which they are inserted
into the political life of their countries, and the manner in
which they are exposed to the contradictory pressures of the
imperialist bourgeoisie (and the general policy of peaceful coexistence) on the one hand and the rise of proletarian revolution
on the other hand.

Once this general complexity of the crisis of Stalinism is

grasped, the basic cause of the erroneous interpretations of the East Berlin conference advanced by so many commentators of the 'right' and the 'left' can be highlighted. *The Soviet bureaucracy must assess everything that is happening within the Communist parties not only in terms of its projects for détente and relations with imperialism, but also in terms of its relations with the toiling masses in the People's Democracies and the USSR itself.*

That is the rub: it is on this point that the dynamic triggered by those Communist parties that are taking their distance from the Kremlin threatens to make the Soviet bureaucracy more vulnerable, to contribute to the ripening of the political revolution.

### What the Kremlin can live with and what it fears

Of course, when Berlinguer, Marchais, and Carrillo renounce the dictatorship of the proletariat, declare themselves in favour of 'parliamentary and electoral roads to socialism', preach alliances with bourgeois parties, and assert that they will even respect the Atlantic Pact when they become ministers in coalition governments, the grimaces of the Kremlin are only for show. The practice of the Communist parties has long since moved in this direction on many occasions, more precisely since the French Communist Party voted for war credits and since the Seventh Congress of the Comintern in 1935. Theory has finally caught up with practice. In this regard, the reformist Communist parties have repeated the process of revision of Marxism initiated by the Social Democrats at the beginning of this century. The Kremlin is in fundamental agreement. Renounce the dictatorship of the proletariat so as to gain a few ministerial portfolios? An excellent deal! Many others of the same type were concluded under Stalin.[1]

---

[1] It suffices to cite a single document, the letter sent by Stalin, Molotov, and Voroshilov to Spanish Prime Minister Largo Caballero, dated 21 December 1936: 'The Spanish revolution is opening a road which is in many respects different from that travelled by Russia. This is due to specific conditions of a social, historical, and geographical order and to the exigencies of the international situation, different from that which confronted the Russian revolution. *It is highly possible that the parliamentary road may prove to be a process of revolutionary development more effective in Spain than it was in Russia.*' (Quoted

Does the Soviet bureaucracy fear that this time integration into the bourgeois state apparatus will go all the way and that in the event of conflict between the European bourgeoisie and the Kremlin, the mass Communist parties will stand squarely in the camp of their own bourgeoisies against the USSR? Most likely, the more the Communist parties recruit on a rightist basis and the more their ideological differences with the Social Democracy narrow, the more numerous will be the functionaries and bureaucrats who would be prepared to make this leap (there were already quite a few in August–September 1939, and there will be more next time). But for the Communist parties as a whole, to break completely with the USSR would be to lose their own identity, which would plunge them into an irreversible process of absorption by Social Democracy. Because of the important material base guaranteed them by their independent existence, it is not likely that the leaderships of these parties will go all the way in the process of social democratization and break with Moscow completely. The present relations with Moscow thus suit them nicely at bottom.

But when Berlinguer, Carrillo, and Marchais speak of a plurality of political parties in the 'building of socialism', when they call for trade-union independence of the state, when they say they are for the right to strike after the overthrow of capitalism, and when they denounce – still in an extremely hesitant and insufficient manner – the violations of and crimes against proletarian democracy and elementary human rights in the USSR and the People's Democracies, then, yes, the Soviet bureaucracy becomes indignant and panics. To see only the aspect of 'capitulation to the bourgeoisie' in Eurocommunism is to fail to understand that the Italian, French, Spanish, and Portuguese Communist parties are now evolving in a prerevolutionary situation, under the pressure of a working class that has understood some of the crimes of Stalinism and is

---

by Santiago Carrillo in *'Eurocommunism' and the State*, p. 157 of the Spanish edition.) Likewise, in 1951 the British Communist Party, with the clear approval of Stalin, adopted a draft programme on the 'British road to socialism' which explicitly identified with the parliamentary road. As of 1947, again with the support of Stalin, Harry Pollitt, the secretary-general of the British Communist Party, had abandoned the perspective of the dictatorship of the proletariat in that country.

firmly resolved to prevent their repetition by any means necessary. To see the pledges of the Berlinguers and Carrillos solely as concessions to the bourgeoisie is to fail to understand the *formidable anti-bureaucratic component* that accompanies the revolutionary upsurge in capitalist Europe. This was already visible in May 1968. It was powerfully revealed during the Portuguese revolutionary process and will be still more powerful in the rising Spanish, Italian, and French revolutions.

The Berlinguers, Marchaises, Carrillos and Cunhals do not like workers' councils any more than do the Brezhnevs, Husaks, or Kadars. But they cannot frontally oppose the emergence of these councils so long as we are in a rising phase of the revolutionary process in Southern Europe. They will be compelled to take evasive action rather than strike openly, to manoeuvre with such councils if they emerge rather than liquidate them. Moreover, this is what makes their role especially dangerous from the standpoint of the fate of the socialist revolution, for these manoeuvres are incontestably aimed at restabilizing the bourgeois order. But to be able to execute these manoeuvres during a period of revolutionary upsurge they must pay an ideological and political price. This is what sows discord within the bureaucracy and has a boomerang effect on the Kremlin. The action of the Polish workers against the price increases in 1976, a temporary success, can only augment the dangers the Kremlin now sees taking shape on various sides to its rule.

The leaders of the Communist parties of Western Europe are now defending some elementary principles of democratic liberties and human rights for the phase of construction of socialism *in their own countries*, while the Kremlin has not excommunicated them the way Tito and Mao were excommunicated. Thus, one can be an advocate of a multi-party system, genuine freedom of the press, and the real right of the workers to strike after the overthrow of capitalism without automatically being dubbed a 'frenzied anti-communist', 'agent of imperialism', or even 'Hitlerite–Trotskyist'. A question is thus immediately posed: suppose a Czechoslovak, East German, Polish, Bulgarian, Soviet (or Yugoslav!) Communist demanded application of these same principles in his or her country as well? Would he or she then be an 'anti-communist', a 'partisan of the restoration of capitalism', a 'slimy viper', or an 'anti-Soviet agitator' for having repeated what comrades Carrillo, Berlinguer, and Marchais proclaimed aloud in East Berlin?

According to information from generally well informed sources (although we have not yet been able to confirm the authenticity of the document), a letter drafted by a number of leaders of the Czechoslovak Communist Party eliminated by 'normalization' (although Dubcek himself is said not to have signed) was distributed to the participants in the East Berlin conference. This letter speaks of a 'faction' of Czechoslovak Communists who agree with the Eurocommunists, whose theses triumphed at the conference. Under these conditions, they call for an end to the repression to which they have been subjected and for the restoration of their rights, since their political line has already been rehabilitated in practice!

In order to escape this embarrassment, Pravda censored practically all the contentious passages in the speeches of the Eurocommunists. Other bureaucracies in Eastern Europe, however, were unable to take exactly the same approach as Moscow. The rulers of the German Democratic Republic, up to now among the most rigid and servile in their subordination to the Kremlin, were compelled to publish the speeches of Berlinguer and company *without a single cut*, for the simple reason that East German radio and television had already broadcast these speeches live and millions of people therefore already knew about them. Once again the revolutionary potential of instantaneous transmission of events at moments of great political and social crisis was verified, this time in East Europe.

Thus, the Kremlin's great fear is not so much that its influence over the Communist parties of West Europe will be further reduced. What it really fears are the effects Eurocommunism, and the concessions to the anti-bureaucratic sentiments of the masses it involves, can have on Moscow's control of the Communist parties and masses of East Europe and of the USSR itself. In its own way, the accentuation of the crisis of Stalinism by the East Berlin conference heralds the tremendous storm that will break over East Europe and the USSR, and even China, after the first victories of the proletarian revolution in Western Europe.

It could then be asked why the Kremlin finally yielded to Eurocommunism if the repercussions in its own sphere of influence threaten to be so negative. The answer is that the cure would have been worse than the disease. A new, third schism in the Stalinist universe, with the open excommunication of the Spanish, Italian, French, and British Communist parties would have unleashed even greater centrifugal forces in the People's Democracies and the USSR. Especially in the light of the great events now looming in Spain and Italy, such an excommunication would have left Moscow with no capacity to intervene in the political life of capitalist Europe and would have weakened it both with respect to imperialism and with respect to the least depoliticized sectors of the masses in the USSR and East Europe. Brezhnev thus opted for what was the lesser evil, from his own point of view.

**One Step Forward, Two Steps Back**

Does this mean that we should applaud the success incontestably won by Eurocommunism and polycentrism at the East Berlin conference? This would be to fall into a one-sided and opportunist assessment of this conference.

To begin with, the increased prestige won at low cost by Berlinguer and others in East Berlin increases their ability to manipulate and thereby betray both the rising proletarian revolution in the West and the rising political revolution in the East. Significant evidence of this is provided by the euphoric commentaries of R. Havemann (who is nevertheless an honest, critical, and left communist and a fierce opponent of the bureaucracy) published in the 5 July 1976 issue of the West German weekly *Der Spiegel*. Enthusiastic about the 'democratic' professions of faith of the Eurocommunist leaders and hoping for innumerable beneficial repercussions for opposition communists and toilers in the People's Democracies, Havemann fails to see the decisive concessions to the bourgeoisie. The abandonment of any struggle to destroy the bourgeois state apparatus and the suppression of the self-organization of the masses, which are inevitable consequences of attachment to bourgeois-parliamentary institutions, imply the risk of defeat of the socialist revolution in Southern Europe. The disastrous consequences this defeat would involve for the working class and for critical communists in East Europe are obvious.

Second, the ideological retreats of the leaders of the mass Communist parties in West Europe also unleash an objective dynamic. They have negative consequences both on Communist cadres and militants and on Communist workers. An entire generation of vanguard toilers who joined the Communist parties because they considered these parties the most combative and anti-capitalist *mass parties* will be systematically misled into confusing the democratic rights of the masses with bourgeois-democratic institutions, opposition to the bureaucratic dictatorship and the one-party regime with opposition to the power of workers' councils, and, possibly, 'austerity' imposed by a government of coalition with the bourgeoisie in order to restore the capitalist rate of profit with 'a stage in the transition to socialism'. This threatens to have extremely serious consequences during a decisive test of strength between the bourgeois state apparatus and the nascent organs of workers' power, such as occurred in Germany in 1918–19 or in Republican Spain in 1936–37.

All this points up the responsibility of revolutionary Marxists, who must combine utilization of the new breach opened in the Stalinist fortress by Eurocommunism with an intransigent struggle for an anti-capitalist revolutionary strategy in West Europe. Widening the breach also means putting pressure on the Eurocommunist leaders on the questions of proletarian democracy in their own bastions.

It is one thing to strut about like great democrats before large audiences in Rome, Paris, Madrid, or even East Berlin. It is quite another thing to practice proletarian democracy where one holds real power. It is the duty of revolutionary Socialists to call attention to this contradiction and to exploit it to the advantage of the working class.

What, then, are these great democrats waiting for to grant the right of tendency in the CGT (the French trade-union federation), the CGIL (the Italian union federation), or the national and regional coordinating bodies of the Workers' Commissions (in Spain), which they control? What are they waiting for to allow the election at all trade-union congresses of delegates elected in general assemblies, chosen on the basis of the presentation of reports and counterreports by each of the organizational tendencies and ideological currents present in the trade unions? What are they waiting for to introduce free-dom of the press in the trade unions, with discussion tribunes open to the various tendencies? Are they prepared once and for all to halt the bureaucratic practice of expelling revolutionary minorities from the unions? What are they waiting for to re-introduce the right of tendency in their own parties?

As for denunciation of the crimes committed by the Soviet bureaucracy against workers' democracy, the rights of the toilers, and human rights, their first timid protests cannot satisfy anyone. Some leaders of the Spanish Communist Party have declared that Trotsky was a great revolutionary.[2] We hail this confession as a step forward. It follows that these same leaders should publicly denounce the crimes committed by the GPU against Andres Nin, the leaders of the POUM, and the

---

[2] The following is an excerpt from a dialogue between Fernando Claudín, former member and leader of the Communist Party of Spain, and Manuel Azcárate, who is presently a member of the Executive Committee of this party. The dialogue appeared in the Spanish weekly *Triunfo* (3 July 1976) under the title 'Azcárate and Claudín Discuss Eurocommunism':

*Claudín:* 'In the USSR a bureaucratic system was created, whatever may be the historic and objective reasons for it. According to Trotsky, there were socialist structures on the one hand and a bureaucratic superstructure on the other (he called it a "deformed workers' state"), with the superstructure in contradiction to this socialist structure. But at the end of his life Trotsky himself affirmed that if it was transformed into a stable regime, this bureau-cratic class would be transformed into a ruling class, not in the sense of a body of private proprietors and a state subject to these proprietors, but rather because of the function its components would fulfill within the state and the party. For these reasons, it does not seem mechanical to me to characterize the USSR as a system that does not have socialist relations of production. On the contrary, it does seem to me mechanical to assert that on the one hand there are socialist relations of production and on the other hand the political and ideological superstructure is not socialist. This is one of the great problems that Marxists have studied and are discussing in order to arrive at the most scientific possible definition of the nature of the Soviet system, which cannot be assimilated to the western capitalist system, but in my opinion cannot be called a socialist system either. . . .

'You said that one of the important problems is the question of the relations between the party and the state. Why do the Communist Party of Spain and other Communist parties maintain that there can and should be various parties, both in the phase of transition and under socialist society? Is it a matter of tactics or is it a deeper question that corresponds to a requirement of social reality in these different phases of the march to socialism?'

*Azcárate:* 'It turns out that I am in greater agreement with Trotsky than you are. (Laughter.) This doesn't bother me. Trotsky was a great revolutionary, a great Marxist thinker. Regardless of the fact that some of his theories, especially during the last phase of his life, have proven erroneous, a good part of his

Trotskyists and left anarchists during the Spanish Civil War. But there is more. One ex-member of the Communist Party of Spain (or is he still a member?), Ramon Mercader, murdered the great revolutionary Trotsky. Today he lives in Moscow, decorated with a high Soviet medal, and whiles away his time writing a history of the Spanish Civil War (who knows, maybe it will be 'critical' too). The leaders of the Spanish, Italian, and French Communist parties should demand that this vile murderer be hauled before a tribunal formed by the international workers' movement. They should demand the public rehabilitation of Trotsky, Bukharin, Zinoviev, Kamenev, Rakovsky, and all the old Bolsheviks. They should demand that the works of these revolutionaries be freely published and distributed in the USSR and the People's Democracies. Otherwise their pledges of socialist democracy have little credibility.

The same applies to the advocates of 'liberal communism' in East Europe. It appears that Tito and Ceausescu now applaud Eurocommunism. But violations of proletarian democracy are on the rise in Yugoslavia (and violations of 'self-management' too – witness the affair of the Marxist professors of philosophy in Belgrade). The internal regime in Romania is one of the most repressive and Stalinist of all the People's Democracies. Let these gentlemen begin to bring their actions into conformity with their words; otherwise the plausibility of their 'democratic' and 'pluralistic' avowals will be undermined even further.

The East Berlin conference reflected a deepening not only of the crisis of Stalinism, but also of its ideological and theoretical

---

critique of the Soviet system has been shown to be valid with the passage of time, especially as concerns the bureaucratic deformation of the Soviet system. Without going into an exhaustive discussion about a theme around which investigation must continue, I would say that the Soviet system is a primitive socialist regime. This is a consequence of its extraordinarily low starting point, the international conditions under which it arose, and a series of enormous deformations, of which Stalinism is the expression, which froze it in this primitive state. I agree that there is an enormous distance between Soviet reality and our socialist ideal. . . . As for our conception of the march to socialism, it must be based on a plurality of parties, both socialist parties and parties which are enemies of socialism, which represent sectors that do not agree with socialism but which, in our view, will be defeated politically because the parties that support socialism will be stronger. Neither in Marx nor in Lenin is there the idea that socialism means one party.'

bankruptcy. At a time when the international capitalist system is going through its most serious crisis since the Second World War, the Communist parties of Europe are incapable of drawing any of the indicated conclusions for the workers of Europe and the world. They have nothing to offer but time-worn neo-Keynesian palliatives, which the bourgeoisie itself is now questioning as less and less effective. At a time when the internationalization of productive forces and class conflict is proceeding at an unprecedented pace, the Communist parties pride themselves on an increasingly pronounced nationalist retreat.

As against this bankruptcy, the Fourth International, legitimate heir of communism and the Communist International, embodies living Marxist thought, proletarian internationalism, and the road to Socialist revolution. With its still weak and very insufficient forces relative to the gigantic tasks of our epoch – but forces that are nevertheless growing rapidly – the Fourth International says to the proletarians of Europe and the world: the combined crisis of capitalism and Stalinism facilitates the accomplishment of your historic task. Forward to the socialist revolution, to the overthrow of the reign of capital, to the democratic power of workers' councils, to the Socialist United States of Europe and the World!

Forty years ago, Trotsky wrote: 'Many things suggest that the disintegration of the Comintern, which has no direct support in the GPU, will precede the fall of the Bonapartist clique and the entire thermidorian bureaucracy in general' (*Transitional Programme*). When Tito, paraphrasing Berlinguer, said of the East Berlin conference that it 'has no past and no future', he confirmed Trotsky's prediction in his own way. In Warsaw it is being murmured that Stalin died for the third time in East Berlin, but that he is not yet dead for good. The victory of the proletarian revolution in Europe will bury him definitively.

# 4
# A New Approach to Stalinism

Of all the important Communist parties of Europe, the French
Communist Party (PCF) delayed the longest in assimilating
de-Stalinization. The tradition of Maurice Thorez had something to do with this, for the secretary-general of the PCF had
long proudly worn the label 'Stalinist' as a 'badge of honour'.[1]
But the law of uneven development holds sway in the realm of
ideas, just as it does in all fields of history. With his book
*L'Histoire du Phénomène Stalinien*, Jean Elleinstein leaps
beyond the criticisms of Stalinism that had previously been
made by the Italian, Belgian, British, and Swedish Communist
Parties, not to mention the Portuguese or West German parties.

The point of departure for Elleinstein – who is, incidentally,
the author of a four-volume history of the USSR[2] which does
not deal with the 'Stalinist phenomenon' at all – is the notorious
insufficiency of the theory of the 'cult of the personality' as an
'explanation' of the 'violations of socialist legality' that cost
the lives of millions of people, among them probably more
communists than were massacred by Hitler. The 'personality
cult' is, after all, an essentially subjective phenomenon: the
personality of Stalin, the weight he occupied in the leadership

[1] Thus, right up to his death Thorez insisted on referring to Khrushchev's
secret report to the Twentieth Congress of the Communist Party of the Soviet
Union in 1956 as 'the alleged Khrushchev report'. In her stirring memoirs (*La
Nostalgie n'est plus ce qu'elle était*, Paris, 1976, pp. 152–59, 169–73, 209–11),
Simone Signoret reveals the tragi-comic contradictions to which this game of
hide-and-seek with history led. She gives an account of the preparations,
vicissitudes, and follow-up of her trip to Moscow in November–December 1956,
during which she had a meeting with the leaders of the CPSU, including
Khrushchev, who spoke at length about his 'alleged report'.

[2] Jean Elleinstein, *Histoire de l'URSS*, Paris.

of the Communist Party of the Soviet Union, his personal dictatorship, the methods by which he established and consolidated it, and so on.

Innumerable personalities within the Communist parties themselves have correctly denounced the scientifically inadequate and profoundly anti-Marxist character of such an explanation. Many anti-Stalinist communist currents, beginning with the Fourth International, had made this same point as early as February 1956, when Khrushchev presented his secret report.

Elleinstein's book, then, constitutes an effort to surpass this subjectivist interpretation of history and to discover a more materialist explanation, one which integrates the 'Stalinist phenomenon' into a general historical context. But a contradiction arises immediately. When Elleinstein speaks of the 'Stalinist phenomenon' instead of the 'personality cult', doesn't he fall into the very mistake he is criticizing? The fact is that the weight of Stalin's personality is decisive throughout the book. Elleinstein strives to explain how phenomena like the stifling of internal democracy in the party and the Comintern, the growing weight of the secret police (GPU, NKVD) in society, the massive terror used as a method of 'resolving' social and political contradictions, the successive purges and extermination campaigns, generalized by Stalin throughout Soviet society, emerged and became dominant. But in the final analysis, he returns to the same point of departure: Why did *Stalin* resort to these measures? Or, to put it another way (but the distinction is slight), why did the central leadership of the party, which had merged with the central leadership of the state and was increasingly reduced to the person of Stalin, supported by his 'most faithful lieutenants', Molotov, Kaganovich, and Voroshilov, resort to them? We have scarcely left the terrain of subjectivism.

The theoretical and political consequences of this methodological error are evident. It is also probable that they are related to the motivations of the author, the reason why he opted for this method rather than another, although this does not mean that he is guilty of bad faith.

If one speaks of the 'Stalinist phenomenon', one can continue to designate the USSR as a socialist country and treat this 'degeneration' as something which falls within the 'socialist universe' but does not flow from it structurally. One can thus denounce Stalinism while simultaneously maintaining special links with the Soviet Union and its present leadership. One can, contrary to all evidence, continue to hope for the application of de-Stalinization from above, self-reform of the dictatorship by the leaders of the Kremlin itself. One can believe that the one-party system is ineluctable in the USSR today – 'The single party in the USSR was an inevitable fact produced by a history which we have studied and which was scarcely possible to reverse. Political democracy could develop only on the basis of this reality of the single, leading party' (p. 243)[3] – but still judge that Stalinism has disappeared, or is in the process of disappearing, and that only a few 'remnants' of it, undoubtedly disagreeable but less and less serious, persist in the Soviet Union. But the one-party system is obviously not suited to 'socialism in the colours of France'.

It is immediately obvious that this is a position which perfectly suits the team around Georges Marchais. The latter is striving, by an increasingly difficult balancing act, to appear super-democratic in France while refusing to go all the way in criticizing the bureaucratic dictatorship in the USSR, so as not to burn its bridges to the 'fraternal parties' of the East. But it is also evident that this balancing act cannot continue indefinitely. Elleinstein's position is only a transitory one. Santiago Carrillo has gone much further.[4] Where Elleinstein has fired a shot at the edifice of Stalinist orthodoxy, Carrillo has dropped a bomb.

One of the consequences of this subjectivism which Elleinstein's analysis has not completely overcome is that he remains a prisoner of an entire conceptual mythology directly inherited from Stalin, the revisionist character of which relative to Marxism and the doctrine of Lenin has been repeatedly demonstrated. Socialism is identified solely with the elimination of private property in the means of production and not with the disappearance of social classes. The survival of market

---

[3] All references to Elleinstein's book are from: Elleinstein, *Histoire du Phénomène Stalinien*, Paris, 1975.
[4] See Chapter Five of the present book, devoted to the work of Santiago Carrillo, *'Eurocommunism' and the State*.

and monetary categories under socialism is proclaimed as inevitable, and Marx's conceptions to the contrary are peremptorily dismissed as 'utopian'. Since social classes survive under socialism, so does the state. Moreover, Elleinstein thoughtlessly repeats Stalin's argument that the survival of the state 'under socialism' is caused by the pressure of the 'foreign enemy'. A classless society with a high degree of social cohesion and technological superiority over its capitalist surroundings would nevertheless have no need for a *special organ of coercion against its own citizens* to defend itself against the foreign enemy. For Marxism the state is just such an organ of coercion.

All these contradictions dissolve the moment we acknowledge that socialism has not at all been achieved in the USSR, that there is a transitional period between capitalism and socialism during which social classes and the state survive, along with market categories, at least partially. The bureaucratic degeneration is rooted in the contradictions that arise in such a transitional society, and not in the 'contradictions of socialism'.

This is precisely the principal theoretical difficulty Elleinstein must confront, and which he fails to solve: *how can the 'Stalinist phenomenon' be limited essentially to the domain of the superstructure?*

Granted, Elleinstein is correct when he answers his critics in advance[5] by noting that the same social infrastructure can give rise to very different superstructures – ideological systems, *forms* of state and government (although all are linked by certain common features).

Thus, the same capitalist infrastructure gave rise to state forms as different as the Nazi Third Reich, the Weimar Republic, and the Bonn republic, to dominant ideological systems as different as the doctrine of equality of all men before the law and the doctrine of the racial superiority of the Aryans. There is no reason for a Marxist to suppose that it is 'inadmissible' for a given infrastructure – that of the epoch of transition from

---

[5] Particularly Professor Steigerwald, major theoretician of the West German Communist Party, who wrote a long critique of Elleinstein's book in the September 1977 issue of the magazine *Marxistische Blätter*.

capitalism to socialism – to give rise to superstructures as different as one of exemplary workers democracy and one of Stalinist totalitarianism.

But Elleinstein goes a step further when he affirms: 'The key to understanding the Stalinist phenomenon will be found in the study of the state' (p. 230). Not only is this inconsistent from a theoretical standpoint, it also does not conform to the facts (some of them revealed, some still hidden, in his own book).

*In the final analysis*, the various superstructures that may arise from the same social base result from the contradictions and transformations of the base itself. The key to the superstructure is never found in the superstructure itself; to suppose that it is means to break with historical materialism. The transition from the Weimar Republic to the Nazi dictatorship cannot be explained exclusively or essentially as a political phenomenon. It had deeper socio-economic roots.

As for the facts, they teach us that the 'Stalinist phenomenon' can in no way be reduced to superstructural phenomena like state terror, the one-man dictatorship, the all-powerful police, or ideological dogmatism. These phenomena are manifestly enmeshed in a totality of *characteristic social relations and relations of production*: the lack of self-management of the producers; lack of self-administration of citizens or control by them over the political and economic administrative system; bureaucratically centralized planning; appropriation and distribution of the social surplus-product by the state outside any control by the producers; the system of a single, omnipotent director in each factory; maintenance of the hierarchical structure of the factories; a system of remuneration assuring privileges to functionaries and subjecting a good part of the proletariat to the horrors of piece-work. How can a Marxist claim that the key to the explanation of all these phenomena is to be found solely at the level of the state and the social superstructure, without turning historical materialism on its head?

Another consequence of unsurmounted subjectivism in Elleinstein's interpretation of the history of the USSR is a dangerous drift towards ideologistic positions which regard this or that 'error' of Lenin and the Bolsheviks as 'primarily responsible' for Stalinism. In the past, Stalinism and Leninism were identified in a positive sense. Now the 'germs' of everything reprehensible in Stalinism are discovered to have dated from the October Revolution itself. Elleinstein does not say this explicitly, but he strongly insists on the excessive weight of the Cheka as early as 1921, on the fact that as of that year 'a certain number of institutions, structures, and mechanisms were established which were to persist beyond the disappearance of the necessities and circumstances that had given rise to them' (p. 25). He returns to the same point in his conclusions (p. 230): 'The dictatorship was a double-edged sword'. The dictatorship was both necessary and the bearer of Stalinism.

The kernel of truth in this reasoning is banal and tautological. If there had not been a certain bureaucracy from the outset, it would not have been able to monopolize power. If there had not been a state, it could not have degenerated. This sort of reasoning does not take us very far. One may likewise say that if there had not been universal suffrage in Germany, Hitler would never have got 12 million votes. But must one conclude from this that the 'germs' of Nazism are to be found in universal suffrage and that without this there would have been no fascism?

The real question raised by the opponents of communism and the October Revolution, one to which Elleinstein does not respond, is whether the dictatorship of the proletariat *inevitably* leads to the dictatorship of the bureaucracy, whether the emergency measures taken by the Bolsheviks against the counter-revolutionary terror inevitably *had to lead* to the Stalinist terror, whether Stalinism is the legitimate offspring of Leninism. If we answer this question, 'No, a thousand times no', it is not solely on the basis of a coherent theoretical interpretation of everything that has occurred in the USSR and on a world scale since 1917. It is also and primarily on the basis of an historical fact which emerges from Elleinstein's book itself: to establish his dictatorship, Stalin had to destroy the party of Lenin physically. The one 'produced' the other only in the sense that life 'produces' death: as its own negation.

## From Subjectivism to Objectivism

Paradoxically, Elleinstein's failure to overcome the after-effects of the subjectivist interpretation of the 'Stalinist phenomenon' leads him to combine a fundamentally subjectivist approach with a mass of interpretations of an 'objectivist' type. Stalinism is said to be 'the product of circumstances': the barbarous past of Russia; the pressure of foreign aggression (or the threat of aggression); the need for a forced-march industrialization of the country; the weight of the peasantry in Russian society; the numerical and cultural weakness of the proletariat; the lack of democratic traditions. All this leads to a famous formula, first used by Brandler-Thalheimer in Germany,[6] later partially taken up by Isaac Deutscher, and now appropriated by a whole wing of Eurocommunist leaders: 'a socialist economy and society were born of the October Revolution and of Stalin's policy. . . . At the same time, totalitarian methods were used' (p. 88). Stalin 'developed socialism, even though he proceeded in a despotic manner' (p. 116). Brandler had been even clearer and more concise: Stalinism is the construction of socialism through barbaric means.

At the root of this reasoning lies an implied axiom: socialism equals the construction of an economy without private property in the means of production (and all its civilizing effects). If this definition is accepted, the rest flows logically. But the definition is false and non-Marxist. The elimination of private property in the means of production is a *necessary but not sufficient precondition* for the construction of socialism, which means a classless society. A great number of additional preconditions are also necessary: revolution in the relations of production; elevation of the level of consciousness, self-confidence, and capacity for self-administration of the labouring masses; transformation of customs, mores, and culture; flowering of the human personality of the producers; progres-

---

[6] Heinrich Brandler was the political leader and August Thalheimer the major theoretician of the right wing of the German Communist Party. This wing led the party during the years 1922–23. Removed from the leadership after the failure of the 'German October' of 1923, the Brandlerites were expelled from the Communist International in 1928. They maintained an international oppositional current during the 1930s and an independent communist opposition in Germany during the 1940s and 1950s. They were always characterized by a highly conciliatory attitude toward Stalin (even approving of the first Moscow trial!). Brandler had some influence on Isaac Deutscher. The last surviving Brandlerite is our friend Professor Wolfgang Abendroth. It is not astonishing that he has hailed the publication of Elleinstein's book enthusiastically.

sive equalization of living conditions and access to information and culture on a world scale.

Considered from this standpoint, the barbaric means not only failed to bring the socialist goal closer, they moved it enormously further off. The formula 'construct socialism by barbaric means' is just as absurd to a Marxist as the formula 'learn to play the piano by amputating the left hand' would be to a musician.

The empirical weakness of this objectivist, fatalistic, and apologetic interpretation ('we' have been attracted to Stalin so long because we saw the socialist achievements and therefore closed our eyes to the barbaric means) lies in its abstract character. When the interpretation is held up against *precise facts*, it explains nothing at all. Was the Comintern policy that allowed Hitler to take power 'the product of the objective circumstances of Russia'? Was it inevitable in the 'construction of socialism'? Was forced collectivization inevitable? Did it serve the construction of socialism? What about the frightful waste of material resources which resulted from the combination of bureaucratically centralized planning and the system of single managers and individual profitability of factories? Was this the product of 'Russia's barbarous past'? Did it serve the construction of socialism? The list could be extended at will. The objectivist interpretation does not succeed in *explaining* what happened in the USSR any more than the subjectivist interpretation. The combination of the two takes us barely beyond the level of common-place observations.

## The Social Key to the Explanation of the 'Stalinist Phenomenon'

All these insufficiencies and contradictions disappear the moment one introduces a *decisive intermediary link* in the chain of the reasoning: *a social force to whose interests* all the 'deviations', 'errors', and 'crimes' of Stalinism in the final analysis correspond: the Soviet bureaucracy.

Stalinism is neither a 'deformation of the socialist state' nor the sum of the 'totalitarian institutions and practices' used to 'construct socialism by barbaric means'. Stalinism is the totality of political institutions, structures of rule, methods of

governing and planning which secure the monopoly of power
of the Soviet bureaucracy and which safeguard its privileges,
in a society of transition from capitalism to socialism. This is
the only explanation of the Stalinist phenomenon that conforms to the method of historical materialism and is capable of
accounting for *the totality* of the contradictory aspects of this
phenomenon.[7]

Elleinstein does not deny the 'bureaucratic phenomenon' in
the USSR. On occasion he even speaks of the 'bureaucracy' (see
especially pp. 92–93). But in general he does not attribute it the
importance it deserves in the explanation of the degeneration
of the USSR. Instead he quickly posits a facile dilemma, which
is not devoid of bad faith for someone as well-read as Elleinstein:[8] either the bureaucracy is a class, or else it is not a *social*
layer (pp. 198–200). He goes so far as to deny the identification
between functionaries and bureaucrats (p. 200) and reduces
bureaucracy to 'bureaucratism' (a concept invented by Stalin
himself). In other words, once again he falls into a subjectivist
interpretation: 'It is true that the Stalinist phenomenon is
bureaucratic, but this means that the role of the bureaux holds
sway over that of the masses, that administrative decision-
making holds sway over economic incentive' (p. 200). No, the
bureaucracy is indeed a well-defined social group: all those who
hold the monopoly of administrative power in the USSR, who
appropriate significant privileges on this basis, and who
ferociously defend this monopoly and these privileges.

It is true that this bureaucracy is not a class. But Marxist
sociology and the historical materialist interpretation of
societies include more than the notion of social classes alone.
There are also fractions of social classes. There are social
layers. There are castes. The bureaucracy belongs to just this
category, as in another way do the scribes and mandarins in

[7] This idea is developed in detail in Trotsky's *The Revolution Betrayed*, in
Trotsky's other writings on the USSR, in the documents of the Fourth International, and in many writings of the present author (particularly 'Ten Theses
on Transitional Society Between Capitalism and Socialism').

[8] Elleinstein polemicizes against 'Trotskyists' who upheld the idea that the
bureaucracy is a class, in particular citing James Burnham and Bruno Rizzi.
He forgets to add that these authors broke with Trotskyism in formulating this
thesis. With similar logic one could assert that the thesis of the new bureaucratic class was formulated by the 'Stalinist' Milovan Djilas.

the Asiatic mode of production.

We said that the social category of the bureaucracy is the key to explaining and understanding 'the Stalinist phenomenon'. For, once we introduce it into the analysis of the evolution of the USSR since 1923, we can see that the great zigzags of economic and international policy, the general features of the denatured state institutions in the USSR (of the dictatorship of the proletariat deformed into the despotic dictatorship of Stalin and then into a collegial dictatorship) *correspond to the social interests of this crystallized layer*, to its contradictory character and situation.

We then also understand why De-Stalinization is not and could not be a 'self-reform of the bureaucracy', the abolition of its monopoly of power and privileges from above, but is simply an *adaptation* of its *methods* of power to modified objective and subjective circumstances. We shall then realize that there will be no socialist democracy in the USSR without a political revolution.

All this is 'Trotskyism'. Elleinstein sprinkles his work with a primitive anti-Trotskyism directly inherited from his Stalinist past.[9] But there is no way to approach the 'Stalinist phenomenon' in a scientific, that is to say Marxist, manner without drawing from the wells of Trotskyism.

[9] See, for example, page 96, where Elleinstein tries to make some use of Trotsky against Trotskyism of 1975, which 'is characterized by its anti-Sovietism and regressive and dogmatic strategy'. Ex-Stalinists of the Elleinstein variety singularly lack a sense of decency in speaking of Trotskyists, whom they slandered and would have willingly sent to Gulag for decades. Now that they have changed their spots, they go so far as to try to make their former victims share responsibility with their own executioners. How much more worthy are the more dignified commentaries of Leopold Trepper, the hero of the Red Orchestra, who wrote in his autobiography: 'But who protested at that time? Who rose up to cry out disgust? The Trotskyists can claim this honour. Like their leader, who paid for his obstinacy with a blow from an ice-axe, they fought Stalinism totally, and they stood alone. By the time of the great purges, they could cry out their revolt only in the frozen vastness, where they had been dragged the better to exterminate them. Their conduct in the camps was dignified and even exemplary. But their voices were lost in the tundra.

'Today the Trotskyists have the right to accuse those who formerly cried for blood with the wolves. Let them not forget, however, that they had an immense advantage over us, for they had a coherent political system that could replace Stalinism and to which they could cling in the profound anguish of the revolution betrayed. They did not "confess", for they knew that their confessions would serve neither the party nor socialism' (Leopold Trepper, *Le Grand Jeu*, Paris, 1975, p. 64).

# 5

# Bombshell from Carrillo

## Santiago Carrillo and the Nature of the USSR

Santiago Carrillo, the secretary general of the Communist Party of Spain, has recently published a book called *'Euro-comunismo' y Estado ('Eurocommunism' and the State)*. The book represents the clearest reflection to date of all the contradictions of Eurocommunism.

## Revisionism

We will not spend much time on the explicit manner in which Santiago Carrillo adopts the neo-reformist revisionism of his party. Nothing is lacking: criticism of the 'excessive' parts of Lenin's *State and Revolution*; references to the famous 1895 preface by Engels to Marx's book *Class Struggles in France 1848–1850*, identical to those used by Bernstein and Kautsky in their polemics against the Bolsheviks (without mentioning the fact that the text had been distorted by the Social Democracy and that Engels himself protested against its falsification); theoretical 'extension' of the 'tactic' of the Popular Front and 'Resistance'; sophisms about the class 'aspects' of the state apparatus and other 'aspects' which are supposedly not class-based; and many others.

What must be stressed is that Carrillo, true to himself, clearly formulates the major theoretical and analytical premises of reformism: the revolution is *impossible* in the industrialized capitalist countries. A comprehensive confrontation with the bourgeoisie and its apparatus of repression must be avoided at all costs, otherwise bloody defeat is *inevitable*: 'The question is whether a democratic transformation of the military mentality can be obtained as a consequence of a social crisis produced by factors other than those of war. If the answer were no, it would be necessary to renounce socialism and resign oneself eternally to the politico-social status quo, or else claim to desire, dementedly, the unleashing of a war' (p. 83).

The idea that a revolutionary crisis can *disintegrate* and progressively *paralyze* the military-repressive apparatus of the bourgeoisie if the proletariat acts resolutely, audaciously, taking the necessary initiatives and mobilizing its enormous strength as a whole (the immense majority of the nation in almost all Western countries) under the leadership of a revolutionary party which is up to its task, is not even considered, let alone refuted.

Equally clear is the manner in which Carrillo exhibits the process of social democratization of his party. It is true that he begins by asserting: 'There can be no confusion between Eurocommunism and Social Democracy in the realm of ideology, at least Social Democracy as it has defined itself up to now. What is vulgarly called "Eurocommunism" proposes to *transform* capitalist society and not to *administer* it, to elaborate a socialist alternative to the system of state monopoly capitalism and not to integrate itself into this system and act as one of its alternative governments' (p. 132).

Let us note that Carrillo does not say *overthrow* capitalism, but *transform* it, which implies progressive, gradual transformation. Now this is the very definition the pre-1914 Social Democratic reformist revisionists gave to their strategy, which Kautsky took up again after 1921. Without noticing it, even when he tries to set himself off from the Social Democracy *today*, Carrillo bases himself on the theoretical acquisitions of *classical* Social Democracy. We have never said otherwise: the process of social democratization is transforming the Western Communist parties (and some others) into classical Social Democratic parties and not into Social Democratic parties like those of Schmidt or Wilson-Callaghan.

But carried away by the ardour of his reasoning, Carrillo goes further and contradicts on page 133 what he has just said on page 132. There we read: 'As far as we Communists are concerned, we take full responsibility for our history, with all its successes, errors, and deficiencies; we do not renounce it or convert it into a triumphalist legend, but approach it in a critical fashion. If the Socialist and Social Democratic parties adopt a similar attitude more or less openly (sometimes political parties make self-criticisms by correcting their strategy and tactics much more than their historical analysis, at least initially), then there is no reason not to overcome the split of the 1920s and move to a convergence based on scientific socialism and democracy' (p. 133).

It couldn't be clearer! The trouble is that 'scientific socialism' confirms the lessons of more than a century of class struggle in the West. Periodically, comprehensive and head-on confrontations between the proletariat and the bourgeoisie are *inevitable*, not as a result of 'adventurism' or of the 'ultraleftist excesses' of this or that 'theoretician', ideologue, or minority group of 'provocateurs', but *as a result of the exacerbation of the internal contradictions of the capitalist system.* Those who attempt, out of fear of this comprehensive and head-on confrontation or for whatever tactical or strategic reasons, to curb and fragment the mobilization of the proletariat do not prepare it for the ineluctable confrontation, but disarm it politically and materially; they do not at all avert the test of strength, nor do they salvage 'peace' and 'democracy'. They simply assure the victory – most often violent and bloody – of the bourgeoisie.

In this sense, the doctrine of Eurocommunism is a doctrine of demobilization and defeat of the European proletariat on the eve of the great pre-revolutionary explosions that are now looming, above all in Southern Europe. It must be vigorously fought if the breakthrough of the socialist revolution in West Europe is to be assured.

### Criticism of the Forms of Power in the USSR

Nevertheless, we do not want to centre our commentary on Carrillo's book on this aspect of Eurocommunism. For the book opens a new stage in the development of the 'second' aspect of Eurocommunism. In it, Carrillo, much more than any other Western Communist leader, moves from episodic and local criticisms of this or that action of the Kremlin leaders and their associates in East Europe to a *systematic critique of the Soviet bureaucracy and the forms of power in the USSR.* In this respect it is no exaggeration to speak of a genuinely sensational literary event which gives important weapons to the anti-bureaucratic struggle in the Eastern bloc and to the anti-Stalinist struggle of revolutionary Marxism in the rest of the world. Revolutionary Marxists should carefully study the relevant passages of Carrillo's book and use them systematically in discussions with Communist party militants, especially in countries in which the critical attitude toward the Soviet bureaucracy still lags well behind that of Santiago Carrillo.

Let us stress some of the most positive aspects of this second part of Carrillo's book.

*On at least two occasions, Carrillo explicitly questions the theory of socialism in one country (pp. 207, 210). It is true that his rejection of this theory is somewhat weakened by an argument tainted by 'idealism': since Stalin and the other leaders of the CPSU opted for 'construction of complete socialism in one country', they were compelled to 'accelerate the pace' and to intensify the drive for accumulation against the consumption of the masses; hence the repression, the lack of democracy, and so on. This idealism has an obvious objectivist counterpart: 'Under the concrete historical conditions, there was no other way out'. We reject both aspects of this reasoning as contrary to Marxism. The Stalinist degeneration was not a result of an ideological choice, nor was it the automatic product of objective conditions. It corresponded to the *interests* of a given social layer, the Soviet bureaucracy. It resulted from the *political victory* of this layer over its opponents.

Even with this reservation, however, it is nonetheless true that the first explicit mention by a leader of a mass Communist Party in the West of the theory of socialism in one country as the cause of the bureaucratic degeneration of the USSR represents a formidable historic vindication of Trotsky and Trotskyism. Fifty years after the fact, it legitimizes the historic struggle of our Soviet comrades, those men and women of iron who were the Bolshevik-Leninist militants of the USSR. It confirms what we have never doubted: history will rehabilitate them all, from the most prestigious leader to the anonymous worker, all murdered by Stalin, and will honour them as giants of lucidity, perseverence, and fidelity to the proletarian cause. In the most difficult conditions in which a vanguard has ever been placed in history, they waged an apparently hopeless fight which in the end permitted the communist programme and banner to be saved, which made possible the new rise of conscious struggle for the world socialist revolution.

*Carrillo explicitly treats the Soviet bureaucracy as a privileged social *stratum* (pp. 199, 206) which is not a social class but does hold a monopoly of power at all levels of social life (p. 208). Further, he adds that this is a genuine phenomenon of 'degeneration' (p. 115) and speaks of the 'horrors of Stalinism' (p. 200). Khrushchev told Simone Signoret, according to her memoirs, that 12 million died under Stalin.

*Carrillo acknowledges that there is no workers' democracy in the USSR, in other words, that the *proletariat*, and not merely the big bourgeoisie and petty-bourgeoisie, has been deprived of the essence of its political rights (pp. 201–202).

*Carrillo admits that the dictatorship of the bureaucracy has formal features in common with fascism and totalitarianism, although in substance it clearly differs from them (especially pp. 199–200). These are the same terms Trotsky and our movement have used for forty years; they, along with terms like 'privileged bureaucratic layer' and 'bureaucratic degeneration', have obviously been borrowed from Trotsky and Trotskyism.

*Carrillo explicitly rehabilitates Trotsky and Trotskyism as the representatives of a current of the workers' movement which was correct on some points (pp. 149–150), although he asserts that this current must be criticized. (He is particularly virulent, not surprisingly, against the Trotskyist critique of the Popular Front policy.) He completely rehabilitates Andres Nin against the slanderous accusations made against him by the Spanish Communist Party and the Communist International and calls his murder 'an abominable and unjustifiable act' (p. 152).

*Finally, and this is not the smallest merit of this theoretical systematization, Carrillo admits that the hopes of self-reform of the bureaucracy raised by the 20th congress of the Communist Party of the Soviet Union were illusory (p. 201) and that the bureaucracy has become practically 'irremovable' (p. 199).

## Santiago Carrillo's Contradictions

But while progress towards a Marxist analysis of the state and Soviet society, towards an *explanation* of the 'Stalinist pheno-menon' in scientific – that is, historical materialist – terms, is evident in *'Eurocommunism' and the State*, the contradictions nonetheless remain many and glaring.

1. In spite of his definition of the social character of the bureaucracy as a privileged layer, Carrillo does not clearly locate the material base of these privileges: the monopoly of administration (of management) of the means of production and of social surplus product in the hands of this bureaucracy. He therefore does not formulate the alternative: democratic management of the means of production and the social surplus product, of the whole of the socialist and planned economy, by the associated producers, by a freely and democratically elected congress of workers' councils.

2. In spite of the fact that he strongly insists on the 'political pluralism' of the West, in spite of his references to 'workers' democracy' for the USSR, there is no precise reference to the necessity of abolishing the one-party system in the USSR, the People's Democracies, the People's Republic of China, and the other workers' states. There is no admission that workers' democracy is impossible without a system of multiple political parties, without the enjoyment of *political* and civil rights for all under the dictatorship of the proletariat (including the right to strike and the right to an opposition press).

3. In spite of the fact that the notion of self-reform of the bureaucracy is rejected, that the bureaucracy is analyzed as practically irremovable, that the question of whether the present form of power in the USSR has become a brake on the development of productive forces and of 'genuine workers' democracy' is raised (p. 208), Carrillo nowhere formulates the obvious conclusion: the necessity for a *political revolution* to overthrow the bureaucratic dictatorship.

4. In spite of the fact that he denounces this dictatorship in severe terms, nowhere does he formulate the obvious alterna-tive: not a return to bourgeois parliamentarism (which he does not in fact propose), but the institutionalization of the power of the toilers, of freely and democratically elected workers'

councils (soviets), with the genuine right to revoke delegates, with real reduction in the incomes of all those who exercise power to the wages of a skilled worker.

5. In spite of his insistence on 'workers' democracy', Carrillo is more than discreet about the obvious implications of this democracy *for the workers' movement of the capitalist countries*, to begin with his own party and the trade-union movement within which it plays a leading role: acceptance of the right of tendencies; return to the democratic centralism of the Leninist era, with full freedom of discussion within all workers' organizations, including public discussions; abandonment and rejection of all practices of bureaucratic manipulation, which run counter to the procedures of workers' democracy.

6. In spite of his explicit rejection of the theory of 'socialism in one country', Carrillo does not at all draw the logical conclusion: an orientation towards the international socialist revolution, rejection of 'national communism', abandonment of all utopias of 'socialist transformation' of the 'Spanish state' alone, orientation towards a Socialist United States of Europe and the World, or necessity for a new mass Communist International not beholden to any state, as an authentic expression of the interests of the international proletariat, and the exploited and oppressed of the entire world.

It is on these contradictions and others which we have not mentioned here that our comrades should centre their criticism in fraternal discussions with the militants of the 'advancing wing' of Eurocommunism. But they will not separate these criticisms from their challenge to the Eurocommunist 'project' as a whole – that is, primarily its reformist strategy, which objectively serves the bourgeoisie and helps to save the capitalist system from a mounting revolutionary crisis. They will not make this separation because there is an obvious link between the contradictions of Santiago Carrillo and his political project. These contradictions are not matters of chance, nor are they the result of deficiencies of 'pure reason'. They correspond to the very nature of the party and leadership that has produced them.

The first four contradictions correspond to the desire not to break definitively and irrevocably with the Soviet bureaucracy. Eurocommunism is a product of the crisis of Stalinism. It has not overcome this crisis, either in a bourgeois or proletarian direction. The three final contradictions correspond to the inability of the Eurocommunist leaders to ride the tiger of workers' democracy (not to mention that of workers' power), while still seeking to remain within the confines of the bourgeois state and the power of capital. The attempt to do so is a dangerous exercise during a period of revolutionary upsurge of mass struggles.

But while these contradictions cannot be overcome by the Eurocommunist leaders, they can be overcome by the militants of these parties. It is towards these militants that we must now turn for an increasingly promising dialogue. Carrillo's book offers every revolutionary powerful ammunition in this regard.

# 6
# The Soviet Response

It was to be expected that the Soviet bureaucracy could not allow the severe critique of the structures of power in the USSR and the People's Democracies developed by Santiago Carrillo in his *'Eurocommunism' and the State* to go unanswered. Nor is the violence of the response, published in the Moscow weekly *New Times* in July 1977, surprising.

The article, entitled *Against the Interests of Peace and Socialism in Europe*, accuses Carrillo of aiding 'the splitting strategy of imperialism and international Social Democracy', of 'counterposing the Communist parties of the European capitalist countries to the Communist parties of the socialist countries', of 'denigrating real socialism, that is, the countries which have already created a new society, the Soviet Union in the first place', of renouncing 'proletarian internationalism, and first of all friendship with the Soviet Union and the other countries of socialism'. The indictment culminates with the following accusation:

'There is no doubt that the interpretation of "Eurocommunism" presented by S. Carrillo corresponds exclusively to the interests of imperialism, the forces of aggression and reaction. Putting it into practice would involve grave consequences, which the Communists of the countries of capital, including Spain itself, would be the first to suffer. Finally, implementing it in practice would lead to a split in the international communist movement, which is the objective to which the reactionary imperialist forces have been aspiring for two decades' (p. 11).

## A Manifest Slander

We will not spend much time on the 'ideological' content of the Kremlin's response. One may respect the Kremlin's military and police power (which is undeniably real). But the power of its ideas is nil. Indeed, more than four and a half decades of the systematic smothering of any real public political and ideological debate in the Soviet Union have produced such a poverty of ideas, including among the leaders of the bureaucracy and its principal spokesmen, that it almost inspires pity.

Thus, the theoretical response of *New Times* to Santiago Carillo is a mixture of falsifications, evident slanders, and ineptitudes which do not present even the semblance of a reply to the argumentation of the Secretary-General of the Communist Party of Spain. For instance, Carrillo is accused of desiring to create an 'isolated grouping of West European countries as a "force" opposed primarily to the socialist states.' *New Times* offers not the shadow of evidence to substantiate this accusation. The falsification is then topped off by a slander: 'It may be noted in this regard that S. Carrillo recently approved the idea of Spain's adherence to NATO, that bloc of aggression whose essential aim is to prepare for war against the Soviet Union and the countries of socialism. This more than bizarre point of view is not repeated in this book. But what is said in the book amply suffices. For it clearly follows that the major idea of the author is the "union" of West Europe on an anti-Soviet platform. It is not surprising that this sort of project of S. Carrillo has won him the approval of bourgeois ideologues. The idea of creating a "united Europe", a "Europe independent of the USSR and the USA", has yet another aspect. It is the idea of splitting the democratic forces and the Communist movement of the continent into two parts. . . . Of course, it is not only the right, but also the duty of the Communist parties of West Europe to coordinate their actions, even if only because of the fact that West European capital has long since acted in a united front against the workers' movement. But one fails to see why it should be necessary to renounce cooperation with the Communist parties of the socialist countries in the name of this coordination, or, what is worse, "revise the principles of internationalism,"' (p. 11).

The slander becomes obvious if one reads the second paragraph attentively. Carrillo *does not defend* Spanish entry into NATO. On the contrary, he implicitly upholds the idea of French and Italian *withdrawal* from NATO. Would this strengthen or weaken imperialism? *New Times*, of course, does not answer this question.

The bad faith of the Kremlin spokesmen becomes even more evident when one remembers that the leaders of the Italian Communist Party openly call for their country to remain in NATO, a position which has not been taken – at least not yet – by the leaders of the French and Spanish Communist parties. Nevertheless, Moscow attacks not apologies for NATO, but calls for a Europe 'neutral' towards the USSR and the United States (although for how much longer no one can say). Must it then be concluded that the Soviet bureaucracy prefers NATO to a 'neutralist' Europe, prefers the presence of the American imperialist gendarme on the European continent to its departure?

But the falsification goes even further. Carrillo does not at all defend the notion of a 'third force' as a system which is neither capitalist nor socialist. Rather, exactly like all the other Communist parties of capitalist Europe, including those which remain solidly indentured to Moscow (such as those of West Germany, Austria, Denmark, or Luxemburg), he presents the idea of a *stage* of 'advanced democracy', of 'anti-monopoly alliance', as a stage in the transition to socialism. We disagree with this strategy completely. Indeed, a good part of the present book is devoted to refuting it. But it is clear that one cannot advocate the 'democratic road to socialism' – which means alliances with Social Democracy and the so-called left bourgeois parties, respect for the electoral process, and the maintenance of parliamentary institutions – and simultandously reject the notion of a grouping of West European countries which refuses integration into Comecon and the Warsaw Pact, as the Kremlin pretends to do. The facts are clear: it is not only the immense majority of the proletariat and the toiling masses of West Europe who now reject such integration, *because of what they know of the political and economic reality of these countries*, but also the majority of Communist workers and militants.

Consequently, the real choice is between the capitalist and imperialist status quo in West Europe and the proposal of an original, new road to socialism which conforms to the traditions, sensibilities, and political opinions of the proletariat and toiling masses of these countries. The only conclusion that can be drawn from the maladroit diatribe of *New Times* is that the Kremlin accepts the defensive coordination of the western workers' movement against the 'international monopolies' if need be, *but in the framework of the maintenance of the capitalist mode of production*. It does not, however, accept a coordination of the efforts of the workers of Western Europe to get rid of the capitalist system through their own resources and along a road that would actually lead to this goal. In other words: the Kremlin prefers a capitalist West Europe; it prefers the bourgeois status quo to a West Europe that would build socialism according to a new model diametrically opposed to the bureaucratic model in force in the USSR. We knew this already. We thank the Kremlin scribblers for having confirmed it once again.

The rejection of integration into Comecon and the Warsaw Pact by the immense majority of the proletariat of West Europe is the product of the crimes of Stalin and the Soviet bureaucracy, of the profound discredit these crimes have heaped on Moscow-style 'socialism'. This discredit is an objective fact of the class struggle today both in Europe and throughout the world.

We are convinced that the victory of the socialist revolution in several key countries of capitalist Europe would modify the situation from top to bottom. It would counterpose the genuinely radiant and attractive face of socialism to the hideous mask the privileged and oppressive bureaucracy of the Soviet Union has clamped on socialism for decades. An immense hope would surge forth again, both East and West, both in the Soviet Union and the People's Democracies and in the United States.

A West Europe in which the power of the workers and the socialized, self-managed, and planned economy held sway, with full enjoyment of political pluralism and individual liberties, would have no interest in cutting itself off from the workers of East Europe and the USSR. It would undoubtedly offer them an alliance, but on an entirely new basis. It would take the political offensive, inviting the workers of the Soviet Union to follow their example. The perspective of the Socialist United States of Europe founded on a genuine regime of workers' councils – of soviets – from the Atlantic to the Urals and beyond, including all the countries which have already abolished capitalism, would then be understood by the toiling masses of these countries as a perspective of ridding themselves of the bureaucratic dictatorship, of establishing the direct power of the workers in their countries too, the regime of the 'associated producers' that we will have established in West Europe. It is understandable that this perspective is scarcely enchanting to the bureaucracy, the end of whose power and privileges it would mean. All the more reason to prefer the status quo, the presence of American imperialism in Europe, the survival of West European capitalism itself.

## A Response of Rare Ineptitude

The great concern of the Kremlin, then, is not the strategy of Eurocommunism. It is Santiago Carrillo's 'denigration' of the system of power that reigns in the Soviet Union and the People's Democracies. Faced with Santiago Carrillo's tight argumentation, which is founded on many pertinent empirical facts and theoretical analyses, even if they remain in part inadequate and incoherent, *New Times* advances only ineptitudes that will convince no one. One may judge by the following excerpts:

'Carrillo asserts that the October Revolution gave rise to a new type of state which, "while not bourgeois, cannot be considered a state of workers' democracy in which the organized proletariat is the ruling class either".

'This is said of the countries in which the working class constitutes the motor force of society, in which it, along with the peasantry and the intelligentsia, assumes the plenitude of power, of the countries in which the leading bodies of power are composed at least half by persons belonging to the working class' (p. 12).

The least one can say is that the sophistry is gross. How many workers still capable of being active *as workers* in production sit in the Council of Ministers of the USSR or the Central Committee of the Communist Party of the Soviet Union today?

Let us recall, then, the recommendation of Lenin's testament that a difference must be made between workers who remain actually engaged in production and members of the Soviet *apparatus* of working-class *origin*, whom Lenin considered so bureaucratized as early as 1922 that they could in no way curb the process of bureaucratization of the regime and the party. That was fifty-five years ago. Everyone can draw his own conclusions.

Where, then, does the Soviet working class assume the 'plenitude of power'? In the factories? Does not the plenitude of power there belong to the manager? Are there democratically elected workers' councils – soviets – that direct the factories? Perhaps at the level of the national economy as a whole? Is the plan submitted to the control and possibility of veto of an All-Soviet congress of democratically elected workers' councils? On the political level? Is political power in the hands of workers' councils, of a congress of soviets, elected the way the first, second, third, fourth, and fifth congress of soviets were, with freedom for all soviet parties, with uninhibited discussion, with different platforms on internal, economic, and international policy among which the workers could freely choose? Nobody really believes that this is how power is exercised in the USSR today.

A new Soviet constitution was adopted recently, one which, we may note in passing, nowhere proclaims that the proletariat 'fully assumes all political power', or that the Soviet state is 'the working class constituted as a ruling class'. On the occasion of the solemn adoption of this constitution by the 4 October 1977 meeting of the Supreme Soviet, Leonid Brezhnev announced that the 'constitutional commission', over which he presided, had received some 350,000 proposed amendments to the draft constitution. A total of 111 of them were accepted (*Le Monde*, 5 October 1977). The others were either altered or rejected . . . by a constitutional commission composed of a handful of persons.

How is it that the working class, which 'fully assumes power' in the USSR, did not even have the right to read these tens of thousands of rejected amendments? Why weren't they published? Why weren't they submitted to public and contradictory discussions? Why didn't the workers have the right to vote for or against some of them? It is a strange sort of 'political sovereignty' which does not even include the right to determine the text of the constitution democratically!

In the same speech, Brezhnev stressed that 'nearly 140 million people, or four-fifths of the adult population of the country', had participated in the 'national discussion' of the constitution. Such a debate, Brezhnev affirmed, proves that 'the regime of the soviets has resolved the problem of mass distrust of whatever comes from the state' (*Le Monde*, 5 October 1977).

Both Brezhnev and other representatives of the leadership of the CPSU and the government stressed 'the unparalleled cohesion' of the Soviet people, who no longer suffer from class antagonisms or deep social contradictions. But at the same time, the Soviet leaders continue to affirm that a 'handful of dissidents', all of them more or less 'in the pay of the foreign enemy', constitute a real threat to Soviet society. To grant them the right to speak or the right to a free press would threaten 'to spread counter-revolutionary subversion'. These theses are as ridiculous and contradictory as can be. When the proletariat was still a minority in the USSR, the regime of the soviets – even in the midst of the civil war – was able to afford the luxury of open and passionate political debate, an opposition press (which existed in the USSR until 1921), and political debate within the government party (including public debate, at least until 1926).

Capitalist countries torn by antagonistic classes and whose regime rests on a socially privileged and exploiting minority have permitted themselves the luxury of allowing even such irreconcilable and subversive opponents of their social order as Marx, Engels, Lenin, Rosa Luxemburg, and Trotsky to write and speak freely. But the Soviet Union, where the proletariat now constitutes the immense majority of the active population, where the 'most homogeneous and united society' ever known is said to exist, where 'four-fifths of the adult population acti ely participate in political life and support the state', this ultra-stabilized society trembles with fear at the prospect of the freedom of expression of a 'handful of renegades'!

Isn't it obvious that if in practice there is no freedom of the press in the USSR, if there is no possibility for any group of citizens to have real access to the means of communication, to express political views and orientations that are at variance with those of the government, it is not because of the 'threat' represented by 'a handful of renegades and spies' (such a threat would be next to nil in a genuinely socialist society), but because of the real threat to the bureaucracy's monopoly of power such a genuine access *by the workers themselves* would pose?

Brezhnev revealed in passing that among the rejected amendments was one concerning the equalization of wages. In all the imperialist countries there is public discussion – especially in the trade-union organizations, but also in the daily press – about wage scales. Why is there no such discussion in the Soviet press? Who can possibly believe that everyone in the Soviet Union agrees that the enormous inequality of monetary remuneration is just, that the privileged should enjoy 'advantages in kind' denied to the masses? Do Brezhnev and company dare to let the workers speak on this? Do they dare let the workers vote, in a referendum, for or against an immediate reduction in the present wage gap by one-half or one-third, including the salaries of the leading personnel of the state, party, and army? And if they dare not, does this not demonstrate, better than a thousand pages of documents, that Carrillo is correct when he maintains that the working class does not exercise power in the USSR?

### Reactions to the Riposte

What were the Kremlin's aims in its public excommunication of Santiago Carrillo? In order to erect a limit to the escalation of criticism of the structures of power in the USSR by the Eurocommunists, the bureaucracy probably sought to divide the leadership of the Communist Party of Spain – setting those nostalgic for Stalinism, Dolores Ibarruri in the first place, against Santiago Carrillo[1] – and to divide the Eurocommunist parties amongst themselves, hoping that the Italian Communist Party, and especially the French Communist Party,

---

[1] It must not be forgotten that several years ago the Kremlin had already attempted to stir up anti-Carrillo dissidence within the Communist Party of Spain, around ex-General Lister. This dissident PCE never grew beyond the dimensions of an insignificant grouplet.

would call upon Carrillo to moderate his attacks and would more or less take their distance from him. This goal was not achieved. The calculation was maladroit. The Soviet bureaucracy underestimated the internal logic of the evolution of Eurocommunism, which for obvious political reasons comprises a number of irreversible trends. Apart from the fact that the leaderships of the Italian and French Communist parties have no desire to approve any excommunication again,[2] they could scarcely afford to give the impression, given their current political projects, that they were yielding to pressure from the Kremlin.

The reaction was therefore quite severe, not only in Madrid, but also in Paris and Rome. On the whole, the Italian and French parties declared their solidarity with Carrillo and not with *New Times*, while the leadership of the Communist Party of Spain, *La Pasionaria* included, declared its solidarity with its secretary-general. The Kremlin for the first time, failed to call to order, not the leadership of a Communist Party holding state power (like the Yugoslav or Chinese Communist Party), but the leadership of a Communist Party operating in a capitalist country.

Even among the Communist parties in power in the People's Democracies, the attack on Santiago Carrillo did not provoke the unanimity that could have been expected. There were differing reactions from almost every party, from the 'unconditional' backers of the Kremlin in Bulgaria and East Germany to the Romanians, who squarely disapproved. There were even different successive reactions from the same party, as was the case with the Hungarians.[3]

[2] *New Times* had the effrontery to write in its July 1977 issue (no. 28): 'Faithful to the principles and policy of its Twentieth through Twenty-Fifth Congresses, the CPSU has never organized, nor is it organizing, any campaign against the fraternal parties, nor does it "excommunicate" anyone from the Communist movement. It could never set itself such an objective, which would be contrary to its principles'. What gall! The CPSU has never excommunicated any fraternal party? What about the excommunication of the Yugoslav Communist Party in 1948? Perhaps it is only since the Twentieth Congress that no fraternal party has been excommunicated? But what about the excommunication of the Chinese Communist Party?

[3] For the reactions of the various Communist parties of East Europe to the *New Times* article, see Guy Desolre's article in *Inprecor*, no. 12 new series, 15 September 1977.

The Kremlin was thus compelled to take a step backwards, publishing in *New Times* (No. 28) a follow-up article taking somewhat different aim. The attack on Santiago Carrillo, of course, remained harsh, as is clear from the following passage:

'For many years, nobody in the USSR criticized Carrillo publicly, even though he published anti-Soviet writings. We took into account that the Francoist regime still existed in Spain, that an intensive struggle to liquidate the remnants of fascism was under way there. It is only now, when the Communist Party of Spain has been legalized and is acting openly, when parliamentary elections have taken place in the country, and when S. Carrillo has published a book in an even more hostile spirit, that *New Times* has criticized the words of Carrillo. . . . For years now Santiago Carrillo has been waging an unconcealed and brutal campaign against the Soviet Union and the CPSU, in no way taking into account that during all these years the Soviet Union has been waging an intense struggle against imperialism, for the defence of peace throughout the entire world. . . . For three or four years now S. Carrillo has barely spoken a word without accusing the Soviet Union, the CPSU, the Communists(?), and the Soviets in general(?) of all varieties of sins. Recently (in his interview with *Der Spiegel*), *he went so far as to call for a fight against the existing order of things in our country*' (pp. 16–17, our emphasis).

The retreat consists in more clearly separating the criticism of 'the conceptions and opinions *in foreign policy*' contained in Santiago Carrillo's book from the strategic and tactical orientation of the Communist Party of Spain, in other words of Eurocommunism generally. In order to avoid a combined attack from the Italian, French, and Spanish Communist parties on this occasion, *New Times* was compelled to explain: the article published in number 26 contained no criticism of the strategy and tactics of the Communist Party of Spain. *New Times* 'stresses once again that the strategy and tactics of the fraternal parties are the internal affair of these parties, which determine them in full independence'. In other words: we can easily accept and live with all the 'rightist' excesses of Eurocommunism; but what we cannot accept are public criticisms of the political regime in the USSR and the People's Democracies, much less 'calls to fight against the existing order of things' in the USSR, that is, calls to political revolution. We say calls to *political* revolution. For to accuse Carrillo, as some have done, of trying to 'combat' the *socio-economic* order of things in the USSR – that is, of speaking for a section of the bureaucracy favourable to the restoration of capitalism, or even of speaking for imperialism – is frivolous and dangerous irresponsibility. Not only is it a slander devoid of all tangible evidence. It would also inevitably lead anyone who desires to conserve the socio-economic foundations created by the October Revolution to the conclusion that critical support must be accorded Brezhnev against Carrillo. But in that case why not support Brezhnev against Dubcek and company, who were no less 'liberal' than Carrillo politically and who, moreover, supported the Eurocommunist orientation with all their might? Must the military intervention in the Czechoslovak Socialist Republic be justified *a posteriori*? Anyone who takes to this road opens a Pandora's box; it is a sidetrack for any proletarian-revolutionary, anti-bureaucratic, and anti-Stalinist current.

The fallout from the Carrillo bombshell strikingly confirms that the conflict between the Kremlin and the Eurocommunist leaderships does not concern the concessions these leaderships have made to their own bourgeoisies in the realm of ideology or economics, or in the domain of internal policy. Nor does it concern their more or less conciliatory attitude towards NATO. It concerns exclusively the more and more extensive public criticism the Eurocommunist theoreticians and leaders have made of the bureaucratic dictatorship in the USSR and the violations of the democratic rights of the broad masses which are the rule there. These criticisms irritate and exasperate Moscow because they stimulate dissident currents not only within society in general, but also within the Communist parties of the USSR and the People's Democracies.

But the Kremlin possesses no effective means of silencing these criticisms. It has no recourse but to respond with verbal blasts and secret pressure. The result is a *modus vivendi* which is constantly challenged, yet constantly reestablished. For an open break would involve even more disastrous consequences than the pin-pricks Moscow must now suffer from the 'fraternal parties'.[4]

A recent incident, limited but significant, has underscored this dynamic once again. At the International Book Fair held in Moscow in the autumn of 1977, foreign publishers were censored, compelled to withdraw from their displays certain books considered 'pornographic' or 'exalting war and racism'. Among the books withdrawn from the stand of the Italian publishing company Einaudi was *Literature and Revolution* by Leon Trotsky, a pornographic work exalting war and racism if ever there was one. Furthermore, the works of the dissident Russian authors Solzhenitsyn and Bulgakov were also withdrawn.

The director of the Einaudi series in which these works had been published had innocently requested a visa to enter the USSR. The visa was refused, in logical application of the Helsinki accords, of course. But it so happens that the director of this collection is one Professor Strada, who has been a member of the Italian Communist Party for thirty-two years! *L'Unità*, the organ of the PCI, reacted sharply, in an article entitled 'A Stupifying Gesture': 'We have expressed, as a newspaper and as a party, our profound disapproval of the rejection of the visa requested by Comrade Strada. After the new seizure [of books], we can only reaffirm our negative judgment of gestures which clearly contravene democratic principles'. In the end, Strada received his visa. But the special envoy of *L'Humanité*, the organ of the French Communist Party, to the trial of four Czechoslovak dissidents on 17 October 1977 was also refused a visa, which provoked vehement protest from the daily of the PCF. In the 19 October 1977 issue of this newspaper, René Andrieu, *L'Humanité* editorialist, criticized the verdict of the trial in these unambiguous terms: 'Although this time the prosecutor did not mention the Charter, it is clear that the four intellectuals brought before the Prague court were indicted for having expressed opinions which do not conform to the policy of the present leaders of Czechoslovakia. If it is objected that they violated the law by distributing abroad leaflets that

---

[4] In this regard see the article by Charles-André Udry and Charles Michaloux, 'Eurocommunists and the Kremlin Face New Times', in *Inprecor*, no. 11 new series, 21 July 1977.

are considered subversive in Prague, we would say that it is quite urgent to change the law. In any case, no one should expect us to sanction, even if only by silence, what clearly appears to us as a denial of justice'.

*Pravda*, meanwhile, censored the speech of the delegate of the CGT (General Confederation of Labour, the largest trade-union federation in France, dominated by the Communist Party) at the last congress of Soviet trade unions, because he affirmed that socialism and liberty were inseparable. This dialectic will continue. It will inevitably foster the rebirth of a communist opposition in the USSR and the People's Democracies. It will objectively accelerate the progress towards an anti-bureaucratic political revolution in these countries, a revolution which will consolidate their non-capitalist socio-economic foundations.

# 7
# Echoes in Eastern Europe

*The Alternative* by Rudolf Bahro[1] is the most important theoretical work to come out of the countries that have abolished capitalism since Leon Trotsky's *The Revolution Betrayed*. From the weak 'New Class' by Milovan Djilas to the 'Open Letter' of Jacek Kuron and Karol Modzelewski to the writings on bureaucracy by former Hungarian Prime Minister Andras Hegedus to the books of the 'liberal' Czechoslovak and Yugoslav Communists to the works of the Pole Włodzimierz Brus to Roy Medvedev's *Let History Judge*, the progression to Rudolf Bahro is striking and undeniable.

Rudolf Bahro's work ties together three strands of the thought and action of our time. Its fabric is woven of threads of three different origins. First, there is the practical experience of the anti-bureaucratic movements, immensely richer now than at the beginning of the 1950s. The winds of the Prague spring and the revolt of the Polish workers in the Baltic ports are felt in the analysis of Bahro.

Next there are the progress and contradictions of international Marxist thought over the past twenty years. Bahro's work resounds with reverberations of the polemic between the Stalinists and the Yugoslav Communists, the Sino-Soviet polemics, the flowering of Western revolutionary Marxist thought, particularly since May 1968, the international debate among Marxists on the 'nature of the USSR', and the debates around Eurocommunism.

Finally, Bahro is also a product of the German theoretical

---

[1] Rudolf Bahro, *Die Alternative – Zur Kritik des real existierenden Sozialismus*, Cologne, 1977. English edition to be published by NLB, 1978.

tradition, which has certainly been weakened, but not extinguished, by the tragic fate of the German workers' movement over the past forty-five years, first in the epoch of Hitler and Stalin, then in its struggle against a second wave of integration and repression in the West and bureaucratic ossification in the East.

This is perhaps the first important lesson – and source of elation – to be drawn from the publication of this astonishing work: the German Marxist theoretical tradition is being reborn in East Germany. We may be sure that the echoes of this renaissance will reverberate for a long time. They will delight the opponents of the exploitation and oppression of man by man in all their forms. They will alarm many other circles, including some unexpected ones.

It is precisely Bahro's solid theoretical heritage – the best traditions of Marx himself, all of Marx, not only the economic works – that lends *The Alternative* a historical, almost 'universal', dimension, an attraction to which any Marxist, any revolutionary, or even any humanist, will respond, whatever critical doubts particular arguments in the work may inspire.

Bahro himself does not succumb to the danger of missing the wood for the trees. 'The devil is generally not found in the details', he writes, not without reason. It is fundamental problems that interest him above all else. Since it is evident that the societies of the USSR, East Germany, China, or Yugoslavia have not achieved social equality, despite the overthrow of capitalism, and since they are not classless societies free of coercive social stratification, two essential questions arise. Is the advent of a classless society a utopia? If not, why has it not yet seen the light of day in the East?

A good Marxist, Bahro answers the first question with a categorical 'No'. His answer to the second goes directly to the root of the problem.

## The Root of the Evil

For Bahro, the ultimate source of social inequality is the social division of labour, which confines one section of society to specific tasks related to the reproduction of material resources for all society. (This notion is a much broader one than that of manual labour. Non-manual labour can be as repetitive and alienating as manual labour.) This social division of labour means that only a minority can enjoy access to spheres of activity which Bahro, like Hegel and Marx, calls 'general labour' (*die allgemeine Arbeit*) as opposed to specific labour – those activities which permit the flowering of the full human personality.

In this connection Bahro uses two concepts which may appear 'idealist' at first sight but are profoundly materialist in reality: 'psychologically productive labour' and 'psychologically unproductive labour'. At the same time, integrating an essential dimension of historical materialism into his study, that of the inextricable unity of 'production-communication' in the *social* activity of humanity, Bahro demonstrates that any social division of labour is inevitably accompanied by differentiated access to information: exclusively fragmentary, specific, and limited information for the 'producers' in the strict sense of the term; general and increasingly universal information for those who devote themselves to 'general labour'.

These two information systems, parallel to the two basic social activities, generate two systems of education of children from the earliest flowering of their intelligence, a stifling one for the children of the toilers, a stimulating one for the children of the privileged. This, in turn, powerfully contributes to the reproduction of social inequality. (Bahro, however, understands quite well that one must not generalize this phenomenon nor attribute decisive importance to it. The ruling classes command institutional and economic mechanisms for the reproduction of inequality, to which the above phenomenon must simply be *added*.)

Hence the vast expansion of the productive forces effected by the industrial revolution of 19th century capitalism, together with the abolition of bourgeois private property in certain countries in the 20th century, are indispensable, but not at all sufficient preconditions for the inauguration of a socialist society. The latter demands, in addition to a social surplus product extensive enough to eliminate the material exigencies that made the existence of the old privileged ruling classes inevitable, systematic and deliberate efforts to abolish the social division of labour. If this division is maintained or petrified, as is manifestly the case in the countries of East Europe, then society itself becomes frozen midway between class society and classless society. The root of the evil, and the historic meaning of bureaucratic dictatorship, is the totality of post-capitalist mechanisms and institutions which maintain the *monopoly of administration and management* in all spheres of social life, the monopoly of 'general labour', *in the hands of a privileged minority.*

Bahro thus reverses the link between material privilege and the monopoly of access to management and administrative functions that mechanistic Marxists have generally attempted to establish, independent of specific historical circumstances. He even strives to effect a parallel 'reversal' when he compares the conditions for the *emergence* of an original ruling class within classless society in decomposition (we would say: during the phase of transition from classless society to class society) to the conditions for the *disappearance* of social inequality in post-capitalist society (we would put it: during the phase of transition from capitalist to socialist society).

It is not the privileges that produce the monopoly, but the monopoly that secretes the privileges. We believe that Bahro is entirely correct on this point. In fact he is restating what Rakovsky, Trotsky, and other Bolshevik leaders constantly repeated during the 1920s and 1930s (although it is clear that Bahro has not read all their works). The masters of the Stalinist apparatus did not 'conspire' to expropriate the working class politically, because they wanted to defend already acquired material privileges. Rather, it is because they expropriated the working class politically, and thus eliminated any possibility of mass control over the mode of distribution, that they were able little by little to appropriate ever more exorbitant material privileges and ended by creating institutions that allow them to conserve and reproduce both the monopoly of power and the privileges.

**A Striking Condemnation of the Bureaucracy**

It is in dealing with the question of the character of the USSR that Bahro's superiority over most 'revisionist' Marxist theoreticians is clearest. Bahro rejects both the thesis of 'state capitalism' and that of the 'new class'. He returns to the original Leninist conception, which distinguishes three phases of post-capitalist society: the phase of transition, the socialist phase (the first stage of communism), and the communist phase. In Bahro's view, the USSR, East Germany, and the other countries of the 'socialist camp' are still in the first or transitional phase, which he defines by the rather academic term 'proto-socialist' (post-capitalist but pre-socialist).

We should not split hairs. In essence, this is the thesis long defended by revolutionary Marxists against hell and high water. That Bahro has arrived at it in spite of insufficient knowledge of the lengthy discussions on this problem that have occurred both in the West and in opposition circles in the East is a further reflection of the exceptional capacities of this Marxist theoretician.

Closely linked to a correct definition of the social (socio-economic) character of the East European countries is the question of a critical scientific analysis of the character of the bureaucracy and its precise articulation with the post-capitalist system as it functions in these countries. Although the formula so dear to Stalinists of all stripes in the East European countries ('actually existing socialism') appears as a subtitle to his work, Bahro forcefully takes the field against this thesis. In this domain as well, he returns to the origins of Marxist thought. A 'socialism' with market production and a money economy, with remuneration paid 'as a function of the quantity *and quality*' of the labour of each person (here Bahro cites the famous passage of *Anti-Dühring* in which Engels denies that there can be such a 'socialism'), with social inequalities and monstrous political constraints is the antithesis of everything the Marxist tradition defines as socialist. Of course, definitions can be modified at will. You can call a piece of furniture on which you put plates a 'chair', or you can call a piece of furniture that serves as a footrest for someone sitting before a fire or watching television a 'bed'. But if you operate that way, then you must at least admit that the society that 'actually' exists in the USSR, China, Yugoslavia, and all the countries of the 'socialist bloc' *is not* (or not yet) the society of the 'freely associated producers' described (too briefly, alas) by Marx and Engels.

There is nothing at all 'moralistic', 'normative', or 'idealistic' about contrasting a *definition derived from a scientific analysis of social structures* (and not ethical axioms) with a reality to which it does not conform. One could equally well denounce as 'moralizers' or 'normative analysts' those Marxist historians who correctly explained that in spite of their progressive integration into the world capitalist market, neither China nor Iran nor Ethiopia was characterized by capitalist relations of production during the latter half of the 19th century. Thought veers from science into moralizing idealism not when it *notes* the difference between the realities of Eastern Europe and the definitions of Marx – which is an obvious one – but when it *contents itself* with condemning it without explaining its origins or seeking the means by which it can be overcome in reality.

The definition of the precise place of the bureaucracy in post-capitalist (or 'proto-socialist') society *today* constitutes one of the most successful and attractive sections of Bahro's work. The analysis is rigorous, the condemnation is brilliant. Many passages could be cited. For example: 'The historic function of the post-Stalinist apparatus lies in its effort to prevent the peoples of East Europe from progressing toward socialism' (p. 402). 'The replacement of the political dictatorship of the bureaucracy is a socio-economic necessity' (p. 306). 'What the Soviet Union suffers from . . . are the misdeeds of apparatchiks and their "superiors" (*natchalniki*), among whom the old patriarchate of the peasantry and the new patriarchate of the industrial despot are combined with party discipline to produce a kind of religious obeisance' (p. 267). 'Just as our pedagogical science has rediscovered the traditional conspiracy of authorities against the independence and imagination of children, in the form of the "united collective of educators", our political education speaks to the people, down to the last street cleaner, *with a single voice*: "We educate you so that you may remain ignorant" (Rainer Kurze). The masses "assimilate" this into their consciousness to the extent that they manifest conformism' (p. 356).

Or: 'Waste and shortages of material resources go hand in hand', under bureaucratic planning (p. 183). 'Edward Gierek deserves thanks for the honesty with which he summed up the problem of our societies after the Polish crisis of December, when he joined the two ends of the problem together: "You work well and we will govern you well"'' (p. 207).

The list could go on: 'The bureaucratic centralist form of planning, under which the summit receives from below only passive factual information and "questions", while active information about what must be produced is transmitted from the top down, determines the manner in which "instructions" are given to individuals. As a matter of principle individuals have no business looking for tasks to perform, discerning problems or seeking to solve them; they simply receive "instructions" to do this or that. Resources are allocated as a function of this method, according to a system of balances which is increasingly a rationing of strict necessity' (p. 252). It is necessary to 'trace a merciless line of demarcation between loyalty to a non-capitalist base and loyalty to an obsolete superstructure' (p. 411).

'Because of the character of our superstructure, it has become the rule that explosive tensions accumulated over a long period is detonated "suddenly", since mounting contradictions find no outlets through which they can express themselves in time. Even in the Czechoslovak Socialist Republic, where many things could have been foreseen in 1966 and 1967, the pace, breadth, and depth of the transformations surprised everyone' (p. 397). 'The possibilities of opposition activity have risen considerably in recent times' (p. 395). 'The need is to develop a socialist model as an alternative [to the existing model], in a thoroughly public manner, without conspiracy' (pp. 359 and 405).

On the question of the specific relationships that determine the positions of the working class and the bureaucracy in the economic system, Bahro presents information which generally confirms the revolutionary Marxist analysis and refutes some of the hypotheses that have been peremptorily advanced by various 'revisionist' theoreticians. For instance, he stresses (as we have on many occasions) that the intensity of labour and labour discipline in East Europe are *inferior* to those prevailing under the capitalist mode of production, precisely because a generalized system of 'right to work' and state guarantee of vital necessities functions on the whole in East Europe (pp. 243–45). 'From the standpoint of political economy', Bahro writes, 'the workers . . . have greater possibilities to blackmail society as a whole than do the trade unions under the capitalist mode of production. Contrary to appearances, they exploit these possibilities, but can do so only in an unproductive manner, by reducing their efforts. This is less true for the lower layers, and least true for women, who do the lion's share of piecework. But the majority of skilled workers determine the work pace in the factories through their own consensus' (p. 245).

The major motor force in the realization of the plan thus has to be 'material incentives' for the bureaucrats, instead of creative initiatives by the masses, which are excluded by the social and political order. But these 'material incentives for the bureaucrats' are oriented exclusively towards attempting to create the *conditions* for the realization of the plan (p. 260), and they increasingly function in a vacuum. Since the structure of the plan is *predetermined* and since material resources are constantly in short supply, 'competition among bureaucrats' arises. They compete not in order to increase economic rationality, but in order to conquer important positions of political and administrative power, which is the only way to achieve greater access to material resources (p. 261). 'The individual bureaucrat may himself be a philosopher, but it is impossible for the bureaucratic apparatus to be a collective philosopher' (p. 258). 'Bureaucratism as the predominant form of management and labour produces a specific human type characterized by conservative mediocrity' (p. 265). Taking up a formula of former Hungarian Stalinist Prime Minister Andras Hegedus, Bahro concludes: 'The bureaucratic system is a system of organized irresponsibility' (p. 134).

Such is a small sample of an anthology that could be expanded at will.

### The Social Content of the Political Revolution

Some of the above quotations may give the impression that Bahro holds that the revolution necessary in the bureaucratized workers' states should be limited to the superstructure. But this is clearly not at all the case. In this domain as well, Bahro remains in the framework of the firmest Marxist orthodoxy. While correctly calling for the maintenance and consolidation of the non-capitalist base of these states, he also perceives, precisely because of his 'totalizing' Marxist analysis, that the coming revolution will make radical changes in the sphere of the infrastructure as well as the superstructure and that it will above all overturn the mediation between the two.

Bahro's contribution in this domain is fertile and impressive, although in the end it is less original than may appear at first sight. What is most striking in his programmatic analysis – the 'alternative' that gives the work its title – is its close relationship to the picture of 'the socialism we want' which revolutionary Marxists have developed in the industrially advanced capitalist countries. This may be seen by examining the central features of Bahro's 'alternative':

1. Generalization of a system of self-management and self-administration, as a process covering *all* aspects of reproduction (p. 523) and organized through a federation of communes founded (although this is not very clear) on councils (*Räte*) (pp. 528–531).

2. A radical struggle against the vertical division of labour, centred on two major fronts: drastic reduction of the duration of mechanical and repetitive work ('psychologically unproductive' labour), particularly through the massive reintroduction of white-collar workers into industrial labour and services for a certain number of hours each week (Bahro offers the following, quite significant, figures on the social structure of East Germany: 3 million workers in production; 1 million cadres of university level and in institutions of professional higher-education; 4 million white-collar workers: p. 504); generalization of university and para-university higher education, that is, extension of compulsory education to 23 years of age (pp. 334–5).[2]

3. A generalized transition to calculation of the objectives and achievements of the economic plan in working hours instead of prices, in order to make the division of social product between funds for consumption and funds for accumulation more transparent (pp. 517–520). Bahro also strikingly establishes the evi-

---

[2] In order to prevent the *habits* of alienated labour from giving rise to practices of alienating and alienated leisure, Bahro insists on the importance of an education for all children which is not solely physical and technical but also scientific-philosophical and aesthetic.

dent correlation between this method of calculating the plan on the basis of quantities of labour and the 'actual expenditure of individual time' by the producers; such a calculation would create a clear and generalized dynamic of socio-economic progress measurable by each individual. Let us add that a *double accounting system*, in both labour time and prices, will most likely be necessary so long as any transitional workers' economy remains related to an international capitalist economy and as long as a monetary system of remuneration persists.

4. Abolition of individual production quotas and piecework, for obvious reasons we need not repeat (pp. 462–68). Bahro demonstrates that the 'savings' made by such production quotas usually do not even compensate for the losses in production caused by the employment of time-keepers who do not participate in productive labour properly so-called.

5. Harmonization of reproduction, particularly by greater emphasis on simple reproduction, repair of machinery, tool maintenance, savings on raw materials and energy, and a radical transformation of 'technological innovation', which should be oriented towards saving time for producers and genuinely improving the quality of life for consumers (pp. 512–513).

6. Elimination of all material privileges, especially those related to the exercise of particular functions and accorded in the form of usufruct or advantages in access to material goods. At the same time, reduction of the wage gap, which admittedly is not as wide in East Germany as it is in the USSR (pp. 458–60).

7. Entirely new determination of priorities in the domain of consumption, ordered from the standpoint of maximum human development and not greater and greater accumulation of material goods (p. 485). Particular priority to spending on education and health.

8. Generalized access of all citizens to centralized information (particularly with the aid of computers to which citizens could be linked by telephone). Complete abolition of 'state secrets' in the realm of economic, political, and cultural information.

9. Demolition of all hierarchical structures based on bureaucratic centralism. These structures exude the generalized phenomenon of 'underlingism', which in Bahro's view is one of

the major characteristics of the societies of the East European countries – the secretary-general himself being merely the first of the underlings.

10. Radical attack on the patriarchal family. Here Bahro centres his criticism more on the nefarious effects of this institution on children than on its function in the oppression of women. The two points of view are obviously complementary rather than contradictory.

When bourgeois and petty-bourgeois commentators (including Stalinists and Social Democrats) insist on the allegedly utopian and even 'demagogic' character of such ideas, they thereby reveal only their own lack of social realism and the hopeless conservatism of their own thought, imprisoned by mental structures that at best correspond to the realities of the 19th century. One may say without risk of error that Bahro's proposals are not only not 'utopian', but that they correspond very accurately to the possibilities of contemporary forces of production, as well as to the aspirations of hundreds of millions of human beings. Indeed in the long-run their realization is a precondition for saving mankind from destruction of material civilization in war and a new fall into barbarism.

## A Refreshingly 'Worldwide' Vision

A similar assessment applies to the other positive aspect of Bahro's analysis, unexpected coming from an East European Communist oppositionist: its resolutely internationalist dimension. We say 'unexpected' because most of the East European dissidents, even those of the left, have reacted to Stalinist-type 'proletarian internationalism' (that is, the identification of the term with blind subordination to the interests of the Soviet bureaucracy), by preaching a nationalist or semi-nationalist introversion which is inevitably sterile and inoperative given the present state of social forces everywhere in the world. We say 'unexpected' rather than 'surprising', since a theoretician who places himself in the tradition of classical German Marxism and has a minimum of practical experience in economic management[3] could not help but inte-

[3] In 1952 Bahro was a candidate member of the Socialist Unity Party of Germany (SED), the name the East German Communist Party has used since

grate into his thought the *worldwide* character of economics, politics, and social contradictions in our epoch. Several aspects of Bahro's analysis in this regard ought to be highlighted.

Rudolf Bahro thoroughly understands the utopian and reactionary character of the idea that the construction of socialism can be completed in one country, although he does not refer to this controversy explicitly. He perceives the political, social and economic pressures the world market exerts on the pace and orientation of accumulation in the East European countries. He presents a gripping theoretical analysis of what underlies the famous theory of 'economic competition between the two systems'. In fact, one of the images he uses repeats a prediction of Trotsky's half a century ago: such 'competition' resembles the fable about the race between the tortoise and the hare in which the hare, in spite of his vastly superior 'cruising speed', is compelled to note that even after ten 'technological revolutions' and a hundred 'new consumer goods', the tortoise is always first at the finishing line.

Bahro likewise fully appreciates the grave and explosive character of the North–South contradiction, and of the key problem underdevelopment poses for the socialist future of humanity. In this regard he pleads for the necessity of rational education in favour of solidarity and non-wasteful use of world resources; many 'ecological' considerations are integrated into his programme.

Bahro has at least a presentiment of the correlation between the rise of the workers' movement in Western Europe and the possibilities of revolutionary overturns in the East European countries. The Prague spring, of which Bahro is in some sense the natural offspring, had already shaken East European society as a whole. The realization of an 'alternative

---

its fusion with the Social Democratic Party of Eastern Germany after the Second World War. He became a full member in 1954. From 1954 to 1959 he studied philosophy at Humboldt University in East Berlin. In 1959 and 1960 he actively participated in the movement for agrarian collectivization. From 1962 to 1965 he collaborated in the national leadership of the trade union of scientific personnel. From 1965 to 1967 he edited the publication *Forum*, a journal for youth and students. Since 1967 he has worked in various enterprises as an engineer specializing in the implementation of projects of industrial rationalization and the scientific organization of labour.

socialist model' in the West would multiply the shock waves tenfold.

But above all, Bahro rigorously opposes any purely defensive or even indifferent attitude towards the Soviet Union on the part of Communist oppositionists in East Europe. He sees the *essential* function of the opposition in East Europe as being to 'detonate' a similar evolution in the Soviet Union. He correctly accuses the ruling bureaucracy in East Germany and elsewhere, in spite of all their pledges of 'friendship with the Soviet Union', of systematically provoking the spread of anti-Soviet sentiment not only among the masses but even within sections of their own party apparatus – sentiments whose consequences for peace in Europe could be disastrous in the event of a victorious political revolution.

Although we do not accept all the premises of Bahro's analysis in this regard, it is clear that it does contain a large kernel of truth.

**Two Stages in the History of the Bureaucracy?**

In sum, important sections of Bahro's book must be assessed positively. But a positive assessment cannot be made of the whole of his analysis, far from it. His book is not a revolutionary Marxist work in the Trotskyist sense. It contains essential weaknesses, much more serious than the spoonful of tar in the barrel of honey in the Russian proverb cited by Lenin. In fact, a central portion of Bahro's 'alternative' is essentially invalid.

The explanation of this contradictory phenomenon – that an author of Bahro's great talent and vision has not succeeded in developing a correct *overall view* of the correlation of contending social forces in East and West – lies in the lack of information from which Bahro suffers (in regard to both facts and theory). It is simply impossible for a single mind to 'reproduce universal reality' on its own, isolated from collective critical work and universal revolutionary practice – in other words, isolated from an international revolutionary organization. But we have too much respect for Bahro's talents and capacities to be content with merely explaining the weaknesses of his analysis. We believe that a critical discussion of them, commensurate with the problems they pose (let us repeat, they are problems that are decisive for the future of humanity), is indispensable. Thus, if we now proceed to a strong criticism of all that we find false in Bahro's theses, it is not at all with the intention of 'shooting him down'. On the contrary, it is in the hope that a real dialogue can occur and that a genuine rectification will be possible, both for him and for those who will be inspired by his writings (and they will not be few in number). In fact, we ourselves will undoubtedly learn much from such a discussion, for in no way do we possess a 'definitive' position on the precise content of the anti-bureaucratic political revolution in the East; it is only the first decisive victories in the struggle that will permit one to emerge.

There are three complementary, mutually inter-related weaknesses in Bahro's theory: a hazy idea of the historic role of the bureaucracy; a confused conception of the historical role of the state; a radically false position on the revolutionary potential of the working class.

Bahro's essential thesis on the bureaucracy is characterized by an 'objectivist', even fatalistic, vision of what happened after the socialist revolution in the less industrialized countries. Since the writings of Preobrazhensky, we have been aware that the USSR, in the absence of a victorious socialist revolution in the West, was condemned to 'primitive socialist accumulation'. But it does not at all follow that the only instrument available for effecting this process was the bureaucracy (the apparatus of the state, economic administration and party, increasingly welded into a single social stratum) or that this accumulation necessarily had to occur at the cost of an absolute decline in the living standards of the workers and the majority of the peasants. Now, a 'materialist explanation' of the Stalinist dictatorship should be based on *these* precise socio-economic features and not on the logic of 'primitive socialist accumulation' *per se*. Thus, the 'inevitability' of a bureaucratic dictatorship cannot be deduced from the particular historic conditions prevailing in Russia in 1917.

Indeed, Bahro acknowledges that the alternative programme of the Left Opposition would have permitted, if not a 'painless industrialization', at least an enormous reduction in its costs and also could have avoided the barbarity of forced collectivization. But he avoids the obvious conclusion through a sleight of hand: 'It is not by accident that this programme was rejected by the immense majority of Russian Communists'.

This brings us to the real issue – the contrast between an 'objectivist' historical fatalism and a correct understanding of the *dialectic of the objective and subjective factors*. From the standpoint of such a dialectic, it is just as absurd to claim that the bureaucratic dictatorship in Russia was inevitable after the victory of the October Revolution 'because of the objective circumstances of Russia' as it would be to claim that Hitler and Auschwitz were 'inevitable' as of 1918, if not since Bismarck, 'because of the objective conditions prevailing in Germany'. A multitude of intermediary links always exist between 'ultimate objective causes' and any final practical result. These intermediary links are primarily expressions of the struggle of concrete social and political forces. To cite but one example: the betrayal of the German revolution in 1918, 1919, 1920, and 1923 by the Social Democratic leadership certainly had as important an effect on the fate of the Russian revolution as did Russia's 'Asiatic' and 'barbarous' past, for it ensured the isolation of the October revolution, contrary to the projects and expectations of the Bolsheviks.

Any fatalistic conception of history involves an apologetic temptation. Although Bahro is perfectly conscious of this danger, he nevertheless in part succumbs to it. For in the end it is his thesis that the bureaucracy was inevitable – *and therefore progressive* – in effecting 'primitive socialist accumulation'. The bureaucracy became reactionary only when the possibility of 'extensive industrialization' was succeeded by the necessity for 'intensive industrialization'. The influence of the tradition of Brandler, who upheld similar theses (recently taken up again by Elleinstein in the French Communist Party), a tradition which has never been wholly absent from the East German Communist Party, is undeniable here.

Bahro commits a flagrant injustice against Trotsky and the Trotskyists when he accuses them of 'historical subjectivism' because of their concepts of 'bureaucratic deformation' and 'degeneration'. In reality, all the objective factors which Bahro believes determined the victory of the bureaucracy were enumerated by Trotsky in *The Revolution Betrayed*. Bahro adds nothing original in this domain.

The difference is not that Trotsky 'underestimated' these objective factors, but that he believed that a politically correct reaction by the worker cadres of the party, the vanguard of the proletariat, could have caused a change in the international and national configuration of social and political forces capable of averting Stalinism. Neither the defeat of the world revolution, nor the depoliticization of the Soviet working class, nor the definitive stifling of Soviet democracy, nor the delay in accelerated industrialization, nor the concentration of the agricultural surplus in the hands of the kulaks was inevitable or irreversible in 1923, 1924, or 1925. Nor were the consolidation and dictatorship of the bureaucracy. A correct reaction by the cadres of the party could have opened the way for developments in the opposite direction, which could have led to cumulative modifications of the trend. The underestimation by these cadres of the danger of Thermidor and bureaucratization and the fact that they understood these dangers too late and in too scattered a manner had decisive effects on the cumulative consolidation of the bureaucracy. A good Leninist, Trotsky believed in *the relative autonomy of subjective factors*. Bahro rejects this in his analysis of Stalinism, although he returns to it, even in an exaggerated manner, in his conclusions. This is a great fault in his method.

## Does the working class have a revolutionary potential?

More serious than this semi-apologetic attitude towards the bureaucracy is the scepticism Bahro manifests towards the revolutionary potential of the working class. Granted, when he stresses the extreme atomization of the working class in East Europe he emphasizes a phenomenon which we and others have noted before him. When he adds that under *present conditions* (that is, under the bureaucratic dictatorship), it is virtually impossible for the working class to reconstitute its organized cadres by itself (pp. 223–4), he is not entirely wrong. But the only conclusion to be drawn from this is that a 'detonator' external to the working class is probably necessary to set the process of political revolution in motion. There are various possibilities: a division in the apparatus, a revolt of intellectuals or even technicians, a major stimulus from abroad, and so on.

Nevertheless, to conclude that because the working class encounters great difficulties in triggering a process of political revolution in Eastern Europe today, it will not be able to play the role of protagonist during the process, and especially at its culmination (p. 388), is to fail to assimilate the real lessons of the Hungarian revolution, the Prague spring, and the Polish events. Now, these are three countries in which the objective social weight and political traditions of the working class were less than those in East Germany or the Soviet Union. In the light of this, Bahro's scepticism has no socio-economic foundation; it simply expresses a political prejudice.

Yet worse, in an attempt to lend greater coherence to his analysis, Bahro extends his scepticism about the working class in the East to the working class in the West and proceeds to a general revision of the Marxist theory of the key role the proletariat must play in the overthrow of capitalism and the inauguration of a classless, socialist society. 'All Marxist discussions since 1914', Bahro writes, 'lead to the conclusion that the interests on which workers actually act are not their real interests' (p. 224). These interests on which the workers actually act, according to Bahro, do not go beyond the limits of a 'petty-bourgeois' and 'corporatist' betterment of their lot. Thus, an 'inherently reformist' (trade-unionist) working class cannot be the bearer of a genuine socialist programme. Such a programme can be developed only by a 'historical bloc' within which intellectuals, technicians, and highly skilled white-collar employees will play a much more dynamic role than workers.

A bridge to Eurocommunism is thereby laid. Eurocommunism justifies its strategy by the same alleged necessity to create a 'historical bloc' capable of achieving the 'alternative' Bahro preaches. This part of Bahro's work does have the merit of a candour which is scarcely to be found among most of the leaders of the Italian, French, and Spanish Communist parties (except, perhaps, such forthright spokesmen as Giorgio Amendola). Eurocommunist strategy is indeed founded precisely on a rejection of the revolutionary potential of the working class. It is highly significant of the dialectic between the rising socialist revolution in the West and the rising political revolution in the East that the contradiction between the immense opportunities now open to humanity and the resistance of the bureaucratic apparatuses to them rends an oppositionist like Bahro between his instinct, which tells him that salvation will come from the revolution in the West, and his reason, which apologetically murmurs in his ear: 'Forget about the Marxist utopia of the supposedly revolutionary role of the proletariat'.

Bahro's argumentation is actually quite weak, apart from a few abstract philosophical flights. It is simply not true that 'since 1914' the *entire* behaviour of the European working class has been confined to a search for immediate material advantages of a 'trade-unionist' or 'corporatist' type. What about the German revolution of 1918, when workers' councils were created throughout the country? What about the general strike against the Kapp putsch in 1920? What about the great strikes and factory occupations in Italy in 1920? What about the general strike of June 1936 in France? What about the Spanish revolution of 1936–37? What about the great battles during and after the Liberation in France and Italy, culminating in the Italian general strike of July 1948? What about May 1968 in France and the 'creeping May' in Italy in 1969? What about the Portuguese revolution of 1974–75 and the rising combativity in Spain today?

After he assimilated the experience of the 1905 revolution, Lenin was more 'realistic', more 'Marxist', and more accurate than Bahro. The practical experience of the 20th century has confirmed that although the working class is 'spontaneously reformist' (trade-unionist) in normal times, it is 'spontaneously anti-capitalist' (revolutionary) during periods of revolutionary crisis. Moreover, it is only this materialist interpretation (and not a conspiracy theory) that explains the *alternation* of 'normal' situations and revolutionary crises throughout the 20th century.

But there we are: preconceived ideas, prejudices, and false consciousness have an implacable logic, even (or especially) for a major theoretician like Bahro. The demon of false systemization lurks quietly behind the angel of necessary systemization. The moment one considers the revolution impossible, 'since there is no revolutionary subject', one is compelled by 'political realism' to curb and stifle a real revolution when it begins to unfold before one's eyes. Thus, Bahro does not reproach Cunhal for his policy of 'anti-monopoly alliance', which enabled Portuguese capitalism to save itself during the worst moments of the capitalist crisis in the first half of 1975. On the contrary, he criticizes him for having provoked a futile polarization between left and right, even within the army. This is the same reproach Eduard Bernstein addressed to the German revolutionaries in 1918, even extending it against the French revolutionaries (and Karl Marx himself) by criticizing their behaviour in 1848. This sort of political wisdom as a substitute for comprehension of the objective dynamic of class struggles is unworthy of Bahro's Communist vision and passion.

## A Confused Position on the Role of the State

In his analysis of the division of labour and of 'general labour' Bahro adopts the general stand-point of historical materialism. But when he considers the nature and role of the state, Bahro's semi-apologetic position on the bureaucracy causes him to lose his footing. He systematically confuses the inevitable emergence of social functions that express the general interests of society in counterposition to particular interests (of groups, sectors, corporations, etc.), with the role of the state apparatus, which fraudulently appropriates this 'expression of general interest' exactly by *separating itself* from the whole of society. The state, of course, does so precisely in the interest of a 'particular group', a ruling class.

All bourgeois theories of the state are founded on this systematic confusion. Social-democratic theories follow suit. So do Eurocommunist ideas. Marxist theory, however, has always denounced the mystification that lies at the root of this confusion. Unfortunately, Bahro resolutely takes to the revisionist road in this regard, which leads him to approve another of the foundations of Eurocommunism.

The state, he claims, is a formidable motor force of civilization (pp. 149–50), indispensable to regulate society and to neutralize competition among particular appetites and interests (pp. 187–88). 'Industrial' society can no longer afford the luxury of dismantling the state apparatus without endangering economic reproduction as a whole. Hence the abandonment of the demand for this dismantlement by the Eurocommunists, a renunciation of which Bahro approves (pp. 160–61). The contradiction between this analysis and the semi-libertarian conclusions Bahro draws from it is striking. Or more precisely: his *combination* of apologetic temptation and revolutionary instinct leads to hybrid solutions which fall rather short of the grand and globalizing vision contained in his critique.

'The division of labour must be overcome before the state can begin to wither away'. Who, then, will *organize* and *assure* this elimination of the division of labour? The bureaucracy itself? Does not Bahro himself demonstrate that the bureaucracy has no interest in doing so; just the contrary? How can the bureaucracy's monopoly of management be overturned (for it is this monopoly that lies at the root of the perpetuation of the social division of labour) without beginning to dismantle the state, without increasingly transferring its competences to congresses of workers' councils, congresses of communes, congresses of health councils, education councils, etc.?

The state is exactly *not* an ensemble of technical, or even technocratic, functions. Bahro himself points this out on many occasions. He derides the so-called leading role of the party, which is merely a clumsy rationalization for the bureaucracy's monopoly of power: 'The party has died of its bureaucratism and hyper-bureaucratism. Its "cadres", the individuals who join the party, are almost entirely allocated to bureaucratic functions in the party, the state, the economy, science, or culture. When the Central Committee of the SED meets, for example, it is an assembly of the highest-placed functionaries of the party, the state, the unions, and the economy. . . . Today they meet as a "Central Committee" and apparently determine the policy of the party. But tomorrow nearly all of them, without exception, can be convoked by the Secretary-General to receive "instructions", since they are all his subordinates, or the subordinates of his subordinates' (pp. 426–27). Bahro eloquently comments: 'The individual members of the party are not communists in themselves, for they are denied the competence to be communists. When they are spoken to as communists, the apparatus appeals almost exclusively to their quasi-military discipline' (p. 427).

But it is these bureaucrats who direct and make up the state!

What does this have to do with 'objective technical imperatives'? Why should this 'power of men over men' – this administration of men, as distinct from administration of things – be
necessitated by 'the present level of technology'? In other
words, why should the self-organization and self-administration of the producers be 'utopian' in the industrially developed
countries (for West Germany, France, and Italy must certainly
be classed in this category)? Why could not the necessary
arbitration among 'particular interest groups' be effected by
collectively elected representatives of the associated producers? Why should this require an enormous apparatus of functionaries and gendarmes (for that is what the state is!), even
under conditions of relative abundance and satisfaction of
basic needs?

Wolfgang Harich, Bahro's compatriot and neo-Stalinist
ideologue (who has perhaps influenced Bahro), is at least more
logical and materialist when he bases the permanence of the
state, the bureaucracy and the single party, even under communism (a strange communism), on the permanence of constraints and the shortage of material goods . . . caused by
ecological exigencies!

## Three Programmatic Ambiguities

These analytic weaknesses determine programmatic ambiguities which would have grave consequences if extended to their
ultimate conclusions. (Let us hope that fraternal discussion,
even if it be conducted through prison bars, will prevent Bahro
from going that far.)

The first concerns the political and social conclusions of
Bahro's whole critique. Yes or no, *does the political power of the
toiling masses* have to be established, or must we content ourselves with hoping for a protracted transformation subsequent
to the substitution of the power of the technocrats for that of
the political bureaucracy?

Bahro is neither hypocritical nor blind. He fully understands
the terms of the problem. In spite of all his enthusiasm for the
Prague spring and the Yugoslav experience, he does not hesitate to write: 'It is no accident that the major economic theoretician of the reform, Ota Sik, wanted *not* real workers' councils,

but a regime of directors to whom the councils would be linked' (p. 116). He comments: 'If the Czechoslovak reform movement had succeeded (in whatever form), the workers would have regained control of their unions, and that would have improved their socio-political conditions. But precisely this restoration would have more clearly revealed their subordinate position in a state maintained by a bureaucracy' (p. 224). Exactly! That is the choice: reform of the bureaucratic system or anti-bureaucratic political revolution. Since Bahro is sceptical of the revolutionary potential of the working class, he does not (yet?) pronounce himself in favour of political revolution, but he does stress the inadequacy of reform. In any event, let us acknowledge that his constant reference to 'cultural revolution' (instead of political revolution) is only a feint which enables him to elude the difficulty but not to solve it. The tragic experience of the Chinese Cultural Revolution permits of only one conclusion. There can be no genuine abolition of the monopoly of power of the 'bureaucratic caste' (the term utilized by Bahro on page 13) without the establishment of the *political power* of the proletariat, of the toiling masses.

The second ambiguity concerns the relationship between the communes, which constitute the 'administrative' basis of the 'state in process of withering away' as projected by Bahro, and the workers' councils. All the passages in the book dealing with this question are suspiciously vague. The 'principle of association' is, of course, highly laudable. But what does it mean concretely, especially in the light of the enormous powers Bahro attributes to the communes? Will they be elected by universal suffrage? Or constituted by delegates of the councils? Territorial councils and factory councils, or only the former? How can it be guaranteed that the non-producers will not again impose sacrifices on the producers? Bahro scarcely furnishes any precise answers to these questions, which nonetheless flow logically from all the premises developed at great length in his book.

The third and perhaps the most serious ambiguity relates to the problem of the one-party state. The most striking paradox in Bahro's thought is that after concentrating his fire, initially directed against the bureaucracy as a whole, solely on the 'political' faction of the bureaucracy (*die Politbürokratie*), he does not clearly come out against the principle of the single party and for a multi-party system. The most he calls for is the creation of a 'League of Communists'. It is not clear whether this is supposed to be a second party, a single party, or not a party at all.

Once again, Bahro is neither naive nor a dupe. On several occasions he reaffirms that in spite of self-management at the factory level and in spite of the 'association of communes', Yugoslavia is still governed by a bureaucracy. Nor does he believe that the state can disappear overnight. He acknowledges the powerful centralizing tendency of contemporary productive forces. He even has an excessive respect for the 'objectively indispensable' role of the state. Who, then, will pin the tail on the donkey? Can thousands of communes acting 'through free association' decide the exact proportions of the division of the national or even international income? How can the toiling masses decide among hundreds of possible variants? Rank-and-file initiative is hailed, all to the good. But if one refuses the necessary institutional means for the masses to be able to make coherent choices among a series of alternative strategies for economic, social, cultural, and political growth – that is, different parties and tendencies – then one is back to the combination of a harmless anarchistic spontaneity at the rank-and-file level and a *regime of a bureaucratized single party at the summit*. These are the only possible solutions, at least so long as the transition from capitalism to communism lasts and the state persists.

Criticizing Lenin's anti-bureaucratic struggle as insufficient, Bahro uses the formula: 'You cannot fight the apparatus with the aid of another apparatus'. Agreed. But the obvious consequence is that bureaucratic dictatorship cannot be abolished if it continues to possess a monopoly of *central* decision-making, which means political decisions. Nor can we harbour the illusion that 'politics' – that is, central decisions – will disappear like magic under the pressure of 'associations'. *Thus, it is the process of central decision-making that must be resolutely democratized.* There is no other way of doing this than by interlocking the political regime of the councils of toilers with the institutions of the communes and with a multiplicity of *parties and associations on a national and international scale.*

Moreover, Bahro himself has pointed out the function and materialist basis of socialist democracy, relating it to the very nature of planning. (We stressed the same idea in *Marxist Economic Theory*.) Describing the planning system in East Germany and the USSR, Bahro affirms: 'At first sight, the major task of the plan seems to be to assure the proportionality of the production of use-values (including services in the broadest sense of the word) as a whole, through matrix calculation. In fact, this work does absorb the lion's share of the time spent by planners at all levels of the hierarchy. It is an enormous figure-juggling operation to calculate, two or three times a year (the draft plan, the final plan, and the corrected plan), the structure of products and labour for innumerable positions . . . and to draw up balance-sheets of all this in terms of expenditure of labour time, machines, and raw materials. At least in principle, our planning is indeed scientific, as it claims to be, as far as the methodological procedures for assuring proportionality are concerned. It may also be supposed that the calculations are "honest", that is to say mathematically correct. . . . But where does the scientific character of the plan break down? In its premises, before it has even begun. These premises, and by this I mean *priorities and preferences* . . . cannot be determined in an objective and scientific manner so long as antagonistic interests exist within society, which result from the uneven distribution of scarce goods of prime necessity and comfort and above all from the unequal distribution of knowledge and labour as a means of self-development and appropriation of culture' (pp. 181–82, our emphasis).

But under these conditions, the essential function of the state in post-capitalist society is to determine *which* priorities and preferences should orient the plan. There are only two possible institutional variants. Either the selection of these priorities is *imposed* on the producers-consumers by forces out-side themselves (including 'market laws' under the sadly famous 'socialist market economy'), or else they are made democratically by the mass of citizens, the producers-consumers themselves. Since there is no material possibility for this mass to choose among 10,000 variants of the plan (nor, for that matter, is there any possibility of their elaborating 10,000 different and coherent general plans each year), the real content of socialist democracy is indissolubly linked to the possibility of their choosing among *certain* coherent alternatives for the general plan. (This could, incidentally, lead to the possibility of much more varied choices, since each general plan, while characterized by internal coherence, would in turn permit a number of subvariants). The formulation of such alternatives presupposes precisely a multi-party system, with free access to the mass media and free debate by the mass of the population. It is only under these conditions that the enormous potential for creative initiative that exists among a highly skilled and cultivated proletariat can be fully liberated.

Having formulated these harsh criticisms, let us conclude by stressing once again the important contribution Bahro has made to discussion of the problems of political revolution. Let us above all reiterate our indignation at the East German bureaucracy, which has put such a thinker behind bars – on charges of spying for imperialist espionage agencies! In a letter to Bebel in which he protested against the censorship the leadership of the German Social Democratic Party was trying to exercise over the publication of the *Critique of the Gotha Programme*, Engels exclaimed: 'What makes you any different from Puttkamer (Bismarck's Minister of the Interior) if you introduce a *Sozialistengesetz* [law against socialists] in your own ranks?' The imprisonment of Bahro is a *Sozialistengesetz* within the workers' movement. It represents a Bastille-style absolutism on the part of the bureaucracy. But the Bastilles will some day be stormed by the toiling masses.

# 8
# The PCI and Austerity

Of all the Eurocommunist parties, the Italian Communist Party (PCI) has gone furthest in adapting to the conjunctural needs of 'its' bourgeoisie and is most prominently playing the role of saviour of a threatened capitalist system in its own country. A more detailed examination of the orientation the PCI upholds in economic policy will serve the useful purpose of revealing tendencies which are inherent in all Eurocommunism but have not yet developed fully in most of the other West European countries or in Japan, Australia, and Mexico.

In addition, such an examination can provide revolutionary Marxist militants with material for discussions with Communist party militants in their own countries. It can help to highlight the contrast – embarrassing for the leaders of the Communist parties – between the apparently determined opposition to austerity policies which the French, Spanish, Portuguese, British, Swedish, and Belgian Communist parties are still evincing (although for how much longer cannot be said) and the brutal manner in which the Italian Communist Party has fully adopted this same austerity policy. Such a discussion also acts as a warning to the workers' movements in these countries, which may well find themselves in situations similar to that of Italy unless trade-union and Communist militants are alerted and mobilized in time to oppose effectively the similar turns now being prepared in their respective countries, and unless the revolutionary vanguard succeeds in time in altering the relationship of forces within the workers' movement and the working class as a whole.

## An 'Explanation' of the Crisis Borrowed from Bourgeois Ideology

The leaders of the PCI have at least one merit: ideological and political coherence. Their strategic aim is perfectly clear: to avoid at all costs a comprehensive and head-on confrontation between capital and labour, a confrontation which they believe could end only in a defeat for the workers' movement. The tactical means are no less clear: to prevent the serious economic crisis now racking Italian capitalism from coinciding with an intensification of the class struggle; to this end to apply a systematic policy of class collaboration at all levels. The economic policy which flows from this project is resolutely to support the austerity policy of the government of Giulio Andreotti.

But if it is to be sold to the most conscious and advanced sectors of the working class, intellectuals, and students, this entire policy needs an ideological cover that presents a structural explanation of the crisis and sketches out some way of overcoming it. It was to this task that Enrico Berlinguer, the secretary general of the PCI, primarily devoted himself throughout the winter of 1976–77.

What is immediately striking in this attempt to establish ideological coherence for the political-social project of the PCI is the increasingly open abandonment of Marxism, with a rapidity that is almost disconcerting when compared to the caution with which the leaders of the German Social Democracy operated in this domain during the period 1914–1923 (for this is the historical precedent that immediately comes to mind). It may be said without exaggeration that the explanation of the economic crisis now being advanced by Berlinguer and repeated by most of the major leaders of the PCI, or at least the explanation of the conjunctural aspects of that crisis, is entirely borrowed from the bourgeois ideology now prevalent in the West, and even from the least 'progressive' currents of this ideology.

In his report to the PCI Central Committee of October 1976 (published in the 19 October 1976 issue of the PCI's weekly, *Rinascità*) Berlinguer limited himself to citing two fundamental causes of the crisis: inflation and the 'transfer of resources' from the industrialized countries to the countries of the 'Third

World' (that is, the rise in the prices of raw materials, especially oil). In his concluding speech to a conference of intellectuals convoked by the PCI in January 1977, he reduced the 'explanation' for the gravity of the crisis solely to the modification of relations with the 'Third World'. (This speech, along with a speech to an assembly of Communist workers of Lombardy on 30 January 1977, has been published by the PCI in a small book under the eloquent title: *Austerity, an Opportunity to Transform Italy*.[1] The following quotations are taken from this book.) In the speech to the intellectuals we read the following:

'We must never lose sight of the general significance of the majestic upsurge of these peoples [the peoples of the 'Third World'], an upsurge which has changed the course of world history and is little by little shaking all past and present balances, not only the relationship of forces on a world scale, but also those within the various capitalist countries. *It is this upsurge, or at least mainly this upsurge, which, acting in depth, is detonating the contradictions of an entire phase of post-war capitalist development and is causing unprecedented crisis conditions in various countries*' (p. 16, emphasis added).

Let us leave aside the 'unprecedented' crisis conditions. Berlinguer rather hastily forgets the crisis of 1929–32, which was far graver than the present one. But to attribute the economic recession, or its gravity, primarily to the rise in oil prices is to parrot the formulae of bourgeois ideology (even though in this case it is camouflaged by a ritual tip of the hat to the 'majestic upsurge' of national liberation movements). This amounts to a Keynesianism so crude that Keynes himself would have disdained it; it plays on ignorance extended to the sphere of the entire international capitalist economy. The rise in oil prices is said to have had deflationary effects on the imperialist economy (through the 'transfer of resources', as Berlinguer put it in his October 1976 report to the Central Committee). Hence the recession.

Unfortunately for the advocates of this theory, the 'transfer of resources' is not at all equal to the sum total of the supplementary income of the countries of the Organization of

[1] Enrico Berlinguer, *Austerità, Occasione per Trasformare l'Italia*, Rome, 1977.

Petroleum Exporting Countries (OPEC), but represents only that fraction of this income which is *withdrawn* from the international circuit of commodities and capital, in other words hoarded by the oil-exporting countries. Those additional resources which these countries use to purchase supplementary goods in the imperialist countries do not have any effect of 'reducing world demand'. On the contrary, they constitute *an additional demand* for goods exported (and thus produced) by the imperialist countries. Now, the balance of payments surpluses of the OPEC countries for 1973, 1974, and 1975 were much lower than initially foreseen: $57,000 million in 1973; $35,000 million in 1974; $34,000 million in 1975. This represents less than 2% of the average yearly gross national product of the imperialist countries; in 1975 it was less than 1%. The rise in oil prices has probably accounted for not more than 1.5–2% of total price increases. It is thus difficult to see how a recession and inflation of the gravity we have seen in the past several years can be 'primarily' attributed to this marginal and secondary factor.

But there is more. Marxists, not to mention Marx himself, have never accepted the theory that attributes economic crises exclusively or mainly to a decline in total demand, whether national or international. In fact, overproduction of commodities *precedes* declines in aggregate demand and does not result from them. If demand phenomena come into the picture, it is because on the eve of a crisis both demand and consumption, *although rising*, do not increase *at the same rate* as productive capacity. Overproduction and its contemporary, late capitalist form of excess productive capacity, are present and visible well before the crisis breaks out. They were visible as of the early 1970s. Berlinguer does not say a word about this, for it is difficult to assign responsibility for it to the emancipation struggle of the peoples of the so-called Third World.

For Marxists, an overproduction crisis is not only *a crisis of overproduction of commodities*. It is also a *crisis of overproduction of capital* in the sense of a crisis of accumulation. Both the decline in the average rate of profit and excess productive capacity lead the capitalists to reduce productive investment. This is the other mechanism which triggers the crisis. It too was visible as of the end of the 1960s and the beginning of the

1970s. Here again Berlinguer hears no evil and sees no evil. A sorry Communist makes a bad Marxist.

It is not gratuitously or simply out of salon courtesy that Berlinguer throws overboard a century of development of the Marxist theory of economic crises. The thesis of the 'transfer of resources' abroad is intended to provide theoretical justification for the inevitability of austerity, the 'sacrifices in consumption' that 'everyone' has to accept.[2] The class struggle has disappeared from the analysis. Instead there are banal references to 'equitably distributed sacrifices', the common watchword repeated by innumerable liberal and reformist demagogues on similar occasions in past decades.

Abandonment of Marxism is necessary in order to lend coherence to the abandonment of the class struggle, to the adoption of a programme for salvaging the capitalist system. The ideology of the 'general interest', of the 'fate of the nation' which must be of primary concern (Berlinguer uses both phrases again and again in the speeches cited), is obviously incompatible with the worn out theory of the 19th century lion of the British Museum that there is an *irreconcilable* conflict of interest between capital and labour, between the bourgeoisie and the proletariat, in each capitalist country. Since strategic and tactical considerations require that the ideology of the 'general interest' carry the day, Marxism can be jettisoned.

The transition from Marxism, which was still formally proclaimed not long ago, to its open abandonment has been so rapid that it threatens to lead party militants and even the most subservient cadres astray. The operation must therefore be camouflaged; the tracks have to be covered. This thankless task was assigned to a member of the PCI economic commission, Sergio Zangirolami. In a hastily patched together book he achieves the *tour de force* of outlining the Marxist theory of crises in the first part (although in a rather summary manner), developing an analysis of the present crisis and the PCI's recommendations for how to overcome it in the second part,

[2] 'It is no accident that in the "Report on the Italian Economy" drafted by the CESPE and published last July, we spoke of the necessity for a "significant reduction" in the share of gross national product destined for consumption. This is necessary not only to reestablish the balance of payments but also and above all to finance investments' (Eugenio Peggio, PCI economist, in the PCI's economic review, *Politica ed Economia*, September–October 1976).

and eliminating any connection whatsoever between the 'general theory' and the 'specific analysis'. The fall of the rate of profit, which plays a central role in the 'general theory', is not even mentioned in the analysis of the present crisis![3]

## Historical Function of the Crisis and Austerity

Although in the final analysis the crisis results from the decline in the average rate of profit, at the same time it constitutes the mechanism by which the capitalist mode of production prepares to restart the mechanism of accumulation, to increase the rate of profit again. The objective function of the crisis is to devalorize capital, to diminish its total value (the weakest enterprises being eliminated) and consequently to augment the rate of exploitation of the working class. This upturn in the mass and rate of profit may now be noted in most of the imperialist countries.[4]

Now it is another significant fact that in the one hundred pages by Berlinguer with which we are dealing here, *profit is mentioned only once* (on page 59), *and that in an entirely positive sense*: 'We affirm', writes Berlinguer, 'that the market, private enterprise, and profit can and must retain a function even in the framework of an economy that develops under the democratic public will and is oriented by this will'. That's all. As quiet as a churchmouse.

Since Berlinguer throws both the Marxist doctrine of crises and the Marxist doctrine of the class struggle overboard, he must also obscure the evidence of reality, namely that *the major function of austerity policies is to modify the division of national income to the detriment of the wage earners and to the advantage of the bourgeoisie*.[5] Under the capitalist system, no recovery of

[3] Sergio Zangirolami, *Economia Politica Marxista e Crisi Attuale* (Marxist Political Economy and the Present Crisis), Rome, April 1977.

[4] Let us cite one example, that of Australia. In 1976 capitalist profits there rose 33%, wages 11.6%, and the cost of living 15%. As a result of this decline in real wages, the share of profits in the national income reached its highest level since 1970.

[5] Nevertheless, the 20 May 1977 issue of the PCI weekly, *Rinascità*, published the account of a discussion among Communist economists during which Napoleoni affirmed in particular that in order to increase productive employment, that is, 'to generate a demand for labour in industry . . . we must, I repeat, deal with the problem of the economic situation of these enterprises in a draconian manner, with particular reference to labour costs'.

the rate of profit, no upturn in productive investment, and no lasting economic recovery is possible without this modification. The Helmut Schmidts and the other aggressive right-wing Social Democrats at least have the merit of frankness. They proclaim from the rooftops: 'The profits of today are the jobs of tomorrow'. But since Berlinguer is confronted by one of the most radicalized and militant working classes of the world, he cannot say this so crudely. He is thus compelled to compound the mortal sin of betrayal of the class interests of the proletariat with the venial sin of hypocrisy and mystification (as were the German Social Democrats in 1918–23).

That is why acceptance of the austerity policy – in other words, the priming of capitalist profits – is embedded in impenetrable phraseology about 'economic programming'. We will return to the real function of this 'programming', which is not mere verbiage, far from it, in the reality of Italian capitalism today. But before examining its economic function, let us unmask its function of mystification.

Berlinguer presents things as though such programming could stimulate a considerable increase in public consumption (mass transit, housing, health care, education or culture), a modernization of agriculture in Southern Italy on a grand scale, the reabsorption of the particularly dramatic unemployment of youth,[6] a spectacular development of scientific research (*Rinascità*, 19 October 1976). In fact, there are two alternatives:

*Either the 'transfer of resources' (as Berlinguer would put it) required to finance all these gigantic projects will be made essentially at the expense of surplus-value, in which case it will be reflected in a new decline in the rate of profit and thus in an even more massive 'investment strike' than that which was conducted during and just after the recession;

*Or else it will be made essentially at the expense of consumption, in which case it implies *a draconian reduction in real wages*, which the working class will scarcely accept, even if called upon to do so by the PCI, so long as it preserves the essence of its organizations and democratic rights. In either case the 'project' of the PCI leads to a veritable disaster for the pro-

---

[6] According to the 21 February 1976 issue of the Milan magazine *Mondo Economico*, as of spring 1975 some 62% of unemployed workers in Italy were less than 25 years old. Of these 775,000 unemployed youth, 620,000 had never had a job.

letariat.

But the most likely possibility, the one which corresponds to the real experience of 'economic programming' in all the imperialist countries during past decades (particularly in France, the Netherlands, and Britain) is that the *reality* of private property in the means of production, of the right and power of the capitalists to command machines and labour power, will put severe limits on the influence and effectiveness of 'economic programming'. The essence of the most ambitious plans will remain on paper. In practice the only projects actually carried out will be those which conform to the interests of big capital, which 'round out' and complete capital's own investment projects and improve their profitability (either directly or indirectly). *Under the capitalist system*, let us repeat, this is simply a way of preventing the 'private sector' from systematically undoing what the 'public sector' has initiated laboriously (and slowly and bureaucratically too, for it is a 'public sector' administered by a bourgeois state; the PCI carefully refrains from demanding workers' management of the nationalized enterprises).

For structural reasons, no 'economic programming' under the capitalist system can be any more than an appendage to the activities of the private companies, above all the trusts and monopolies. To entice the workers with the prospect that the contrary could occur is to deceive them. It is to suggest that the supposed 'mixed economy' could somehow miraculously emancipate them from the imperatives of profit and competition, that is, that this economy would differ structurally from the capitalist economy, that it would evolve under the effects of laws of development which differ from those of the capitalist mode of production. This is a gross illusion, a hundred times belied by history.[7]

[7] The leaders of the PCI deliberately stress the lamentable failure of the 'economic programming' applied in Italy up to now. The 1965–70 'programme' had called for a net increase of 800,000 jobs; in fact there was a reduction of 172,000. It called for a reduction in the difference between national per capita value-added and per capita value-added in the South from 22% to 15%; in fact the difference increased from 22% to 24% (Zangirolami, op. cit., p. 92). But instead of explaining this failure by the contradictions inherent in the very nature of *capitalist* 'programming', which cannot be separated from the imperatives of profit, competition, private enrichment, and private profit, they attribute it to the 'weakness' and 'inefficiency' of the Centre-Left governments.

**The Real Content of the PCI's Economic Policy**

Does this mean that 'economic programming' is nothing but a trick? Were that the case it would be difficult to understand why it has been introduced in one imperialist country after another. It would also be difficult to understand the meaning of the twofold bid the leadership of the PCI is now making to the bourgeoisie of its country.

In Berlinguer's speeches there is a vigorous denunciation, which sometimes even takes on pathetic overtones. But it is not a denunciation of the capitalist mode of production. It is not a denunciation of the profits of individual firms as the motor force of economic development. It is not a denunciation of the *model of capitalist accumulation.* No, it is a denunciation of the *model of consumption* of the 1950s and 1960s, based on the acquisition of durable consumer goods and symbolized by the private automobile. This indictment is combined with denunciation of all that is archaic, backward, and underdeveloped in Italian capitalism:

'Austerity, depending on its content and on the forces which govern its application, can be used either as an instrument of economic depression, political repression, and perpetuation of social injustice or as an opportunity for new economic and social development, rigorous pruning of the state, profound transformation of the basis of society, and defence and expansion of democracy' (pp. 44–45). Elsewhere, Berlinguer declares: 'In fact, it seems obvious to me that these objectives will contribute to forging a social basis and an economic and financial policy organically directed against waste, privilege, parasitism, and dissipation of resources. They will thus embody what must constitute the essence of what is by nature and definition a genuine austerity policy. Better, it may be observed that injustice and extravagance have often been combined, are combined in decadent societies, whereas justice and frugality go hand in hand in ascending societies' (p. 27).

Should anyone hesitate to share our severe judgment of Berlinguer, should anyone detect a socialist project or a project for the overthrow of capitalism – even if in an obscure, or even perverse, manner – behind vague formulas like 'transformation of the basis of society' or 'new social development', Berlinguer himself misses no opportunity to dot the i's. His concern is to reassure the bourgeoisie, and he allows no trace of ambiguity. Here is what he says in his report to the conference of intellectuals: 'Our initiative is not an act of propaganda or exhibitionism on the part of our party. It is intended as an act of confidence. It is intended, once again, to be an act of unity; it is a contribution which solicits the unity of the other parties so as to permit real work and to appeal for common commitments which will involve all the democratic and popular forces [which for the PCI includes the Christian Democracy, the major party of the Italian bourgeoisie – E.M.]. Similarly, because of its unitary character and intentions, our project, I believe, *is not intended to be and cannot be a programme of transition to a socialist society*. More modestly and concretely, it must propose to trace out a development of the economy and society whose characteristics and new forms of functioning can win the adherence and consensus of all those Italians who do not hold socialist or communist convictions but who are acutely conscious of the need to free themselves and the nation of the injustice, distortions, absurdities, and lacerations towards which the present basis of society is diverting us' (pp. 24–25).

That is clear enough. We do not want an immediate transition to socialism, the PCI says. Our proposals do not aim at such a transition. But since there is no such thing as a society which is simultaneously capitalist and non-capitalist, since the 'mixed economy' is a fairy tale, what 'we' therefore propose (without saying so in such a way that the workers understand it clearly, although the bourgeoisie, with its infinitely greater political experience, has obviously understood it) is to replace an *'irrational', archaic, and absurd capitalism* under which a good part of surplus-value is wasted by the 'patronage' and 'parasitism' so dear to the Christian Democracy, with a *modernized, rationalized, competitive, expansionist, and dynamic capitalism.* It is only in the framework of such a 'rationalized' capitalism that the workers' movement will be able to consolidate and extend its gains, that the living standards of the toilers will be able to rise again after a phase of 'inevitable sacrifices' ('equitably distributed', of course). This, once again, is a pure and simple repetition of the classical Social Democratic project formulated by the German trade-union leader Tarnow during the great crisis of 1929–32: to be the bedside doctor of ailing capitalism, for if the patient does not recover the cake will not expand and the workers will get fewer crumbs. Is the economic policy the PCI is proposing to the bourgeoisie credible? Does it have any chance of success? Yes and no. Undoubtedly, the big Italian monopolies would not be hostile to using the austerity policy, with the active participation of the unions and the PCI (that is, utilizing their pressure), to get rid of many elements of waste and extravagance with which Italian capitalism has been plagued ever since the country was unified (because of the historically peculiar manner in which this unification occurred) and particularly since the period of fascism. The reign of the Christian Democracy has scarcely eliminated these elements, in spite of twenty years of economic expansion. Nothing here is incompatible with the production, realization, and accumulation of surplus-value, which is the nature and rationale of capitalism. *In a favourable economic and social context* this project could even win a general approval from big capital (with the exception of retrograde and parasitic sectors), comparable to the endorsement received in France by the scheme developed by De Gaulle with the creation of the Fifth Republic, which was analogous on the whole.[8]

But there is the rub. The PCI project comes twenty years too late. It presupposes that vigorous economic expansion of Italian capitalism is possible, primarily on the world market. Now, the most likely possibility is on the contrary that there will be a lasting slow-down in the rate of growth of world trade and an exacerbation of international competition, in which Italian capitalism is at a marked structural disadvantage because of its past (as the representatives of the PCI are aware). In the best of cases an enormous investment effort over a whole historical period would be needed simply to compensate for this disadvantage and to retain the country's current competitive position. To win a qualitatively superior portion of the world

[8] On the attempts of the PCI to link its austerity policy to more long-term projects, crystallized in a report entitled *Proposta di Progetto a Medio Termine* (Draft Medium-Term Project), written by an economic commission of the Central Committee in June 1977 and published with a preface by Giorgio Napoletano, see the article 'The Medium-Term Economic Project of the PCI', by Livio Maitan, in *Inprecor*, no. 13 new series, 29 September 1977.

market than Italy presently commands appears completely utopian. The Italian capitalists themselves do not even believe it.

The prospect of 'modernization' and 'rationalization' thus leads to the prospect of a lasting, long-term reduction of the share of consumption in a national income which can now grow only slowly. It thus leads either to tension and a grave and lasting social crisis or to a defeat and demoralization of the working class, driving the entire workers' movement to a lower level. Both eventualities would represent failure for the PCI project.

But precisely because the project of modernizing Italian capitalism occurs within a particular international context, it involves another dimension which is scarcely noted in the analyses of the PCI. Because of the exacerbation of international competition, because of the vast gap between the arena of operation of the big expansionist and profitable monopolies on the one hand (of which Fiat and Pirelli are the prototypes in Italy) and the public or mixed companies condemned to survive on the strength of repeated and growing public subsidies on the other hand, the activity, orientation, and interests of the 'multinationals' of Italian origin will tend increasingly to spread beyond the national borders. It follows that there will be a growing trend towards the international interpenetration of capital, through mergers or absorption: Fiat–Allis Chalmers and Pirelli–Dunlop are examples of this sort.[9] It also follows that any capitalist 'national economic programming' – that is, any programming which respects private property, the profit imperative, and market laws – will be decreasingly able to have any effect on the scope, orientation, and localization of the investments of such monopolies.

The leaders of the PCI sense this vaguely (without drawing any strategic or tactical conclusions from it). In the 1976 election programme of the PCI we read the following passage in the chapter on 'How to Overcome the Economic Crisis': 'Our choice is still to accept an "open" market system, a system of open competition in the international domain. . . . But there is no

[9] The share of Fiat's turnover realized abroad, which was still 40% in 1973, has now surpassed 50% and should reach 60% soon (see Arturo Cannetta in *Consigli*, No. 27/28, August–September 1976).

contradiction between an anti-protectionist option and the adoption of an investment policy which aims at increasing, at competitive prices, Italian production of agricultural and industrial goods which have been imported in growing quantities and at rising prices during past years. . . . An investment policy must be applied which moves Italy into sectors that are more highly skilled technologically, so as to strengthen and renew export capacity' (*l'Unità*, 16 May 1976).

But since *all* the imperialist powers are seeking to reduce imports and increase exports, what will the overall result be? Isn't it a lost cause for Italy (still supposing that there is no crushing defeat for the working class)? It is therefore necessary to go further. The result is the following miserable 'solution', formulated by Luciano Lama, the leader of the CGIL (Italy's largest trade-union federation) and one of the leaders of the PCI itself: 'It is clear that the interdependence of economic policy in the various countries increases constantly as time goes by. . . . I therefore exclude *a priori* the idea that we can achieve or approach full employment by applying a policy of autarky. . . . On the contrary, we must act within international groupings, including economic ones, to induce the countries of Western Europe and of the advanced capitalist world to understand that it is in everybody's interest to resolve the problem of employment in Italy'.[10]

Would it be possible to fall any lower into banality and the diffusion of stupid illusions within the working class? Lama begins by admitting that the crisis is exceptionally serious, continues by stressing the violence of capitalist competition, and finally acknowledges that the Italian capitalists are at a pronounced disadvantage in this crisis. He admits that these capitalists are seeking to reduce 'labour costs' in order to 'prime' production. Isn't the *essential* function of unemployment precisely to achieve this end?[11] But Lama concludes by

[10] Luciano Lama, *Intervista sul Sindacato*, edited by Massimo Riva, October 1976, p. 101.

[11] This is another instance of abandonment of an elementary thesis of Marx. For Lama the periodic reconstitution of the industrial reserve army of labour is no longer an objective necessity for capital. This, he claims, is simply a thesis which 'bourgeois ideologues' advance from time to time and could just as easily be replaced by the opposite contention (op. cit. pp. 103–104).

trusting in foreign capitalists, who will undoubtedly surrender part of the world market in order to aid dear Italy 'to resolve the problem of employment'. Although the normal behaviour of the bourgeoisie in the capitalist jungle has always been to try to *export unemployment* to neighbouring and competitive countries in time of crisis (which is just what the Swiss, German, and Benelux capitalists have done again this time, sending Italian immigrant workers home), Lama pretends to believe that the predators will suddenly agree to *increase unemployment in their own countries during a period of crisis* for the benefit of Enrico Berlinguer. This ridiculous analysis is presented as a sample of Communist wisdom.

It is true that the PCI does not always speak with a single voice. Its representatives express differences, not only in the Central Committee, but also in public. For instance, Giorgio Amendola, the leader of the right wing of the PCI, did not hesitate to write an article in October 1976 (suggestively titled 'Coherence and Rigour') expressing a position in nearly frontal opposition to the Communist trade unionists: 'When we speak of the necessary sacrifices the workers must accept in order to overcome the crisis, it would be erroneous to conceive of these sacrifices as "concessions" to the capitalists and the government, as is sometimes done, or as the "price" of a supposed Communist manoeuvre aimed at getting into the government at any cost. On the contrary, the sacrifices are necessary if the country is to extract itself from the crisis in a manner consistent with the interests of the workers, if the youth are to find jobs, if the living conditions of the people are to be improved. . . . That is why it is not correct to discuss what compensation should be demanded in return for the sacrifices needed for the effort towards change' (quoted by Henri Weber in *Parti communiste Italien: Aux Sources de l'Eurocommunisme*, p. 68).

The 'Communist' and 'Marxist' Amendola seems to have been unable to foresee or realize that the sacrifices imposed on the workers increase *capitalist* profits and bring the *bourgeoisie* out of the crisis without finding jobs for the youth, while the people's living conditions deteriorate rather than improve.

Moreover, isn't it part of the most obsolete bourgeois ideology to assert blithely that it is 'inevitable' for the workers to make 'sacrifices' in their living standards during periods of crisis?[12] These 'sacrifices' are about as 'inevitable' as the economic crises themselves. They do not result from any 'fatality' or 'iron law'. They flow from the existence of the capitalist mode of production, which is neither 'fatal', nor 'inevitable', nor eternal, but survives because of a given relationship of socio-political forces. In other words, it can be overthrown by a working class which is strong, conscious, and united enough. Even in the framework of this mode of production, the precise division of the national income between wages and profits is not pre-determined and does not flow automatically even from the level of employment. It is determined by the 'relationship of forces between the contending classes', in other words, the ups and downs of the class struggle.

One is almost ashamed to remind someone who still calls himself a communist of these elementary truths. But Amendola pretends to forget that the original and historic purpose of the Communist Party was not at all to convince the workers of the 'inevitability' of crises and the 'sacrifices' they 'necessarily' impose on the proletariat, but rather to educate, organize, and mobilize the workers to defend their interests intransigently, to prepare the overthrow of the capitalist system as the instigator of crises and unemployment, precisely taking advantage of the moments of weakness and grave crises of the system in order to achieve this end.

The PCI trade-union leader Trentin, however, takes pains to speak an entirely different language. He affirms that: 'an alternative policy must inevitably lead to a qualitative modification of the system. Not to a more rational capitalism, but to a transitional economic system. When the collectivity manages not through decrees, but through mass action, new forms of workers' control, new relationships among the traditional

---

[12] 'The damage caused by demagogues of various extraction who claim that we want to impose the burden of sacrifices on the workers is immense. The damage is to the working class, not to our party. This is not only because the sacrifices are inevitable whether we like it or not, but also because they conceal the essential point in this way ... namely the fact that these sacrifices will be decided either by political determination guided by a conscious plan of equity and reform, or by the market, which means by a capitalist mechanism' (Alfredo Reichlin, in *Rinascità*, 3 December 1976).

representative institutions, and new forms of rank-and-file democracy . . . to determine a new allocation of investments, a policy of reconversion of the sort supported by the trade-union movement today, then one cannot speak merely of restructuration or capitalist rationalization. I think, and Italian capitalism is quite well aware of this, that it is the power of capital to command a profit which will then be challenged' (ibid., p. 120).

Let us leave aside the irreconcilable contradictions between a policy of sacrifices and reduction in living standards imposed on the workers and mass actions pressed to the point where they could win workers' control of production and investments from the capitalists. Trentin fails to notice that if profits are to be *shared* according to criteria of 'social utility' established by the trade unions and the workers' parties, they must first be *produced*. In other words, there must first be a sufficient volume of productive investments and employment. Now, the capitalists do not invest in order to serve 'social utility' or the 'collectivity'. They invest to maximize private profit and to dispose of this profit freely (within the limits of fiscal constraints, attenuated by fraud and institutionalized tax evasion). If their aspirations and expectations in this respect are not satisfied, they go on strike: they refuse to invest. Employment levels decline. All the beautiful projects of the plan go up in smoke. Further, the aggravation of social tension that would inevitably flow from the amplification of 'mass action', not to mention 'new forms of rank-and-file democracy' and the generalization of workers' control, could only lead to the same result.

In other words, the 'transitional economic system' vaunted by Trentin amounts to the same mystification as the 'mixed economy'. Nobody has ever worked out how to compel the capitalists to make factories run against their own interests. Either the law of profit – private profit, understand – reigns supreme, in which case the system functions, to the benefit of capital and (during and after the crisis) *to the detriment of the toiling masses,* or else an attempt is made to impose an order within the factories and the economy as a whole which is contrary to the interests of the bourgeoisie, in which case *the bourgeoisie must be deprived of the right to own the means of production,* which means that factories must be nationalized, profits must be confiscated, the volume and direction of investment must be determined by the collectivity, and all necessary resources must be amassed to *impose* this plan. This can never be done through 'consensus'. It is known as initiating the socialist revolution. To attempt to straddle these two possibilities is to sink into utopia once again. It is to rush headlong into depression and a decline of productive activity:-

## The 'New Model of Consumption'

The centrepiece of Berlinguer's apology for the austerity policy demanded by big capital is his plea for a 'new model of consumption' which will replace spending on private consumption by spending on public consumption. In a rather demagogic manner, the leadership of the PCI is thus seeking to coopt, more or less in passing, some of the themes of the intellectual dissent of the 1960s. All this is presented by Berlinguer as the development of 'elements of socialism' within capitalist society (*Rinascità*, 19 October 1976). Once again, we are dealing with a barely altered reproduction of classical Social Democratic theses on 'municipal socialism' and 'political wages'.

An initial contradiction is immediately apparent, which reveals the mystified character of the entire project: among the products to be removed from individual consumption (which is 'alienating', it appears) is beef, since Italy imports too much of it, to the detriment of the balance of payments. Since the only mechanism that mediates consumption under a system of money economy and capitalist property is purchase, the only way to 'reduce consumption' is to raise prices. But raising prices reduces consumption only for people with modest incomes. The logic of the entire bombastic tirade about a 'model of consumption' is thus to take away the workers' steaks without stopping the bourgeoisie from feeding at will. (Let there be no talk of 'equitable rationing', which in a country like Italy would inevitably lead to a black market, afflicting the workers and the poor while benefiting speculators and capitalists.) The 'trade unionists' who defend such injustices have the impudence to accuse workers who try to defend themselves against such exactions of 'corporatism'. Cynicism decidedly has no limits.

142

Another striking contradiction is that the development of
'public consumption' obviously presupposes an expansion of
public expenditure. Yet Berlinguer repeats the allegation,
widely diffused by the bourgeoisie, that public spending is
'excessive' in Italy[13] and that an 'austerity policy' should be
applied in the public sector as well (pp. 41–42). The problem,
then, is to reduce and increase public expenditure simultaneously. The embarrassed economists of the PCI respond that
public spending has to be 'rationalized', which means that
'wasteful' public spending (in which category military expen-
ditures are not placed, since the PCI respects Italy's 'international commitments', meaning NATO) must be replaced
with public spending 'that directly or indirectly stimulates
economic development'. But this is only a subterfuge which
dodges the real question: does the entire economic programme
imply a growth or reduction in the share of the gross national
product represented by the budget? No person of good will
could deny that it implies an increase, even a considerable one.
Is the bourgeoisie prepared to accept this increase and pay for
it? How can it be forced to do so? Will the essential portion of
this enormous burden be imposed on the working class (which
already pays more than 60% of direct taxes in Italy)? Would
the working class accept this, regardless of the disastrous consequences for its standard of living? The 'Communist analysis'
does not even run the risk of posing these problems, let alone
resolve them.

But this entire programme is doubly invalid. Historically,
the development of those public services in bourgeois society
from which the toilers primarily benefit is always linked to
periods of rapid expansion of production, incomes, and capitalist profits. This is an insurmountable constraint. The bourgeoisie has an interest in making such concessions in order to
accentuate the weight of reformism within the working class.
In addition, the 'indirect by-products' of such concessions are
generally more advantageous to the bourgeoisie than are direct
wage increases. Nevertheless, the capitalists can make these

[13] In reality, according to EEC statistics, state spending represented 42% of
gross national product in Italy in 1975, as against 44.2% in Belgium, 46.4% in
Britain, 48% in West Germany, 53.1% in Ireland, and 55.3% in the Netherlands.
It was only in France that the percentage was lower, very slightly (41%).

concessions only when the economic situation is good. To hope for such increases of social services in an atmosphere of economic crisis and decline in the rate of profit is an idle illusion. The only sort of public spending the bourgeoisie seeks to increase in such an atmosphere is direct and indirect subsidies to capitalist companies, in other words 'state guarantees of capitalist profit', especially profit for the monopolies. This hardly encourages a 'new model of consumption'.

It is true that even during periods of slow-down in economic growth the toilers can win new social gains through direct and vigorous struggles (how long they can conserve such gains if they do not continue the struggle through to the overthrow of capitalism is another question). The general strike of 1936 in France won paid holidays for all, an example of a 'change in the model of consumption' if ever there was one. But it took precisely a general strike and the fear of revolution it generated among the bourgeoisie to win this conquest. Thus, even the most important reform won by the international workers' movement in the 1930s appears as a by-product of a mass struggle that was objectively revolutionary in scope. The PCI breaks and stifles attempts at generalized strikes in Italy today. It scarcely wants to extract reforms under the threat of revolution. Rather, it wants to negotiate with the employers under the ensign of 'common interest'. We would wager that in this manner the PCI will never win the reforms of 'socialist consumption' it is now dangling before the naive.

The worst contradiction of this policy is that while it understands that the 'model of consumption' of the 1950s and 1960s obviously corresponded to capitalist logic (Berlinguer, op. cit. p. 26), which is the logic of the massive production and sale of *commodities*, of the universal drive toward *private* enrichment, it nevertheless blithely proposes to alter this 'model of consumption' without breaking out of the capitalist system. In its fundamental dynamic, the 'model of consumption' of public services preached by Berlinguer is based on the logic of the satisfaction of needs. Even a Galbraith has understood *that for this very reason* it can only be marginal under the capitalist system. Does Berlinguer seriously believe that an economy based on profit can integrate as an *essential element* an economy that fundamentally negates profit? The Catholic mystery of transsubstantiation is nothing compared to this mystery.

## A Provisional Balance-sheet

When all the verbiage is eliminated and all the smokescreens are dissipated, one essential and immediate point remains: *the leaders of the PCI have surreptitiously drifted toward a thesis that tallies with that of the employers, namely that wage increases are one of the essential causes of inflation*, that the struggle against inflation is the top priority, and that this struggle demands *an incomes policy that drives down real wages* by no longer adapting them to the dizzying increase in the cost of living. Such is the unabashed content of the austerity policy.[14]

In October 1976 Luciano Lama still rejected this thesis 'energetically', although he nonetheless upheld the idea that 'automatic' wage increases (not a sliding scale, but seniority increases, extra-legal pensions, and so on) would be contrary to the interests of the workers' movement (op. cit. p. 83–90). But Berlinguer is much more brutal. Speaking before the Communist workers of Lombardy, he began by saying that rising labour costs were not the sole cause of inflation (p. 41). Then he continued, unveiling his artillery: 'We say that on the whole the problem of the dynamic of labour costs in Italy compared to those in other European countries must be taken into account and resolved, but that this must be done on the basis of broader criteria that better correspond to reality' (op. cit. p. 42).[15]

[14] The theory that wage increases cause inflation is closely related to the thesis that reductions in real wages are inevitable if 'the national economy is to be cleansed'. This theory has now been cheerfully adopted by some Communist economists, such as Ezio Tarantelli (see, in particular, his article 'Scala mobile e inflazione') who completely adopts bourgeois attacks on the sliding scale as a mechanism that allegedly fuels inflation. His article was published in the September–October 1976 issue of *Politica ed Economia*. It also resorts to the Ricardian theory which sees a direct and immediate relationship between wage increases and declines in the rate of profit, without the mediation of the organic composition of capital, discovered and introduced by Marx in his critique of Ricardo. The neo-Ricardian economic theory associated with the Cambridge school and Piero Sraffa, which has profoundly influenced the PCI, is thus now having disastrous practical effects on the defence of the interests of the workers, for it is serving as pseudo-theoretical justification for a bourgeois offensive that blames the unions for the crisis.

[15] Not once does Berlinguer mention the responsibility of the monopolies, of their pricing policies and the banking and monetary practices which serve their interests, as among the causes of inflation, although these are given some importance in the first part of Zangirolami's book.

Berlinguer then summed up the action recommended by the PCI: 'What is the most significant fact about the present crisis from the political and class standpoint? It is that the capitalist world, and with it the old political personnel who still occupy some (sic) positions of power, have been compelled to turn toward us – toward the working class, the toilers, and the Communists – as a force which has now become indispensable for setting things in order, for making the machinery of the economy and the state function, for bringing efficiency to the entire Italian social system. . . . This reveals something which is genuinely new from the historic point of view. The old ruling classes and the old politicians are no longer in a position to *impose* sacrifices on the working class; today they must *ask us* to make them, and they are asking us' (op. cit. p. 52).

This at least has the merit of frankness. Capital is no longer capable of *imposing* wage cuts on the workers. It has to *'ask'* the PCI and the trade-union leaderships to grant them. The Communist Party bureaucrats toe the line, without reticence o ' second thought: 'But in whose name do the old ruling groups ask our aid? They certainly do not say that they are asking us to salvage capitalism, to preserve their class privileges. They say that the sacrifices of the workers serve to attain three objectives of general interest: redress the national economy, accentuate the upturn of production, maintain and extend employment. What response must we give to these objectives? We have no doubt: we answer 'yes' to all three, but we must immediately add something else' (op. cit. p. 53).

In other words, in their attempts to facilitate the betrayal of the interests of the workers by the reformists, the intelligent capitalists claim that salvaging the capitalist system means salvaging the 'national economy' and not the capitalist system itself. Berlinguer naively takes the bait. Capitalism? 'We are not traitors, we will not save it'. But the national economy? That's different. If you invoke noble sentiments, if the fatherland is in danger, then we answer, 'Present and accounted for'. It is naive, but perhaps not quite so naive as all that. You need precisely this mixture of naïveté, cynicism, and insolence to have a chance of persuading disoriented workers to accept all this and hope to win the benevolence of the employers at the same time.

But our supposedly naive politicians also assume swaggering

airs now and then: 'Pay heed or I'll make trouble'. Berlinguer says, for example: 'If you try to attain these objectives while maintaining the Italian social system as it now exists, with its economic structures and basic ideas, then that won't work. . . . Today there is only one way to achieve these three objectives of general interest: we must move away, even if only gradually, from the mechanisms and values that have governed Italian development during the past twenty-five years . . . and we must introduce into Italian society and the economy at least some objectives, values, and methods which conform to the socialist ideal' (op. cit. pp. 53–54).

The bourgeoisie might be nervous for about fifteen seconds, long enough to read to the end of the paragraph. Salvage capitalism? Never. Salvage the 'national' economy, even though it is capitalist? Of course! But not under any old pretext or ideological cover. We will salvage the capitalist economy only if you allow us to do so under the cover óf the introduction into this economy – gradually, you understand, very gradually – of values borrowed from the 'socialist ideal': programming, expanded public services, greater rationality, etc. Capitalism 'cleaned up and modernized' by borrowing from 'socialist values'. This is not a bad synthesis of what has actually happened during past decades. On the whole, it conforms to the definition Karl Marx gave of stockholding companies: going beyond private property in the context of private property; going beyond capitalism in the framework of the capitalist mode of production.

But what is the balance-sheet of this operation, if we come down from the sky of great spiritual values and enter the realm of our miserable planet, afflicted as it is with private selfishness and class interests? According to official statistics, which do not express the whole truth, the cost of living in Italy rose 1.4% in January 1977, 2.3% in February, 1.5% in March, and 1.1% in April, which amounts to 6.3% in four months (or nearly 20% per year). But the sliding scale granted the workers only a six-point increase in May, which amounts to a maximum of 3% in compensation for cost of living increases during the first four months of 1977. Workers making less than 6 million lire a year, about £3,500, received increases of 14,334 lire a month. Workers who make between 6 and 8 million lire a year received only half this sum, which means that some workers got less than 2% increases from the sliding scale. *In other words, real wages actually began to decline.*

Moreover, *Rinascità* (25 March 1977) has acknowledged that since February 1977 the sliding scale has guaranteed the full maintenance of the purchasing power only of those workers earning about 300,000 lire a month, which is less than the average wage in industry. The French bourgeois daily *Le Figaro* offered a good summary of the situation: 'The historic compromise concluded between Christian Democracy and the PCI has its homologue on the economic plane, for the two parties have understood the danger involved in allowing inflation to run rampant too long. The result is an agreement reached at the beginning of the year between the employers (Confindustria) and the union federations. The unions made serious concessions, and it is probable that they would have gone further had the rank and file been willing to accept, which was not the case. Seven paid holidays were eliminated. . . . The second, and principal, point: the sliding scale, once as sacrosanct as paid holidays . . . was modified, its effects attenuated' (31 May 1977). Thus, sacrifices were made, but the 'old capitalist structures' did not disappear.

What about jobs? This is the basic argument used to justify sacrifices to the least conscious workers. During the first quarter of 1977 employment declined 1.1% compared with the first quarter of 1976, in spite of a 10.9% increase in production (*Neue Zürcher Zeitung*, 24 May 1977). An erosion of purchasing power plus a loss of jobs resulted in a pronounced increase in productivity. In other words, there was an increase in relative surplus-value, which means an increase in profits. Such is the balance-sheet. Does it reflect 'values borrowed from the socialist ideal'? Or is it a classically, crudely, and entirely capitalist balance-sheet?

During a period of serious economic crisis the workers' movement cannot resign itself to purely defensive battles to protect real wages. That is the rational kernel of the theses of Berlinguer and Lama. If unemployment spreads and becomes stabilized, wages will give way in the end. The working class and the workers' movement then run the risk of being weakened by the division between those who are prepared to lose some of their purchasing power in order to keep their jobs and increasingly desperate unemployed workers who are prepared to leave the unions and abandon class solidarity in order to get jobs at any price. *Thus, a comprehensive working-class response to the crisis is needed.*

The essential elements of such a response must combine the demand for the maintenance and strengthening of the sliding scale (in order to defend purchasing power) with demands aimed at achieving full employment: radical reduction of the working week (35 hours immediately); division of available work among all the toilers (sliding scale of hours), with no reduction in weekly pay; confiscation of companies that shut down and the restarting of production under workers' control; nationalization of basic industry under workers' control with no compensation and no resale to capitalists; development by the workers' organizations of an economic plan centred on satisfying the needs of the masses; creation of modern public enterprises in that framework; centralization of the entire credit system in a single public bank under workers' management; workers' control of production and investment; elimination of financial and banking secrecy; immediate establishment of a wealth registry to combat flight of capital and tax fraud; a workers' government that breaks with the bourgeoisie and the bourgeois state.

Such a programme can never be agreed to by Christian Democracy or by any sectors of the bourgeoisie. It is an anticapitalist programme of class confrontation and not conciliation. It is a programme which does not lead to the demobilization of the working class or to the curbing and fragmentation of workers' struggles; on the contrary, its implementation demands a general mobilization of the working class and all the toiling masses, as well as working-class initiative and increasingly advanced self-organization.

Is the relationship of forces ripe for the realization of such a programme in Italy today? It is here that the Berlinguer–Lama argument falls into its most glaring contradiction. They paint us the picture of a decadent, fatally ill bourgeois society and economy. They further assert that the working class has become so strong and united that it can become the decisive force in Italian society today (Berlinguer, op. cit. p. 52). *In that case, why couldn't the working class insist on its own anti-capitalist solution to the crisis, a solution that points in the direction we have indicated?* If the working class can do this objectively, why do the Berlinguers and Lamas refuse to take this road? Perhaps because they have chosen to salvage capitalism, because of the strategic choices that lie at the very root of Eurocommunism itself?

Is all this really as new as Berlinguer claims? In reality, Berlinguer's innovations are just as misleading as his innocence. He is only repeating what German Social Democracy did in 1918–19 and what the French and Italian Communist parties did in 1944–47. During these periods, like that of today, capitalism was too weak to impose sacrifices on the workers. The reformists took care of that. In return they were given their cards and sent on their way. The same thing will happen again this time, unless the workers prevent Berlinguer from extracting the Italian bourgeoisie from the tight corner in which it is now trapped.

# 9
# The PCF and the State

At the end of April 1971, the Week of Marxist Thought, supported by the French Communist Party (PCF), organized a colloquy entitled 'One Hundred Years After the Commune – Problems of the Socialist Revolution in France'.[1] Speaking at this colloquy in the name of the Political Bureau of the PCF, François Billoux summarized the classical position of Marx and Lenin on the character of the bourgeois state and bourgeois democracy:

'Can one speak of democracy in general, apart from economic and social realities, *from class relations*? We do not think so. In a class society, any state is by nature the instrument of the domination of one class over another. Only socialism, by putting an end to the exploitation of man by man, will create conditions that permit the abolition of societies divided into antagonistic classes and will thus be able to develop democracy continuously' (p. 79).

It is true that this definition, correct on the whole, was immediately combined with ambiguous elements that tended to render it contradictory. Billoux added this formula to the definition of the state as an instrument of class domination: 'We have the example of the present state in France, in the service of the big monopolies'. The 'big monopolies' are in fact only a fraction – albeit the dominant one – of a class, the bourgeois class. The French bourgeois state acts in the service of the bourgeoisie, and not solely of the big monopolies. The manner in which it arbitrates inter-bourgeois conflicts – particularly

---

[1] The transcript of this colloquy was published under the same title by Editions Sociales, Paris 1971.

those among French 'big monopolies', multinationals of European inclination, multinationals dominated by American and Japanese capital, 'small and middle-sized' French companies, and so on – depends on many factors, among which the relationship of forces between them *in the particular conjuncture* is an important element, although far from the only one.

Furthermore, between the bourgeois state and the 'socialist state' (it would have been better to say 'workers' state' or 'dictatorship of the proletariat') Billoux inserted a transitional phase, which he called 'advanced democracy', during which the working class must undergo an apprenticeship in 'directing the state'. He did not explain that this could occur only through an experience of *dual power* or that the working class, thoroughly capable of administering a workers' state, is incapable of administering a bourgeois state, by its very nature.

Apart from these reservations, however, it may be noted that as of 1971 the PCF still maintained 'formal orthodoxy' on the question of the state, at least as far as abstract theoretical proclamations are concerned (in terms of political practice, its drift towards opportunism dates from 1935, with increasingly revisionist repercussions particularly during the period 1941–47).

Moreover Billoux, a representative of the Stalinist 'old guard', was not the only PCF member to recall 'orthodoxy' at this colloquy. Lucien Sève also presented an interesting analysis, demonstrating the relationship between the alienation of the toilers, including their political alienation, and the very nature of the capitalist mode of production (not simply the 'rule of the big monopolies'): 'The more one thinks about this problem, in essence a very simple one, the more one realizes that there is no other road, and especially that *there is no short-cut, or supposed short-cut, that can avoid the socialization of the means of production and exchange* – neither traditional reformism, which imagines that one can at least partially eliminate the effects of alienation without touching their ultimate cause, namely a system of private property in which the mass of individuals are deprived of control over the social conditions of their labour, and thus of their entire lives; nor anarchism, which confuses piecemeal recovery of some products or *some immediate liberties within alienated society* with genuine and

general emancipation from the objective conditions of alienation; reducing anarchism, in practice, to a boisterous variety of
reformism' (ibid. p. 30, emphasis added).

Today, six years later, the same Lucien Sève, in collaboration
with Jean Fabre and François Hincker, has published a book
devoted to the state which upholds theses opposite to those of
the April 1971 colloquy.[2] We are now offered a 'democratic
state' which is supposedly neither a bourgeois state nor a
workers' state; in other words, precisely a state which is no
longer 'the instrument of domination of one class over another'.
We are likewise presented with a working class in the midst of
a process of disalienation, becoming master of its conditions of
life, *without* the prior abolition of the capitalist mode of production and *without* the elimination of private property in the
means of production and exchange, but simply by 'recovering
some liberties within alienated society itself'.

There is no point in retracing here the intermediary theoretical stages which led from the apparently 'orthodox' positions of
1971 to the overtly revisionist ones of 1977. That is a study we
recommend to Marxists interested in demonstrating how
Marxist theory, petty-bourgeois ideology, and reformist practices in the class struggle can be closely intertwined in capitalist
society. The fact is that the revisionism of the PCF in regard to
the question of the state does not originate in the purely
theoretical domain (any more than did the revisionism of
Bernstein). Rather, it is a *post festum* theoretical codification of
reformist practice, of long-established class collaboration.
Theory has been remodelled to serve practical opportunism,
which is born not of lack of theoretical clarity but of social
pressures, integration into prevailing circumstances and
stratification within the proletariat (workers' bureaucracy,
labour aristocracy, predominant weight of official apparatus,
growing fusion of this apparatus with petty-bourgeois social
layers, and so on).

One of the intermediary links in the passage from 'formal
orthodoxy' to open revisionism of the Marxist theory of the
state on the part of the PCF, however, deserves to be highlighted. That is the articulation of this revisionism with the

[2] Fabre, Hincker, Sève: *Les Communistes et l'Etat*, Paris 1977.

theory of state monopoly capitalism. The chapter on 'State Monopoly Capitalism' in the second volume of *Traité Marxiste d'Economie Politique* (Paris 1971) defends at length the thesis that there is a symbiosis between the state and the monopolies such that the state more and more assumes responsibility for surmounting the contradictions of the accumulation of capital *for the monopolies*. The result is allegedly to aggravate the contradictions between these monopolies on the one hand and the non-monopolist sectors of the bourgeoisie and the rest of society on the other. Behind this apparently descriptive thesis lurks a sizeable theoretical revision. The specific forms of the contemporary state in Western Europe are in effect held to be no longer determined by the capitalist mode of production, but by technical and conjunctural imperatives of economic development. The state, according to this theory, becomes purely 'functional' and socially 'neutral', capable of utilization by other social classes, depending on the evolution of the relationship of social forces. Thus: 'By modifying the content of the state bequeathed by state monopoly capitalism, advanced democracy, which liberates the dynamism of the classes and layers exploited and dominated by finance capital, permits a fundamental and progressive modification of the forms of the state, as well as an assault on social relations at their roots' (ibid. p. 264).

In other words: let us place a new ruling elite at the head of the state apparatus, and the immense weight of this apparatus (with its tax structure, nationalized industries and credit system) can be used more or less automatically in the service of the toiling masses. Of course, up until the most recent congress of the PCF, this underlying revisionism was still combined with public professions of faith in 'orthodox' theses, as can be seen in the previous quotations from Billoux and Sève.

It will be useful to dissect the arguments with which Sève and his co-authors justify their present revisionism, to reveal their sophistry and their similarity to the reasoning that led to the theoretical degeneration of classical Social Democracy. In doing so, we shall indicate the disastrous practical political results of them for the workers' movement and the working class.

## The Character of the State Apparatus

The first momentous confusion in these arguments is the way in which they put the thousand and one social functions that the state – any state, and particularly the bourgeois state in the era of late capitalism – fulfills in order to satisfy certain *objective* needs of the material process of production, on an equal footing with the apparatus of the state as an instrument for the maintenance, consolidation, defence, and reproduction of the domination of one class over another.

Distribution of mail, guarantee of natural gas installations, provision of education, vaccination against epidemics, construction and maintenance of roads: these are useful and indispensable functions given the present development of productive forces and social needs, regardless of the class nature of the state. Today they are fulfilled by a bourgeois state. Tomorrow they will be fulfilled by a workers' state, without prior modification of nearly all the personnel who effect these tasks. No communist with a modicum of sense has ever proposed 'breaking up the postmen, railway workers, and teachers' on the grounds that the apparatus of the bourgeois state has to be smashed.

Of course, we must immediately add that the *content* of the education guided and controlled by the bourgeois state, the *hierarchical structure* of the postal system, railways, and public utilities, the *interlacing* of the administration of public works and the private capitalist interests which take charge of their realization, and even the *exact placing of roads* (greatly influenced by the pressure of real estate groups and industrialists representing fractions of the ruling class) will undergo profound upheavals after a socialist revolution, after the seizure of power by the proletariat. Nevertheless, in all these areas the idea of 'breaking the state' may well appear irrelevant and unreal.

But this question acquires burning and decisive importance when we pass from the functions of material reproduction fulfilled by the state to its functions in the *reproduction of a given social structure*, the reproduction of class rule. To claim that the generals, commanders of the CRS (the French political police), chiefs of police, high functionaries in the Ministry of

Finance and the Quai d'Orsay serve the interests of 'material reproduction', the interests of 'society as a whole' in the same way as teachers, postmen, railway workers, or employees in the social security system is obviously a gross sophistry. These personages, far from serving the interests of 'society in general', serve the interests of the ruling class *against* the immense majority of citizens. It is they who represent the 'parasitic body' feeding off the 'social body' of which Marx and Engels spoke. It is they who constitute the famous 'state machine' which, as Marx and Lenin stressed on innumerable occasions, the working class must smash,[3] since it can in no way use it for its own purposes. Nothing that has happened since 1914 – not the experience of the *Reichswehr* under the Weimar Republic, nor that of the Spanish army under the 1931–36 republic, nor that of the generals of the French army in the 1930s and 1960s, nor the role of the army and the *carabinieri* in the 'strategy of tension' used against the rise of workers' struggles in Italy since 1969, nor that of Pinochet and company in Chile, to cite only the most striking and best known examples – suggest that this conclusion should be modified.

This conclusion is not the product of biased dogmatism. It results from an analysis of the mechanisms of recruitment of the leading personnel of this apparatus; from an examination of the inevitable consequences of its hierarchical structure; from an understanding of the link between ideological internalization and capacity to fulfill certain functions (one cannot be an effective prison guard desirous of promotion if one systematically organizes escapes of prisoners; history has never known a convinced and practising pacifist chief of staff). It is inevitable in bourgeois society that the summits of the state apparatus, the people who represent and incarnate the 'state machine', regardless of their individual origins, are absorbed and integrated into the bourgeois class, even if only through the size of their incomes and the inevitable accumulation of capital to which they lead. On the whole, then, they can only serve the interests of the bourgeoisie.

Sève is of another view. He writes: 'In this sense, there is un-

---

[3] See, in particular, Karl Marx: *The Civil War in France*; and Lenin: *State and Revolution*.

doubtedly something to *eliminate* in the present state: the power of big capital. This task is *decisive*: the fate of political and social change depends on it. The process begins with a change in the parliamentary majority and the establishment of a democratic government charged with applying the Common Programme of the Left. The great transformations of political and economic structures, nationalizations for example, must then begin immediately. A sufficient *threshold* must be reached to weaken monopoly rule immediately. Beyond that, democracy must be pressed forward so as to render the conquests which correspond to the will and the vote of the majority irreversible, at once in their aims and their methods. This is how to make the revolution in the conditions of France today' (*Les Communistes et l'Etat*, pp. 148–9).

This reasoning simply begs the question. For Sève and his colleagues assume resolved exactly what must first be achieved. Is there any way to attain a 'sufficient threshold' in the dismantling of the 'power of big capital' (that is, *the political and economic power of the bourgeoisie as a class*) while leaving the hierarchy of the army, police, the CRS, and the ministries essentially intact? Can they in fact be 'democratized' gradually, a piece at a time? Is it not inevitable that this 'state machinery' will sabotage and block by any means necessary, including violence and illegality, any attempt to 'render democracy irreversible', that is, to break the class power of the bourgeoisie? Is that not the lesson of the entire history of capitalism, especially since the workers' movement acquired a mass force capable of inspiring fear in capital? Can Sève cite a single historical example in support of his thesis? The bourgeois state apparatus does not respect the 'will and vote of the majority' whenever they come into irreconcilable conflict with the fundamental class interests of the bourgeoisie. Such is the lesson of history on which the Marxist theory of the bourgeois state is founded. To insinuate the contrary is to lead the working class into a bloody trap.

The contradiction in the position of Sève and his colleagues explodes in a single sentence when, under the suggestive title 'Break Up the State?' (note the question mark), they write: 'The Giscardian regime . . . is striving(!) to convert the police into a mere cog in the monopolist order. Encountering diffi- culties in doing so, it is now seeking ever more to use the gendarmerie to this end, since the latter, being part of the army, are subject to military discipline. In this situation, what are the interests and demands of the popular masses, of the workers' and democratic organizations, joined today by the police unions on some points? A democratic regime would assign the police the sole(!) mission of guaranteeing liberties and assuring per- sonal security and the protection of property, respecting the legality and institutions with which the people have endowed themselves. What this places on the agenda is not the "suppres- sion" of the police, but their profound democratic reform, placing them exclusively at the service of the people and the nation. This coincides with the interests of the police personnel themselves' (ibid. p. 148).

Lucien Sève has forgotten a small detail: we are still under the capitalist system, which he himself contends should not be abolished during the phase of 'advanced democracy'. Now, under the capitalist system, 'legality' protects capitalist *private property*. It conserves and sanctions hierarchy and blind disci- pline within the army, gendarmerie, and police. A 'deep democratic reform' of these institutions, if the word is to have any meaning at all, would inevitably involve a challenge to this hierarchy and discipline, that would precisely provoke the *progressive disintegration* of these apparatuses of repression, of this 'state machine'. We completely agree that such a disinte- gration is an essential, primordial form of their destruction, especially after the living example of Portugal. Let the soldiers exercise the democratic right to meet in daily assemblies to discuss (and reject if need be) the orders they receive! Let them replace appointed commanders with elected ones! That would indeed be an excellent extension of democracy!

But does anyone believe for a moment that the officer corps will passively observe such a process of disintegration of *its* army? Isn't it obvious that the old army would be replaced by a new one through such a revolutionary process? How can Sève fail to understand that it would exacerbate political and social contradictions to the maximum? Isn't it absurd to claim that all this could occur 'under law and order', simply through the passage of laws by parliament?[4]

Most important of all: how can anyone fail to see that processes as revolutionary and tumultuous as these cannot possibly unfold without constantly attacking private property, without repeatedly violating the famous 'protection of goods' for which Sève and company have blithely assigned their 'democratic police' responsibility? Or that they will impose on every policeman and soldier a decisive choice: either support (or at least refuse to suppress) the impetuous initiatives and mobilizations of the masses (including those of the most revolutionary soldiers), or prepare for repression (including attempts at bloody repression) of these initiatives?

The most recent proof of the accuracy of this analysis is provided by what happened in Portugal in 1975. At the end of such an evolution there is no 'democratization' of the state apparatus. There is either its break-up (and obviously, the proletariat will greet with open arms all those, officers included, who come over to its side in the struggle for the overthrow of the bourgeois regime) or the restoration of its 'integrity', over the bodies of the proletarians, revolutionaries, and 'rebel soldiers' suppressed by the upholders of bourgeois order.

### Democratic Rights and Institutions of the Bourgeois-Democratic State

A second fundamental confusion which lurks behind the revision of the Marxist theory of the state concerns the identi-

---

[4] Back in 1968, in a book rendered odious by its insinuations of 'complicity' between the Gaullist regime and the protagonists of May 1968 in France, René Andrieu wrote: 'It would be parliamentary cretinism to believe that a revolution is made once more than half the votes in an assembly are won. Although as we have already stressed, universal suffrage can give a majority to the parties considering themselves socialist, it does not have the virtue of thereby according them real power so long as the life of the nation remains dominated by bourgeois oligarchies. Indeed, to form a government is not necessarily to hold real power. It is still necessary to put an end to the de facto dictatorship of the bourgeoisie, that is, to the domination of the masters of the monopolies who hold all the commanding levers of the state and the economy, can impede production, organize the flight of capital abroad, torpedo the franc, use the high functionaries of the administration, along with the high officers of the army and the police, for purposes of sabotage' (*Les Communistes et la Révolution*, Paris 1968, p. 248).

fication of the democratic rights of the masses with the institutions of the bourgeois state in its parliamentary democratic form.

Parliament is not an institution 'imposed' on the bourgeoisie by the struggle of the toiling masses. It is an institution of typically bourgeois origin, originally designed to control the use of the taxes paid by the bourgeoisie. This is why the bourgeoisie traditionally opposed universal suffrage, preferring to restrict the right to elect parliament deputies to the owners of capital.[5] All the other institutions of the bourgeois state have the same origin and the same function of protecting the interests of the owners (against semi-feudal absolutism, of course, but also against the dispossessed masses).

Universal suffrage, on the other hand, was (with a few exceptions – Germany being the clearest case) a conquest imposed on a recalcitrant bourgeoisie by the workers' movement.[6] The same goes for freedom of association, freedom to demonstrate, unrestricted freedom of the press, and the unregimented right to strike. The bourgeoisie attempted to limit the scope of fundamental democratic rights to prevent them from conflicting with the defence of private property. Only the rise of the organized workers' movement imposed their extension, that is, eliminated some (but not all) of these limitations.

Moreover, in conformity with the logic of the bourgeois system, universal suffrage and the extension of democratic rights have a twofold corollary: an increasingly heavy fiscal drain on the incomes of the workers (who now pay more than 50% of direct taxes, as they have always paid the greater part of indirect taxes in all the advanced capitalist countries); and a continual extension of the powers and weight of the executive branch of the state, outside the control of parliament. These executive apparatuses constitute the ultimate guarantor of the

[5] The most representative and consistent ideologues of the revolutionary bourgeoisie were all opposed to universal suffrage, which they saw as a threat to freedom (the freedom of capital, that is). This was particularly the case for Locke, Montesquieu, Voltaire, Fichte, Kant, Turgot, for example. Even the 'Levellers', the far left of the English bourgeois revolution of the 17th century, accepted this point of view. (In this regard, see Leo Kofler: *Zur Geschichte der bürgerlichen Gesellschaft*, Halle/Saale 1948, pp. 444–45, 455–56, 462.)

[6] Göran Therborn (*New Left Review*, No. 103) recalls the late date at which universal suffrage was generalized in most of the advanced capitalist countries: just after the First World War.

bourgeois order. The more representatives of the workers' movement gain admittance into parliament, the more the role of parliament in the ensemble of mechanisms of the bourgeois state tends to narrow.

Obviously, this does not imply that the working class and the organized workers' movement should be indifferent to the precise form taken by the bourgeois state and to the degree of extension of the democratic rights of the masses within this state. Compared to more repressive state forms (military or bonapartist dictatorships, fascist dictatorships), the parliamentary-democratic form of bourgeois state permits a freer and more organic development of the struggles and organization of the workers, a greater rise of the workers' movement, and an accumulation of experiences and possibilities for education which serve the development of class consciousness. Paradoxically, even from the standpoint of the necessary struggle against electoralist illusions, conditions of protracted bourgeois democracy permit more conclusive results in the long run, provided the revolutionary vanguard is sufficiently broad and influential among the masses and sufficiently experienced in the political arena. These illusions tend to strengthen their hold on the broad masses under dictatorial regimes, according to the well-known formula: How beautiful the Republic was under the Empire!

The European proletariat's disastrous experience of fascism and Stalinism has had a genuinely traumatic effect on it, undoubtedly rehabilitating bourgeois democracy in the eyes of the masses (a form of regime which was rather discredited during the period 1929–1939). One of the major ideological campaigns of the bourgeoisie is its hammering home the false axioms: no political and individual freedom without bourgeois-parliamentary democracy; no political freedom without free enterprise. International social democracy vigorously propagates this ideological mystification, the West German Social Democratic Party in the lead. The Eurocommunist parties are now increasingly joining this new Holy Alliance.

The mystificatory character of the enterprise is not difficult to demonstrate. If the institutions of the bourgeois-democratic state are really the 'natural' and 'tailored' framework for the consolidation and extension of democratic rights, why doesn't the bourgeois world demand the generalization of the *principle of electability* at all levels of the state institutions? Why not demand the election of judges, officers, and directors of state ministries? Why not write into the constitution the right to work and the right to a *guaranteed* vital minimum for *all* citizens? Wouldn't this be 'democratic'? Or is it rather because it would not be compatible with the function of the bourgeois state, which is to guarantee capitalist property, the valorization of capital, and the production of surplus-value?

Why not combine the *principle of revocability of elected officials at the will of the voters* with the principle of generalized election of all administrative 'chiefs'? Is it because this would undermine 'technical competence'? But what about the 'competence' of members of parliament and senators, who are supposed to decide problems not in a single domain but in a hundred specialized ones? Isn't it rather because this principle would no longer allow the state apparatus to be *independent of the working people*, which is precisely the precondition for its defence of the class interests of the bourgeoisie?

In the same order of ideas why not demand the general limitation of the salaries of high functionaries, army commanders, ministers, and members of parliament to the wages of a skilled worker, a principle applied by the Paris Commune and defended by Marx and Lenin?[7] Perhaps because the application of this principle would prevent the process of selection of high-ranking state personnel from occurring in a bourgeois manner (by eliminating competition for personal enrichment, by preventing the automatic integration of such personnel into the bourgeoisie through its accumulation of capital)?

It is thus no accident that neither the Common Programme nor the programme of the PCF itself ('Le Socialisme pour la France' or *Le Défi Démocratique* by Georges Marchais), nor the commentaries of Sève, Fabre, and Hincker[8] call for any of these genuine revolutionary transformations of democracy. *All of them respect the existing structure of the bourgeois-democratic state, which is precisely the expression and guarantor of its bourgeois character.* In other words, *all of them accept the*

---

[7] To cite just one example: *The Civil War in France*, by Karl Marx.
[8] See especially all of Chapter 2 of the second part of *Les Communistes et l'Etat* (pp. 153 and following).

*decisive limitation of the democratic rights of the masses which flows from this state structure*, even though they recommend some extension of democratic rights – precisely those which do not deal blows to the very foundations of the bourgeois state apparatus.

Our position is diametrically opposed to theirs. We uphold the consolidation, extension, and qualitative transformation of the democratic rights of the masses. But we know that every move in this direction clashes with the structures of the bourgeois state, whether parliamentary-democratic or not. A conflict between this process of extension and the defence of the institutions of the bourgeois state is thus inevitable. This conflict constitutes the very content of the period of dual power, of the revolutionary situation proper. From a pedagogical and political standpoint, the effect of this process will be progressively to destroy the legitimacy of the bourgeois state in the eyes of the masses, as they gain practical experience of a higher form of democracy, of a flowering of rights and freedoms which are denied them under bourgeois democracy. It is thus that a new and higher democratic legitimacy can be founded, that of proletarian democracy, of workers' councils. Without the victory of this second legitimacy over the first in the eyes of the majority of the population, there will be no real overthrow of the bourgeois state and no real socialist revolution in the industrially advanced countries.

From a practical and institutional standpoint, such a conflict will lead to the establishment of organs of workers' and people's power which embody a *new* state, a *new* class power, which cannot be the same organs of class power as those of the bourgeoisie. But they can and must be organs that assure an extension of the *political and individual rights and freedoms of the masses*, and not only an extension of their economic and social rights (right to work, to social security throughout their lives, that is, a guaranteed vital minimum, genuine equality between men and women, between immigrant and indigenous workers, and so on).

If they are not, then the enterprise of socialism has no chance of success in the industrially advanced capitalist countries, given the level of experience and consciousness of the toiling masses. That is why we are resolute partisans of a multi-party system and of free expression for all ideological, political, and cultural currents.[9] Our differences with the Eurocommunists relate not to this principle, but to the inevitable and explosive contradiction between the institutions of the bourgeois-democratic state and the extension of the political, economic, and social rights and freedoms of the toiling masses. Once a certain threshold of mass mobilization is reached, that contradiction becomes irreconcilable and poses a precise choice: either supersede and break the bourgeois state apparatus, or violently restrict and repress the freedom and action of the masses (what Mario Soares, Melo Antunes, and company called 'anarcho-populism' during the rise of the Portuguese revolution in 1975).

## Indirect Democracy and Direct Democracy

It is here that we encounter another striking contradiction in the Eurocommunist theses on the state. The Eurocommunist leaders and ideologues talk at great length of 'the extension of the democratic rights of the masses', of 'the growing participation of the masses in the management of the nationalized sector and the state'.[10] They are even prepared – at least in France, where the self-management current is most powerful – in part to 'coopt' the idea of the self-administration and self-management of the masses, which is the most popular antidote to the mortal danger of bureaucracy, of which the workers are increasingly and rightly aware.[11] But nowhere do they highlight the tendential, and in the long run irreconcilable, conflict between the representative institutions of *indirect democracy* and the manifestations and institutions of *direct democracy*.

A parliament, even if elected by universal suffrage, remains

---

[9] See in this connexion the draft theses of the United Secretariat of the Fourth International, 'Socialist Democracy and the Dictatorship of the Proletariat', in *Inprecor*, No. 10 new series, 7 July 1977.

[10] See especially *Les Communistes et l'Etat*, pp. 164–66.

[11] 'This would transform their relationship to the state progressively and very profoundly. *Partial forms of social self-organization* are conceivable immediately or in the short run. They will be part of a movement whose perspective is, in our view, to lead to *overall national self-management*. . . . In view of today's conditions and their foreseeable evolution, this would prefigure what the classics of Marxism called the *withering away of the state*' (*Les Communistes et l'Etat*, p. 167).

the prototype of an institution of indirect representative democracy and thus the expression of a *deep distrust* in the capacity of the toiling masses and the people to manage their own affairs. An assembly constantly renewed at the will of the voters would be subject to auctioneering and demagogy, say the extollers of the virtues of bourgeois parliamentarism (including Social Democrats, Stalinists, and Eurocommunists). If we remove the hypocritical veil in which this claim is shrouded, its real nature becomes clear immediately: 'Let the people elect members of parliament on the basis of rhetorical and deceitful election "programmes" and promises. But please, do not prevent these ladies and gentlemen from subsequently "governing" with a "sense of individual responsibility", without being under the "constant pressure of the street". In other words, let them dupe the voters, betray their promises, and legislate in the interests of the bourgeois order'. The whole business turns out to be rather unsavoury.

The more the direct impetus and action of the masses increases, the more their mobilization broadens, the more their initiatives of self-organization and direct democracy in the most varied domains will multiply – from workers' control of the factories to the organization of 'people's markets'; from the takeover of public services to the establishment of cultural institutions and 'unofficial' crèches. But the more the arena of direct democracy expands in this manner, the more the conflict with the institutions of the bourgeois state will widen and become irreconcilable. This is not merely a matter of a conflict with the repressive apparatus proper and the summits of the 'state machine'. Potentially it is also a matter of a conflict – barring completely exceptional conditions – with the organs of indirect representative democracy, which will desperately defend their monopoly of 'sovereignty', their ultimate right to make decisions, and the 'authority' of the government that emanates from them, against the authority of the new majority and the new popular sovereignty arising from the mobilized masses.

This real conflict is founded primarily on the fact that within indirect representative democracy the 'citizen' – including the wage-earning citizen – is an *atomized and alienated individual*, subject to the thousand and one pressures not only of bourgeois ideology but also and more important of patterns of labour and consumption which are fashioned by capital and dominate his entire existence. This 'citizen' is neither a protagonist nor even an actor in the political drama. He can only have a walk-on part, as a spear-carrier.

By contrast, once the self-organization of the masses is set in motion, and varied mechanisms of direct democracy are created, the 'citizen' – and primarily the wage-earning citizen – is no longer isolated and is less and less alienated. He becomes conscious of his strength through force of numbers. He transcends his individual prejudices by participating in collective decision-making. He is not content merely to drop a slip into a ballot-box. He participates in processes of decision-making, in the application of these decisions, and in the verification of their application (of their conformity with the majority will). He is no longer a spear carrier but a real actor, a protagonist, in the political drama.

That this is a formidable leap forward in democracy no one of good faith lending the word a real content could deny. (Those who do so simply confess that for them 'real power in the hands of the people' is a utopia or a threat. Their 'democracy' amounts to giving the people a semblance of power, not its substance.) That it permits the transformation of formal democracy into genuine democracy, in which power is truly in the hands of the masses, is also evident. That it is incompatible with an accentuation and reinforcement of the power of the representative organs has been confirmed again and again by all the revolutionary periods we have seen in Europe and elsewhere, from the Paris Commune and the Russian revolution to the Portuguese revolution.[12]

The Eurocommunists are caught in a dilemma. To proclaim

[12] We do not rule out the possibility, improbable but not impossible, that a very high level of development of political consciousness among the masses, a qualitative expansion of the political influence of revolutionary organizations, and a crisis of fragmentation of the reformist parties could result, after a prolonged revolutionary period, in a coincidence between a parliamentary majority and a majority in the organs of direct democracy. All the better. But what seems to us inadmissible and contrary to the interests of the proletariat is to subordinate the realization of the revolutionary programme to a prior and durable attainment of a stable parliamentary majority, even when that programme is supported by a clearly expressed majority of citizens.

on the one hand the necessity for the 'extension of the democratic rights of the masses' but to demand on the other hand the 'strengthening and extension of the powers and prestige of parliament' is to seek to reconcile fire and water. In practice it is impossible. The logic of the Eurocommunist acceptance of the 'progressive' role of the 'bourgeois' democratic state is an eventual option, like that of the Social Democrats after 4 August 1914, for the capitalist state and against the freedom of action of the masses, as soon as social tensions and class contradictions produce a rise in popular combativity and therewith a real and irreconcilable conflict between the two.

Thus far, it has been the Italian Communist Party that has travelled furthest along this road. The programmatic agreement the PCI concluded in summer 1977 with the five other 'parties of the constitutional arc' – including Christian Democracy, the major political party of big capital – contains an entire section on the defence of 'public law and order'; it grants very broad discretionary powers to the bourgeois police. The police in Italy can now resort to preventive detention of suspects, proceed directly to interrogation of arrested persons without the presence of a lawyer, search housing claimed to be a 'subversive hideout' even without a warrant, and engage in telephone tapping at will. Obviously, this is a *restriction* and not an extension of democratic freedoms. Likewise, carried away by the logic of the 'defence of parliament',[13] the PCI has changed its attitude towards referenda. It is now seeking to *limit* and not extend the right of the masses to initiate referenda, for this right 'would undermine' the authority of parliament (a popular majority opposed to the parliamentary majority could emerge, as happened in the case of the referendum on divorce).

Moreover, the leaders of the PCI have not failed to draw all the revisionist ideological conclusions of their turn towards a

---

[13] The following quotation, which comes from the pen of a former 'leftist' of the PSIUP (Italian Socialist Party of Proletarian Unity) who has now joined the PCI and its parliamentary caucus, indicates just how far the parliamentary cretinism of the leaders of the PCI has gone. The writer hails the fact that the Communist Pietro Ingrao, who is now President of the Chamber of Deputies, 'has reestablished, in an extremely strict manner, the practice of wearing ties' (*Quale Parlamento?*, Turin, 1977, pp. 68 and 43).

'historic compromise'. Since a Marxist cannot say 'yes' to a bourgeois-democratic state without saying 'yes' to its apparatus of repression, the *class character* of this apparatus must necessarily *be denied.* Bufalini, one of the major leaders of the party, told the Central Committee in March 1977: 'The workers' and people's movement must collaborate with the forces prepared to safeguard the democratic order and must support them morally and publicly. The police have never been the enemy for us, not even during the 1950s and 1960s, when they were used to defend class privileges and when we clashed with them. But today the situation has completely changed, been overturned. Today the police are called upon to defend the democratic order against the attacks of gangs that are enemies of this order, enemies of the Republic born of the Resistance' (*France-Nouvelle*, 1 April 1977).

Bufalini no longer argues that the police always defend a *socio-economic* order, that is, the domination of one class and predominant mode of production. He has forgotten that this class domination in Italy is bourgeois class domination, that this mode of production is the capitalist mode of production, that history has furnished innumerable – and suicidal – illustrations of a 'democratic' police which supposedly defends a 'democratic order' standing above classes, beginning with the example of Social Democracy under the Weimar Republic. (Severing, the Minister of the Interior and Chief of Police of Prussia, ruled over a 'democratic' police for nearly fifteen years, until he was removed from power by a handful – a lieutenant and ten soldiers – during the Von Papen coup in July 1932, without the slightest action 'in defence of democracy' on the part of this police.)

**The 'Left' Variant of Eurocommunism**

These contradictions in the doctrine of the major leaders and ideologues of Eurocommunism are so flagrant and so contrary to the lessons of history that intelligent defenders of Eurocommunism feel compelled to take some distance from their more glaring sophisms. Two cases in point are Bruno Trentin, the leader of the Italian metalworkers' union, and Fernando Claudín, former leader of the Spanish Communist Party, who may be considered typical representatives of the left variant of Eurocommunism.[14]

We have already seen how Trentin has tried to present Eurocommunist strategy in economic policy not as an attempt to rationalize Italian capitalism, but as a bid to transform the capitalist nature of this economy. His positions on the state are not dissimilar: 'I believe that we must do a lot of thinking about the question of pluralism and the dialectic of powers, from an angle that is completely different from the division of powers in bourgeois society. From this standpoint, the strength of the councils in a transitional society should derive from the fact that they remain an autonomous and conflictual power, that is, are not an institutionalized power. Here I think that Gramsci's distinction between the public nature of the council and the private nature of the trade union and party should be re-thought and deepened. The council can become a second power, or as Adler said,[15] a real second chamber of a socialist democracy, to the extent that it remains a force of control, and of conflictual control, complementing the action of other democratic institutions, including elected institutions' (*Parti Communiste Italien: Aux Sources de l'Eurocommunisme*, p. 134).

Trentin goes on: 'The decentralization of the powers of the state at the territorial level and the multiplication of instances of confrontation between the institutional structures of the state (national and regional legislative assemblies) and the more or less institutionalized forms of direct democracy (factory councils, zonal councils, neighbourhood committees, committees of users of public utilities, school and university councils) which may emerge at the local and national level

[14] In his youth, Jean Elleinstein himself leant towards this 'leftist' version of Eurocommunism: 'The point is not to repose confidence in the bourgeoisie not to launch a civil war, but to tie its hands so as to prevent it from doing so' (*Problèmes de la Révolution en France*, p. 189). Indeed. But how can the bourgeoisie's hands actually be tied without disarming it, that is, without dismantling and disintegrating its army and without arming the proletariat and the toiling masses?

[15] The reference is to Max Adler: *Politische oder soziale Demokratie*, Berlin 1926. See also *Die soziale Staatsauffassung des Marxismus*, Vienna 1922, by the same author, in which he explicitly approves the idea of the destruction of the oppressive state machine, the idea upheld by Marx (pp. 275–80). The Eurocommunists, even 'left' ones, stand to the right of the Austro-Marxists – a sufficient indication of their theoretical poverty.

appear to me to be in the process of becoming the new terrain of initiative of the workers' movement, for a transformation of the state during the phase of transition' (ibid. p. 135).

Let us leave aside the fact that Trentin openly acknowledges his kinship with Max Adler, that is, with Austro-Marxism, which sought to 'combine' soviets with bourgeois democracy, the class domination of the proletariat with the class domination of the bourgeoisie, a notion Lenin and Trotsky implacably derided. Let us also leave aside the fact that among the 'institutional structures of the state' are enumerated only the elected and representative organs, whereas the entire permanent machinery of the state – the police, gendarmerie, army, high functionaries, irremovable judges – is forgotten, as if by accident (but is it an accident?). The confusion lies in the fact that Trentin drifts imperceptibly from the functions of *contestation* of bourgeois power exercised by the councils and committees of embryonic direct democracy in the context of a *bourgeois state in decomposition* (that is, in the context of a pre-revolutionary situation), to the role of 'co-management' played by these same councils (about which there is much to be said, but that is not the subject of this book) in the context of a 'socialist democracy' (that is a workers' state), without telling us the secret of *how to pass from one to the other*, which is precisely the subject of all the controversy.

We could calmly discuss whether or not an assembly elected by universal suffrage is necessary, alongside a congress of workers' councils, in the framework of a socialist democracy. Once the economic power and state apparatus of the bourgeoisie are broken, this is a conjunctural question and not a matter of principle.[16] But the question that stirs passion, since it is a life-or-death question for the workers' movement, is whether it is possible to pass from the bourgeois state to the workers' state ('socialist democracy'), from the class power of the bourgeoisie to the class power of the proletariat, 'through the peaceful road', that is, without dismantling and breaking up the bourgeois state machine, above all its apparatus of repression. *On this decisive subject Trentin breathes not a word.*

---

[16] See the plea for the maintenance under a workers' state of a representative assembly elected by universal suffrage, in Nicos Poulantzas: The State and the Transition to Socialism in *International*, vol. 4, no. 1, p. 5.

That is why all his flights of fancy about workers' councils are so lacking in credibility. Workers' councils 'tolerated' by the bourgeois state apparatus? In peaceful symbiosis with it? Sharing the crumbs with Messrs. Von Seeckt, Von Schleicher, Badoglio, Mola, Franco, Pétain, Salan, Spínola, Eanes, and Pinochet, the innocent lambs?

Fernando Claudín is incontestably more lucid and refined in his analysis and argumentation. He understands that the alternative is between acceptance of the legitimacy of the bourgeois (democratic) state and support of the impetuous, anti-capitalist movement of the masses. He understands the terrible implications of this alternative of *repression or self-defence* of the mass movement, even – in fact especially – when the movement represents the absolute majority of the nation: 'The mighty PCI is at a crossroads today. Not a few now believe that the most likely outcome of its democratic road will be a role analogous to that of the British Labour Party or German Social Democracy – mere collaboration with Christian Democracy to administer the crisis and carry through yet another rationalization of the decrepit machinery of capitalism. The only difference would be that for such a function to be exercised in a country like Italy, a Noske-style repression would have to be unleashed against the workers' movement. That would be impossible without profound splits and rents in the fabric of the party. This is not in our opinion the most probable outcome. The Italian workers' movement has a rich history of struggle and has repeatedly demonstrated its combativity and creativity. Already there are signs within its ranks of a vigorous reaction to the dangers that threaten it and Italian democracy. The same is also true of the PCI, which possesses very close links with the masses and the workers' movement and is very sensible to pressure from them. . . . The crucial need today on which any successful solution to the crisis depends, is to formulate a policy that unites all these forces in action for a thoroughgoing transformation of the country, *which accepts the inevitability of a show-down with the present ruling group that represents monopoly capital.* . . . If this great task is to be accomplished, a new strategy for the principal party of the Italian Left is an urgent necessity. Between the adventure of extremism and the adventure of the 'historic compromise', space must be found for a realistic policy of advance towards the democratic socialist transformation of Italian society. The tempo of the crisis does not allow for a very long delay.' (*Eurocommunism and Socialism*, London 1978, pp. 118–119; emphasis ours.)

The least one can say is that the inception and the conclusion of the argument are singularly contradictory. Does not the 'inevitable show-down' with the 'present ruling group that represents monopoly capitalism' also imply an inevitable confrontation with its state apparatus? How can you effectively prepare for this confrontation by lulling the masses with illusions about a 'peaceful road to socialism', or even a 'historic compromise'? Yet if it is necessary to *break* with the 'adventure of the historic compromise' (and to hope that even the leadership of the PCI will effect this break, 'under the pressure of the masses'), will that not provoke precisely the 'profound splits and rents' to which Claudín first alludes but later discounts as improbable, forgetting the *integration* of innumerable PCI cadres into the bourgeois state and para-state apparatus which is exactly what accounts for the 'historic compromise'?

Let us repeat once again: the difference between revolutionary Marxists and Eurocommunists does not concern the need to reject any putschist notion that power can be seized against the majority of citizens (which implies, given the present socioeconomic structure of Western Europe, against the will of the majority of the proletariat). Nor does it concern the need to respect the democratic rights of the masses *in words and in deeds* (which, once again, in the concrete conditions of Western Europe implies complete respect for political, ideological, and cultural pluralism). The notion of the 'peaceful road to socialism' and the rejection of the 'dictatorship of the proletariat' have nothing to do with this necessarily democratic nature of the socialist revolution. Their function is to instill the illusion of a 'neutral' state apparatus kindly adapting itself to the view of the majority of voters, allowing itself to be gradually 'democratized', transforming itself without a shot from an instrument for the defence of private property and capitalist exploitation into an instrument for the suppression of private property and the abolition of capitalism. We reject this perspective as a utopian dream. The least one can say is that the verdict of history pleads in favour of our thesis, and not in favour of that of the Eurocommunists.

## The Real Transitional Stage: Dual Power

Does this mean that in our view the socialist revolution can be reduced to insurrectionary action alone and that the real alternative is either 'insurrection' or 'elections'? It would be a caricature of revolutionary Marxism to do so. An insurrection is only the final point of a revolutionary process, and if the relationship of forces is favourable, it can be effected practically without casualties, provided the armed apparatus of the bourgeoisie has first been morally and politically disintegrated and the legitimacy of workers' and people's councils has been acknowledged by the immense majority of the population, including the soldiers.

For us, it is inconceivable to pass in one fell swoop from the 'normal' state power of the bourgeoisie to the new state power of the workers. The transition from one to the other requires time, especially in countries in which the state institutions of bourgeois democracy preserve enormous prestige and legitimacy in the eyes of the majority of workers. *The masses must undergo an apprenticeship in new and higher forms of democracy.* They must have the time to assimilate the meaning and value of the new state organs they are in process of creating. At the same time, the institutions of the bourgeois regime – above all its armed apparatus – must undergo a process of decomposition and progressive paralysis, without which, moreover, the *generalized* establishment of the organs of power of the workers is inconceivable.

The concrete historical stage during which this combined process of decomposition of the bourgeois regime and emergence of workers' power occurs is called the stage of dual power. That is the real 'stage of transition' between the stable state power of the bourgeoisie and the victorious socialist revolution. We counterpose this phase of dual power to the Eurocommunist concepts of 'advanced democracy' and 'democratic stage'.[17] This counterposition, once again, reflects the

[17] Claudín clearly sees the contradictions and risks of the 'electoral road' and the 'anti-monopoly alliance' conceived as an alliance with bourgeois

fundamental strategic (and analytic) division between Marxism and reformism.

For us, dual power is the expression of the class struggle brought to its paroxysm: the struggle between antagonistic state (or pre-state) apparatuses contending for *de facto* power and the allegiance of the majority of citizens over a given territory.

For instance, when the Spanish generals unleashed their *coup d'Etat* in July 1936, the workers of Catalonia, and to a lesser extent of the Levante, Andalusia, Madrid, Asturias, Aragon, and the Basque country, responded not only by defeating and disarming the fascist insurgents in their regions militarily. They also armed themselves, formed workers' militias, occupied factories, railway stations, and electrical and telephone installations – all the nerve centres of 'real power'. They re-initiated production under their own leadership, covering the territory of the Republic with a multitude of committees that directed wide areas of economic and social life, at least for the first several months after their local victory over the generals.

The legitimacy of these committees was acknowledged by the immense majority of the workers. For weeks, they frequently exercised full powers on the local level. On the national level, however, they coexisted with a government, and other institutions of the bourgeois state (including the remnants of a regular bourgeois army). In this sense, there was a real *duality of power*. It was the workers' inability spontaneously to centralize their

---

parties: '[This tactic] subordinates all forms of mass action and social struggle to a quest for alliances with one or several fractions of the bourgeoisie (and we must not forget that the 'non-monopoly' bourgeoisie comprises the greater part of the bourgeoisie and is responsible for the exploitation of a large part of the working class) for fear that such struggle will develop autonomous and unitary organizations of the working-class and popular masses, thereby jeopardizing the sacrosanct "leading role" of the Communist Parties' (*Eurocommunism and Socialism*, p. 108).

He goes on even more clearly: 'What we do wish to suggest is that for all the reasons we have given a strategy of "two stages" tends to produce a dissociation of the social struggle from the political struggle – very much in the Communist tradition – and to give primacy to the political, and within that to the electoral arena, with a tendency to play down working-class self-organization and struggle, which might upset alliances with the "non-monopoly bourgeosie"' (op. cit. p. 109).

committees, and the refusal of all parties, including the anarchists, to promote this centralization, which then proved fatal. In the end the committees were reabsorbed, integrated, and finally extinguished by the bourgeois state within the Spanish Republic.

The Eurocommunists today are pursuing the chimera of a qualitative change in the socio-economic system (initiating the transition from capitalism to the construction of socialism) without any general confrontation between classes or even an exacerbation of class struggle. They hope to achieve this mirage by manoeuvre, conciliation, and systematic curbing of popular mobilizations. We say: if the initial stage of socialism is to replace capitalism, the state machine of the bourgeoisie must be dismantled, with the agreement of the majority of citizens and the overwhelming majority of the proletariat. That is possible only through an immense mass mobilization, accompanied by generalized self-organization. Such is the real meaning of the period of dual power. By contrast, the Eurocommunists speak of the 'democratic state' of 'advanced democracy', which will allegedly 'dismantle the power of the monopolies'. But they remain absolutely silent about the class nature of this state and about the place and function of the apparatus of repression within it.[18]

Nicos Poulantzas believes that the repetition of a revolutionary crisis, precipitating a situation of dual power, is extremely improbable in the West (he forgets that such situations were not at all peculiar to the Russian revolution of 1917; they were repeated in Germany in 1918–19, in Northern Italy in 1920, in Spain in 1936–37, and partially in Chile in 1972–73 and Portugal in 1975).

He therefore argues: 'Now, as far as the question of the rupture is concerned, this moment of test of strength you are talking

---

[18] On this question the book of Fabre, Hincker, and Sève contains only empty platitudes, lacking any precise meaning. For example: 'The functions of the judicial system, the police, and the army are consequently redefined.' 'As for the army . . . it is confirmed in its mission of national defence, to the exclusion of any other'. 'A profound restoration(!) of the administration, of its rules and methods of functioning, will follow, guaranteeing the public interests, as well as those of the citizens' (op. cit., pp. 176, 177, 179). Thus do the authors cheerfully dispense with the class nature of the state, indeed of the class struggle itself.

about could be located only between the state and its absolute exterior, which would be the centralized organization of rank-and-file popular power. . . . I agree on the necessity for the rupture. But in the end, it is not evident that the test of strength can occur in a genuinely revolutionary manner only between the state as such on the one hand and its absolute exterior(?). . . that is, the movement, the popular powers, centralized at the rank-and-file level into a second power. . . .

'. . . The revolutionary break does not inevitably occur in the form of a centralization of a counter-state confronting the state itself *en bloc*. It can pass through the state, and I think this is the only way it will happen at present. . . . The organs of popular power at the base, the structures of direct democracy, will be the elements which bring about a differentiation inside the state apparatuses, a polarization by the popular movement of a large fraction of these apparatuses. This fraction, in alliance with the movement, will confront the reactionary, counter-revolutionary sectors of the state apparatus backed up by the ruling classes.' (*International*, volume 4, no. 1, p. 5.)

These observations call for a reply on a number of levels. First of all, on the empirical level: the entire history of revolutions in the countries in which the proletariat is the majority of the population during this century indicates that the trend towards the self-organization of the toiling masses is *spontaneous and inevitable* in revolutionary situations. Should revolutionaries then encourage and stimulate the centralization of these organs or not? If they do not do so, the restoration of the bourgeois state power is fatal, regardless of all initial victories (and illusions) in the rising phase of the revolution. This is the tragic lesson particularly of Catalonia in 1936–37, Chile in 1970–73, and Portugal in 1975.

Poulantzas's charge that revolutionary Marxists typically view the proletarian revolution as a process 'absolutely outside' the bourgeois state is unfounded. We attach enormous importance to the disintegration of the bourgeois state *apparatus*, in which entire sectors of this apparatus will escape from *central bourgeois authority* and come under proletarian-popular authority, through the emergence of mechanisms of self-organization. One need only think of the potential contribution to the revolutionary process to be made by the self-organization of the employees of the electrical system or the banking system, or of the workers, technicians, and journalists of the television networks to understand that we attach crucial importance to socialist struggle 'within the state'. Let the banks, power stations, and television networks cease to follow the orders of the government and instead work alongside a central strike committee, or even a central workers' council, in determining their daily behaviour, and the bourgeois state would be 80% paralyzed; power would already be in the hands of the proletariat to a large extent.

But such a scenario could only occur if these committees were structured as a counter-power, while the *central apparatus* of power of the bourgeoisie was disintegrating, as workers in the public services concerned refused to accept the operative hierarchy, laws, rules and procedures which reproduce capitalist authority. Without such a process, there can be no 'crisis of rupture' but at most the substitution of a 'left elite' for a 'right elite' at the summit of the *bourgeois state*.

On the analytical level, Poulantzas rather rapidly discards the positive teachings of the Gramsci of 1919–1920 on the sociological or, so to speak, structural links between *the nature of the working-class and the character of proletarian power*. He does not answer the critical question of whether the proletariat, *by its social nature*, can ever establish itself as a ruling class, fully conscious of its own interests as a class, and exercise real state power through 'representative assemblies' elected by atomized citizens. In no way does he examine the deeper social reasons for which the masses of wage-earners have spontaneously constituted committees and councils in all revolutionary situations in which they had full freedom of action, nor the links between this freedom of action and the council form of organization. Let us put it bluntly: any attempt to fragment and stifle the centralization of the organs of workers' and people's power which arise in the course of a revolutionary process can only mean a limitation and repression of the freedom of action of the masses; that is, it is precisely incompatible with a 'democratic road to socialism'. Such an attempt may, of course, take the form of what Lenin and Trotsky called a 'democratic counter-revolution', as it initially did under the Weimar Republic, the Negrin government in Spain, or the

Soares government in Portugal. *In those countries in which the proletariat is the majority of the active population, a democratic socialist revolution implies precisely that supreme political authority must not be external to the self-organization of the masses, but must be integral to it.* Poulantzas, however, scarcely speaks of this 'externality'.

Finally, on the practical level, the emergence of a situation of dual power will undoubtedly be accompanied by lacerations within the bourgeois state apparatus. In this sense, we agree with Poulantzas when he emphasizes that a revolutionary situation implies an 'articulation' between the emergence of a new power and the struggle within the old one. But apart from the fact that this struggle can only be a by-product of the emergence of the dual power situation (this was very clearly the case in Portugal), Poulantzas's way of posing the question evades the real alternative. Is it a matter of a simple struggle to 'reorganize' the bourgeois state machine (to 'democratize' it)? Or is it a *process of decomposition of this machine*? Is it possible to imagine a genuine socialist revolution which triumphs simply by 'substituting' 'democratic' generals for 'reactionary' ones, leaving the structure of the army intact, with its traditional hierarchy, discipline, and so on? The question is not whether the revolution will 'pass through' the army or not. Obviously it *will* pass through it, otherwise its victory is unlikely. The question is whether, in order to triumph, the revolution will have to destroy *the structure of the bourgeois army* and replace it with the people in arms, with elected commanders, regardless of how many officers of the old army cross over to the side of the people (the more the better, obviously).

Let us repeat: this is an eminently practical question. If, in an attempt to obtain its (illusory) 'neutrality', one refuses to attack the hierarchical structure of the army, passively allows the reestablishment of 'discipline' within it, or stifles the inevitable attempts at self-organization by soldiers, *one does not avert the test of strength but precipitates it under the worst relationship of forces*, through a merely marginal and rudimentary 'class struggle' that 'runs through' the army. If, on the contrary, one encourages in every way the introduction of the political and class struggle 'into the state apparatus' – including the army – then one promotes a decomposition of the old structure, which can ultimately be replaced by new structures generated by revolutionary mobilizations and self-organization. The case of Chile is the most eloquent in this regard. But the verdict of Portugal is no less clear. There is no middle way between the terms of this alternative, precisely because the state, like the mode of production, is an integrated *structure*. It cannot be 'a little bit bourgeois and a little bit proletarian' any more than food can be a little bit fish and a little bit fowl.

## The Famous Engels Preface

Up to now, we have refrained from any reference to the so-called 'sacred texts' of Marxism, in order not to lend our analysis a dogmatic tone that can deter militants today. But such references are obviously not useless, if one believes, as we assuredly do, that the writings of the classics – that is, the corpus of historical materialism – furnish a scientific systematization and generalization of 150 years of experience of the real proletarian class struggle on a world scale.

The preface written by Engels in 1895 for Marx's work *Class Struggles in France, 1848–1850* played a prominent role in debates between Marxists and reformists within the international workers' movement during the years preceding and following the revolutionary explosions of 1917–1920. The reformists made abundant use of the arguments of Engels to defend an electoralist tactic of gradual accumulation of forces leading 'irresistably' to the fall of capitalism, and rendering recourse to insurrection 'outmoded'. It is no accident that the major representatives of Eurocommunism now frequently refer to this same preface in their justification of the 'peaceful, democratic, and electoral road to socialism',[19] exactly as Bernstein, Ebert, and Scheidemann did before them, against Luxemburg, Lenin, Trotsky, and their companions.

Now, few Communist militants today recall – such is the quality of much Marxist education in Western Europe, despite its incontestable diffusion – that the old Social Democratic attempt to make Friedrich Engels an advocate of a legalist

[19] See, for example, Santiago Carrillo: *'Eurocomunismo' y Estado*, pp. 118–122; Fabre, Hincker, and Sève: *Les Communistes et l'Etat*, pp. 44–45.

strategy at any price was a manipulative fraud, as is its Euro-communist successor today.

The text of the preface published by German Social Democracy in 1895 was a version that had been *shortened and censored*, supposedly in order to avoid legal prosecution. Bernstein and Kautsky in fact never published the entire Engels manuscript, despite the fact that it was in their possession. It was published for the first time by the Marx–Engels Institute of Moscow in 1930.[20]

Engels protested vehemently against the cuts that had been imposed (not to mention the cuts he had not accepted but which Wilhelm Liebknecht made anyway in *Vorwärts*). The terms of this protest leave no doubt about what Engels really thought about the essence of the question: 'Liebknecht played a dirty trick on me. He took from my introduction to Marx's articles on France between 1848 and 1850 everything he could use to support a peaceful tactic at any price, which rejects any use of violence, which is a tactic he has found opportune to preach for some time now, especially since emergency laws are being prepared in Berlin. But I recommend such a tactic only for *Germany today*, and *even here with strong reservations*. For France, Belgium, Italy, and Austria this tactic as a whole is not appropriate, and for Germany it may become inapplicable tomorrow' (Letter to Paul Lafargue, 3 April 1895, *Marx–Engels Werke*, volume 39, p. 458, Dietz-Verlag, 1968).

The letter of protest Engels sent to Richard Fischer, a member of the leadership of the German Social Democracy, is no less eloquent: 'I can nevertheless not believe that you have decided to accept absolute legality body and soul, legality under all circumstances, legality even in face of the violation of laws by their own authors, in short, the policy of turning the other cheek. *Vorwärts*, it is true sometimes repudiates revolution with all the force with which it used to preach it. . . . It is my view that you will gain nothing by preaching the absolute renunciation of direct action (*Dreischlagen*). Nobody will believe it, and *no* party in any country goes so far as to renounce resistance, arms in hand, to illegalities (which are imposed on

---

[20] For the facts, see Marx–Engels *Werke*, volume 22, p. 645; for the full text of the Engels preface, see pp. 509–527 of the same volume.

it). . . . You are trying to transform a temporary tactic into a lasting one, a tactic of relative application into an absolute one. This I will not do, I cannot do, without discrediting myself forever' (ibid. pp. 424–25).

It is interesting to note that among the sentences censored in the Engels text that was published in *Die Neue Zeit* are two which profoundly modify the text's apparent opposition to insurrectional action. On page 523 we find the suppressed phrase: 'everywhere the *unprepared* launching of an attack has been relegated to the background'; while on page 521, the passage: 'Even in the classic time of streetfighting, therefore, the barricade produced more of a moral than material effect. It was a means of shaking the steadfastness of the military. If it held out until this was attained, victory was won; if not, there was defeat', was followed in the Engels manuscript by the following sentence, censored by *Die Neue Zeit*: 'This is the main point, which must be kept in view, likewise, when the chances of possible future street fighting are examined' (our emphasis).[21]

These excerpts show beyond any doubt that the old Engels, on the eve of his death, in no way ruled out recourse to insurrection and did not at all defend a peaceful, legalist, gradualist, electoralist road to socialism. He remained what he had always been: a genuine revolutionary. It is instructive to compare other texts drafted around the same time, to grasp his real thought.

For example, Engels's preface to *The Civil War in France*, Marx's essay on the Paris Commune, which was written on 18 March 1891, the twentieth anniversary of the Commune, concludes with the following passage, which permits of no equivocation: 'From the very outset, the Commune was compelled to recognize that the working class, once come to power, could not go on managing with the old state machine; that in order not to lose again its only just conquered supremacy, this working class must, on the one hand, do away with all the old repressive machinery previously used against itself, and, on the other hand, safeguard itself against its own deputies and officials, by declaring them all, without exception, subject to

[21] See Marx and Engels, *Selected Works*, London, 1970, p. 652.

recall at any moment. . . . In reality, however, the state is nothing but a machine for the oppression of one class by another, and indeed in the democratic republic no less than in the monarchy; and at best an evil inherited by the proletariat after its victorious struggle for class supremacy, whose worst sides the victorious proletariat, just like the Commune, cannot avoid having to lop off at once as much as possible until such time as a generation reared in new, free social conditions is able to throw the entire lumber of the state on the scrap heap. Of late, the Social-Democratic philistine has once more been filled with wholesome terror at the words: Dictatorship of the Proletariat. Well and good, gentlemen, do you want to know what this dictatorship looks like? Look at the Paris Commune. That was the Dictatorship of the Proletariat' (Karl Marx and Frederick Engels: *Selected Works*, volume 1, pp. 483 and 485).[22]

In a letter to Karl Kautsky on 3 November 1893, dealing with the general strike, we find the following prophetic words (whose historical importance Trotsky correctly underlined): 'You yourself say that barricades are outmoded (but they could be useful again, if the army is composed one-third or two-fifths of socialists and it is important to offer it an opportunity to yield); but the political strike must either triumph immediately . . . or end in colossal failure, *or lead directly to barricades*' (*Marx–Engels Werke*, volume 39, p. 161).

One can see how coherent Engels's positions were and how appropriate they remain today. The conquest of power by the proletariat is impossible without the destruction of the bourgeois state machine. The proletariat cannot renounce violence under all circumstances, particularly when it must oppose the enemy's attempts to use violence to prevent the masses from fully mobilizing their forces. Any head-on confrontation between classes will provoke an internal disintegration of the army, and opportune conditions must be created for the soldiers

---

[22] In Engels's manuscript, the words 'Social-Democratic philistine' had been crossed out and replaced by 'German philistine', in a handwriting that was not Engels's. In the editions of this preface published by the Marx-Engels Institute of the USSR, as well as those published by the various publishing companies controlled by the Communist parties of Europe, the words 'Social Democratic philistine' were used during the 1930s, 1940s, and 1950s. In the complete edition of the works of Marx and Engels published in the 1960s, however, the version 'German philistine' reappears without explanation.

to pass to the side of the toiling masses. Here we come to the pivot of the controversy between Eurocommunists and revolutionary Marxists: the necessity for the self-defence of the masses and the necessity to disintegrate the bourgeois army.

## Overwhelming Testimony

Some official representatives of Eurocommunism have imprudently invoked the example of Chile to justify their tactics and strategy. According to them, the Chilean experience demonstrated that any attempt to confront the bourgeois army inevitably leads to a defeat of the working class. Allende is said to have been brought down because he was too radical, because he allowed himself to be influenced by the 'criminal provocations of the ultra-left', because he did not conclude a rapid enough compromise with Christian Democracy and the army.

Such a description of the experience of Unidad Popular is a complete distortion of the real historical facts. *The truth is that Allende applied a strategy similar if not identical to that of the Eurocommunists.* It was in the nature of things that during a phase of objective exacerbation of the class struggle growing sectors of the proletariat outflanked his government from the left and escaped the control of Unidad Popular. This will also occur in South-West Europe if left governments come to power and apply policies inspired by Eurocommunism. The fundamental orientation of Allende, however, was to respect the framework of bourgeois legality and representative institutions, to accept the constitution and parliament, to compromise with Christian Democracy, and to proclaim from the rooftops that he would maintain the integrity and structure of the army, since it was 'democratic' and would itself respect the constitution.

It has been widely forgotten that it was during the Allende government that the Chilean army received the right to 'reestablish order' in the factories by searching them for stocks of arms; and that the army 'reestablished order' in its own ranks by arresting and torturing sailors and soldiers who had committed the 'crime' of informing the legal government of the putschist plans of their officers. It was Allende himself who introduced army commanders – *including Pinochet* – into his

Cabinet, just as Martinez Barrio, *immediately after the Spanish putsch*, invited General Mola, one of its military and political chiefs, to enter a 'republican government of national union'. The Eurocommunists are preparing to repeat this suicidal policy, to the detriment of the workers of Western Europe, if these workers allow them to do it.

There is, however, overwhelming testimony to the real lessons of the Chilean experience, from a source that cannot be suspected by Communist cadres: Volodia Teitelboim, the major theoretician and second-ranking political leader of the Chilean Communist Party. The January 1977 issue of the Spanish edition of *Problems of Peace and Socialism* (published in Prague), contained an article by Teitelboim entitled 'Reflections on the Thousand Days of the Unidad Popular Government in Chile' – which mysteriously disappeared from the French edition of the same review, although normally all the versions are identical. Long excerpts of this article could be cited. We will limit ourselves, however, to three particularly eloquent passages. Firstly, here is what Teitelboim has to say on the 'peaceful and electoral road to socialism': 'In our view, the events in Chile demonstrate in the final analysis that under given circumstances, as the result of a vast and complex historical evolution, through a laborious process of accumulation of forces and unification of sectors interested in social change, it is possible to achieve through the ballot box *something which is much more than a pure and simple electoral victory, but which is at the same time much less than real power*. . . . It was probably an error to have elevated certain forms of struggle within the Chilean revolutionary process to an essential category, rendering recourse to a single road absolute in practice. . . . Although the peaceful development of the revolution corresponded to a real possibility and reflected the will of the Chilean popular movement, it was still necessary to take account of the adverse reaction of the enemy, who was prepared to prevent the revolution by any means necessary' (emphasis added).

Secondly, Teitelboim writes of the social character of the state under the 'anti-monopoly alliance' and 'advanced democracy': 'But Salvador Allende's accession to the post of president of the republic could not in and of itself alter the class nature of the state, nor the character of the armed forces,

police, and public administration. For this reason, it is necessary to insist on the fact that a capital objective of any process
by the peaceful road(!) must be also to guarantee a relationship of military forces favourable to the development of the
revolution. Indeed, this is a key aspect. . . . Towards this end, it
was necessary to establish a state apparatus under the organized pressure of the people, to be able to place it increasingly in
the service of the people. Even more, it was necessary to
develop an active democracy with mass participation, depriv-
ing the reactionary sectors of parts of their empire, transferring
them to the direction of the workers, of the progressive sectors
of society'.

The language is hazy and ambiguous. It is the language of
pseudo-centrism, which sketches timid criticisms of reformism
but can relapse into the old errors again at any moment. The
peaceful road which is reflected in a relationship of military
forces; the pressure which detaches parts of power from the
hands of the 'reactionaries' (is mere 'pressure' enough?); a
reactionary state power which is placed 'in growing manner'
in the service of the people: all this is marked with the stamp of
confusion. But for anyone who really wants to listen to this
voice, steeped in a guilty conscience, the message is clear:
*power must be wrested from the hands of the bourgeois apparatus
of repression and transferred to the direct democracy of the
masses, that is, to organs of workers and people's power.* The rest
is only bad prose, a smokescreen to cover the tracks of an
operation that led to disaster.

Finally, Teitelboim comments on the attitude of Unidad
Popular towards the army: 'One of the major weaknesses of the
Chilean popular movement was that this problem [the army]
was wrongly posed, in a poor and shameful manner, in terms of
personalities, excluding the participation of parties . . . and of
the masses themselves. Army and police chiefs who did not seem
prepared to accomplish their duty were generally left in command. . . . We sincerely believe that we Communists suffered
from a historic deficiency because of the inadequacy and weakness of our military policy and our policy towards the armed
forces. . . . *It is utopian to believe in the political neutrality of the
army.* It is another thing to produce, in a given situation, a
period of neutralization *as the result of a struggle outside and*

*inside the armed forces* to prevent the plans of the fascist sectors for a reactionary coup from coming to fruition. . . . The class origin of the members of the army is a fact of prime importance: but in the end, the fact that the majority of its members are the sons of workers and poor peasants can achieve manifest external expression and can be brought to bear massively and openly only under the impetus of a revolutionary conjuncture and *on the condition that organization and work has been done in the barracks*' (emphasis added).

These eloquent conclusions have even greater weight in that they come from a leader and a party which *acted in exactly the opposite manner*; which constantly, right up to September 1973, sang the praises of the 'unity' and 'political neutrality' of the army and its alleged respect for the constitution; which, for this reason, refused to organize any work within the army and denounced revolutionary militants as the 'Trojan horse of reaction' when they, with their extremely limited and modest resources, attempted to begin such work.[23]

Teitelboim's veiled polemic against Eurocommunism (is he in the process of becoming a 'left Eurocommunist'?), however, appears strikingly equivocal, when we notice that he keeps complete silence about the fact that the Chilean Communist Party today is preaching an even more rightist orientation than it did at the time of Unidad Popular. The only *practical* policy that accompanies his self-criticism is the quest of the Chilean party for an alliance with Christian Democracy, that

[23] Let us limit ourselves to some quotations from an interview granted *Nouvelle Revue Internationale* (December 1972) by Luís Corvalán, Secretary-General of the Chilean Communist Party, which illustrate the lamentable failure of the political orientation and perspectives of this party, then shared by Teitelboim:

'The very great majority of the country rejects the sedition and civil war that reaction, and more particularly the fascist groups, would like to impose on us. That is, despite the regroupment of the opposition within a "Democratic Confederation", not all its participants are seeking to overthrow the government. If a relatively limited(!) but no less dangerous portion of the opposition takes the road of sedition, another portion, more numerous, intends to remain within the framework of the constitution'.

'The political activity of the MIR and the other ultraleftist groups, to whom the reactionary press is affording such great publicity, is most prejudicial to the government of Unidad Popular. Their policy of frontally attacking the bourgeoisie and the opposition en bloc, their occupations of the factories and small and middle-sized agricultural units, their provocations and ostentatious

is, an Italian-style 'historic compromise'. This certainly does not allow for work in the barracks to dismantle the authority of the corps of reactionary officers.

How is it possible to miss the imperative lesson that emerges from this compelling testimony to a tragic experience: that any confusion about the class character of the state machine threatens to cost the working class thousands of victims as well as all its civic rights and economic gains? Let the workers of Western Europe and the imperialist countries in general, let Communist militants ponder the words of Teitelboim, and let them remember that an ounce of prevention is worth a pound of cure. It is better to prevent the victory of the Pinochets of Europe than to make resounding self-criticisms after the fact.

The coincidence of a grave economic and social crisis in Western Europe with – contrary to the years 1929–33 – a rise in workers' combativity, accompanied in several countries by a popular political radicalization, is today creating conditions propitious for the transformation of defensive struggles by workers, against attacks on their living standards and past conquests, into pre-revolutionary and revolutionary explosions. The vanguard of the proletariat and of all the forms of the mass movement, however, will only be able to prevent these struggles from being diverted into various forms of class

---

adventures with firearms, their insistence on the inevitability of an armed confrontation, their opportunist exploitation of this or that weakness of the people's movements are grist to the mill of the opposition in general and the conspirators in particular'.

'In conformity with the constitution, the army does not engage in politics. Of course, the army is primarily men, and man, whether in uniform or not, is a social being. The revolutionary process exacerbates the class struggle, affects all citizens. It would thus be illusory to think that the armed forces remain impermeable to the influences of our epoch. The diversity of classes and political attitudes which characterizes Chilean society is also reflected and manifested in the armed forces. But whatever the differences may be, *the military men feel united by a certain number of values: respect for the constitution and the law, obedience to the legitimately constituted government.* Granted, the possibility of the entry onto the political scene of a military chief greedy for power is not excluded, as ex-general Viaux, for example, rebelled against the previous government at the end of 1969 in an attempt to prevent the victory of Unidad Popular. The present situation will not be able to continue indefinitely. Nevertheless, in the conditions of our country, changes can be made not only by strictly following the classical roads taken by other revolutions, *but in the framework of the law, given the evolution occurring in the way the officers conceive of their role in the society the people want to construct*' (Emphasis added).

collaboration and parliamentary coalition with the bourgeoisie – salvaging the capitalist system from its crisis once again – if it is possessed of all necessary clarity about the structural character of the bourgeois state and if it orients resolutely towards a popular seizure of power by the workers.

# 10
# The Strategy of Eurocommunism

Eurocommunism conceives of itself as a common strategy applicable by all the Communist parties in the advanced capitalist countries. Indeed, it is striking to note the similarity with which most of these parties modified their political orientation during the 1960s and 1970s, and not only in West Europe. The same positions are now shared by the Japanese and Australian Communist parties, to mention only two examples. If the Communist parties of the United States, Canada, and West Germany still seem to present exceptions to the increasingly general Eurocommunist rule, this can easily be explained by their relative isolation and by the special conditions of class struggle in their respective countries. For it is simply not credible for them to pose the question of a strategy for power in the medium term. The corollary of this weakness is their complete material and political dependence on the CPSU (or the bureaucracy of East Germany in the case of the West German Communist Party). This does not (yet?) permit them to go all the way in the evolution that has produced Eurocommunism. An attentive analysis of their political *tactics*, however, demonstrates that these have many more points in common with Eurocommunism than is generally supposed. The only essential distinction is their systematically uncritical attitude towards the Soviet bureaucracy.

The principal theses of Eurocommunist strategy may be summarized as follows:

1. It is impossible to achieve socialism in the industrialized countries without the consensus of a large majority of the population.

2. In order to win this consensus, bourgeois-parliamentary

institutions, which manifestly enjoy the support of the majority, must be preserved.

3. The nature of these institutions is such that they can be progressively emptied of their class content; that is, they can cease to be props for the class rule of the bourgeoisie. This is a consequence particularly of the constant extension of the role of the state in economic life, which transposes the major contradictions of society into the state itself, transforming it into a field of battle on which the monopolies and the 'union of progressive forces', if not the bourgeoisie and the proletariat, can contend.

4. A head-on confrontation between the bourgeoisie as a whole and the isolated proletariat must be averted at all costs, not only because such a confrontation would surely end in the defeat of the working-class, but also because it would inevitably lead to the destruction of bourgeois-parliamentary institutions and would thus postpone any chance of a 'breakthrough' towards socialism for a protracted period.

5. In order to win significant parliamentary majorities (supported by the pressure and mobilization of the masses), the workers' movement can and must fight for structural reforms which will transform the nature of the capitalist system by stages and will eventually alter its very nature.

6. The essential stage now before us is that of the anti-monopoly alliance, or 'advanced democracy', which, first weakening and then abolishing the power of the monopolies, will deal a decisive blow to capitalism and will enable the weight and power of the toiling masses in society to grow qualitatively, through various mechanisms of democratization of economic life and through the participation of the masses in the administration of the state. This stage is a decisive transitional one towards the abolition of capitalism and the advent of socialism. In itself, however, it constitutes neither one nor the other.

7. In order to isolate the great monopolies, this anti-monopoly alliance must include, in addition to the working class and the mass of employees (including functionaries, technicians, and cadres), a good part of the peasantry and a considerable portion of the small and middle bourgeoisie. That is why it is inappropriate to challenge the system of private property during

this initial stage.

We believe this constitutes an objective summary of the fundamental strategic premises of Eurocommunism, to which, incidentally, the Kremlin has accorded general approval.[1] They deserve and require a comprehensive response, which must include an analysis of the dominant features of the evolution of the class struggle in the advanced, industrialized countries. We have already dealt with the particular problems raised by this strategy in regard to the nature of parliamentary-democratic institutions and the role of the state in the contemporary class struggle in general.

### The Historic source of Eurocommunist strategy: Kautsky's 'Attrition Strategy'

What is most striking about the Eurocommunist strategy is that it is scarcely new. It was first formulated in a coherent form in 1910, by Karl Kautsky in his debate with Rosa Luxemburg in the German Social Democratic Party. At the time, Kautsky defined two strategies for the struggle for power of the German workers' movement (and by extension for the workers' movement in all the industrially advanced countries): the so-called strategy of assault and the 'attrition strategy' (*Ermattungsstrategie*). He opted resolutely for the second.

According to this strategy, the workers' movement, rather than seeking to take the enemy fortress by assault in one fell swoop, thus putting everything at stake and risking all the gains of forty years of partial progress and accumulation of forces, should begin by encircling this fortress and undermining it, compelling the enemy to make repeated and costly sorties resulting in defeats. The workers should divide the enemy and provoke a gradual erosion of his will to win, and

---

[1] 'There can be no success unless the working class, all the toiling masses, transform parliament from an instrument of domination of the bourgeoisie into a representative of the interests of the working people. . . . The programmes for profound transformation of the economic structure of society, the construction of a state of democratic alliance, a government of a bloc of left forces, an anti-monopoly democracy, and others, which have been proposed by several Communist parties in Europe and in other parts of the world today, are intermediary stages and transitional forms on the road to socialism, which take account of the concrete conditions in each country' (*Pravda*, 1 March 1977).

even his will to fight. The fortress can then eventually be taken at low cost, although not without firing a shot.[2]

To trace the historic source of Eurocommunist strategy is not simply an exercise in erudition. On the contrary, it enables us to confront the advocates of Eurocommunism with the teachings of practice, the lessons of history. The Kautskyist strategy failed miserably. It led not to the collapse of the capitalist fortress, but to the collapse of the German workers' movement, through the well-known stages of 4 August 1914, the suffocation of the revolutions of 1918 and 1923, and the capitulation to the advent of the Nazis to power in 1933. Successive applications of a similar strategy by the French and Spanish Communist parties between 1935 and 1938 likewise led to bloody defeats. A similar strategy was again applied by the Communist parties in France, Italy, and other, smaller countries of Europe between 1944 and 1947; they also failed. The same strategy was applied under the particular conditions of a semi-colonial country, but one endowed with a powerfully organized and independent workers' movement: in Chile at the end of the 1960s and beginning of the 1970s, under the Unidad Popular. It resulted in a bloody defeat, the Pinochet coup of 1973. The least one can say is that the Eurocommunist strategists do not seem inclined to draw the lessons of these repeated defeats.

The case of Portugal is particularly eloquent. The Portuguese Communist Party, while maintaining an uncritical attitude towards the Soviet bureaucracy, also strictly applied the strategy of 'anti-monopoly alliance' and 'advanced democracy' between April 1974 and November 1975. It even participated in coalition governments with bourgeois forces. The great monopolies were effectively excluded, not by a conscious plan of the Communist Party, but under the pressure of impetuous mass mobilizations. But capitalism was not at all abolished. The nationalized sector accounted for barely more than 25% of either industrial production or gross national product. The

---

[2] Karl Kautsky: 'Was Nun?' in *Die Neue Zeit*, 8 April and 15 April 1910 (year 28, vol. 2). It should be noted that Kautsky's attrition strategy also provided for passage to a strategy of assault (*Niederwerfungsstrategie*) and to the struggle for power, either when the enemy sought to suppress the proletariat's freedom of organization or when the enemy has been so weakened that his overthrow could be effected without great cost.

bourgeoisie, far from withering away, moved to an aggressive and increasingly arrogant counteroffensive. The working class, far from streaking from victory to victory, was disoriented, thrown onto the defensive, and divided (although not defeated; it is still capable of taking the offensive again, but this is not at all due to the 'success' of the 'attrition strategy', far from it).

Why these repeated defeats? To respond to this question is to put one's finger on the essential weakness of Eurocommunist strategy, on the grave defects in the Eurocommunist analysis of class relations in industrialized capitalist society and their dynamic, on its lack of understanding of the *structural character of bourgeois relations of domination*, which cannot be abolished gradually.

The very image utilized by Kautsky is symbolic of a profoundly mechanistic and erroneous view of the relations of bourgeois domination. The power of the bourgeoisie is represented as a fortress standing *outside* the social body properly so called. The workers' movement is represented as capable of gradually and tranquilly assembling the living forces of this social body, independent of and against the bourgeois regime. The reality of capitalism, however, is quite different.

So long as the bourgeoisie commands political and economic power, the workers live and act under conditions of material dependence on the ruling class. Their jobs, incomes, and living standards are determined in the final analysis by economic mechanisms which function on the basis of the objectives pursued by the bourgeoisie: valorization and accumulation of capital. Likewise, the political power of the bourgeoisie, which includes not only the apparatus of repression but also the apparatus of ideological manipulation, is not external to the political action and behaviour of the proletariat, not to mention the petty-bourgeois masses, but stands in permanent interpenetration with it (to varying degrees, of course, depending on the political situation and the vicissitudes of the class struggle).

Under these conditions, the notion that all the living forces of society can gradually be assembled for a long, perhaps even permanent, siege of the 'capitalist fortress' is an idle dream. Capitalism commands innumerable machine-gun nests stationed around its 'fortress', within the very social body that is supposed to be besieging it. These defences permit no lasting assemblies or sieges of long duration. They can be dismantled, but only at precise moments, when a juxtaposition of circumstances momentarily weakens or even paralyzes the enemy's ability to make use of them. But this moment never lasts very long. It is called a 'revolutionary crisis'. For any attempt to dismantle the bourgeois defences disorganizes and unravels all the mechanisms of the functioning of society and the economy and provokes extreme tension. Far from the image of a calm and untroubled siege, this evokes precisely the inexorable, head-on test of strength the strategy was designed to avert in the first place. This test of strength can be averted only if the machine-gun nests are left intact. In that case, however, there is no question of a siege, nor even of assembling the bulk of the forces required for a siege.

## Crisis of Domination of the Bourgeoisie and Economic Crisis

Intimately linked to the false image of a bourgeois political power standing outside society itself is the concept that a gradual conquest 'of powers'[3] could occur, not only without provoking a general confrontation between labour and capital, but even without fundamentally upsetting the normal course of economic and social life. This presupposes an economy functioning independent of specific relations of production and class interests, another idle dream.

Under the capitalist system, economic life functions normally only to the extent that the owners of the means of production are able to utilize them with the aim of realizing the intended profits. When the rate of profit falls, when profits realized are inferior to profits anticipated, the capitalists' possibilities of accumulating capital decline and their immediate interest in the productive investment of newly accumulated capital is placed in question.

Investment, production, and employment thus decline for a time. A crisis then breaks out, not primarily because of bour-

---

[3] The book *La Conquête des Pouvoirs*, by Gilles Martinet, constitutes the most coherent and sophisticated presentation of the 'attrition strategy' yet produced, going far beyond the very general theses of Kautsky and the Eurocommunists.

geois 'bad faith' or a desire to hatch 'conspiracies' against a 'left government' (although these motivations do play a role), but essentially because of the very logic of the system. It is utopian to expect capitalists to increase investments and stimulate economic growth when the rate of profit is on the decline; and it is quite simply impossible to compel them to act against their own interests, whether private or class.

Now, the entire sequence of reforms of any real substance affecting the living standards and quality of life of the toiling masses, and even more any general attack on the mechanisms of domination of the bourgeoisie (of the 'power of the monopolies'), inevitably implies a decline in the average rate of profit. They thus inevitably undermine the basic mechanisms of the capitalist economy. A capitalist reaction – investment strike, 'destabilization', flight of capital, accelerated inflation – is then equally inevitable. This in turn involves a deterioration of the living standards of the masses, which can only provoke an exacerbation of the class struggle and a deep social crisis, especially when it occurs at a time when the masses feel that the relationship of forces has shifted in their favour, that capitalism has been weakened.

A genuine economic and social earthquake is then touched off. Under the conditions of this earthquake, the idea that a protracted and tranquil 'siege' is possible becomes thoroughly absurd. The besiegers risk being buried in the debris of the fortress if they do not act with speed and resolution.

At the root of the utopian 'strategy of attrition' which has been adopted by the Eurocommunists lies an incomprehension of the structural character of capitalist relations of production. These relations of production cannot be modified gradually, piece by piece. Either they function on the basis of their own logic or they do not function at all. They cannot function half way, just as a woman cannot be a little bit pregnant. The concept of a 'mixed economy' is a delusion, or a myth deliberately propagated to deceive the masses. The nationalized sector in a capitalist economy is not an 'island of socialism'. It is an instrument for subsidizing and stimulating the valorization of private capital.

In this sense, when bourgeois society is shaken by a profound socio-economic crisis, there are only two possible outcomes that reestablish 'normal' economic life:

§Either all the conditions for the satisfactory valorization of capital are reassembled, which means a substantial rise in the rate of profit, which in turn requires austerity, the dismantlement of social reforms, and a green light for an offensive against employment and for speed-up in factories. This undoubtedly permits 'normalization' on the basis of capitalist logic, but it has nothing whatever to do with 'advanced democracy' or the 'dismantlement of the power of the monopolies'. On the contrary, it strengthens their power and their grip on all society, at the expense of the working class.

§Or else all the conditions for a recovery of production on the basis of the logic of a socialized and planned economy are assembled. This demands that the proletariat take over the essential means of production and exchange and suppress any bourgeois force capable of impeding this socialist 'normalization'. This is called socialist revolution, and it cannot be accompanied by any respect for private property or any servility to bourgeois legality. Once again, this has nothing whatever to do with a stage of 'advanced democracy' or an 'anti-monopoly alliance' that avoids attacking capitalism as a whole.

The first outcome is that recommended by the right wing of Social Democracy ('acting as bedside doctor for ailing capitalism') and implemented by Social Democrats when they are in power (Helmut Schmidt, Wilson–Callaghan). The second is the perspective of revolutionary Marxists. The Eurocommunist strategic project, like that of Kautsky or the Unidad Popular in the past, straddles two chairs and is completely unrealistic. Abandoned to its own logic, it leads straight back to the first outcome in practice, unless the masses themselves go beyond it. Its talk of a 'transition to socialism' typically proves to be a smokescreen behind which the consolidation of the capitalist economy and the power of big capital is effected.

## Crisis of Domination of the Bourgeoisie and Social Crisis

The lack of realism of the 'attrition strategy' becomes equally evident when one broaches the problem from the angle of the evolution of the socio-political relationship of class forces. Any project of 'dismantling the power of the monopolies' must presuppose a dramatic modification in this relationship of forces. Better: the Eurocommunist project, like similar ones in the past, generally arises only when this modification has already begun to manifest itself. Objectively, the project then represents a method of diverting the rise of workers' struggles towards objectives compatible with the maintenance of the capitalist system.

The bourgeoisie inevitably must react to any deterioration of the conditions of its own domination. Its reaction will be both economic and political. We have already spoken of the economic reaction. The typical course of the political reaction is also well known: 'strategy of tension' (physical attacks and terrorism), within which the far-right groups (Cagoule and the 'synarchie', SAC and company, 'Guerrillas of Christ the King', the Spinolists) operate in intimate symbiosis with the bourgeois state apparatus – primarily, but not exclusively, the repressive apparatus; hysterical intoxication of the petty-bourgeoisie and the less politicized layers of the proletariat with the spectre of the 'red menace'; progressive paralysis of parliamentary institutions and overt sabotage of the public administration; preparation of a *coup d'Etat* if need be.

A working class in the midst of a rise in its own combativity and an advance of its own forces, motivated by a great surge of desire for unity and sensing that the enemy is on the defensive (which sentiment the entire Eurocommunist strategy must inevitably consolidate) will most assuredly respond to these reactions of the bourgeoisie, both to defend its living standard, jobs, and past and present conquests and to defend the project of 'dismantling the power of big capital through the legal and peaceful road', the project the reformist leaders have held up as the only 'realistic' path. The workers will thus move against the owners of big capital, who now begin to act through increasingly overt sabotage and illegal conspiracy. Hence, the historic phase during which the Eurocommunist strategy acquires all its credibility in the eyes of the masses is precisely the phase in which the exacerbation of contradictions, tensions, and class struggles inexorably places a frontal test of strength between capital and labour on the agenda.

Now, the essential aim of the Eurocommunist strategy is precisely *to avert* this confrontation at any price. Its capacity to influence the behaviour of the bourgeoisie, however, is virtually nil. The coups of Kapp, von Papen, Mola-Franco, De Gaulle, Pinochet, and Eanes have never been warded off by the pledges of Ebert-Noske, Otto Wels, Prieto, Thorez, Allende, or Mario Soares that the army is 'national' and 'democratic' and 'stands above the class struggle' and 'respects the constitution'. The reformists have never been able to paralyze, or even curb, the anti-worker and counter-revolutionary projects of the capitalists through tricks, deceit, manoeuvre, or the restriction of workers' struggles. Their capacity to influence the behaviour of the proletariat, however, has unfortunately been much more real. Inasmuch as their efforts are wholly centred on the goal of averting a direct confrontation, there can be only two results. Either they fail, that is, the Eurocommunist leadership is increasingly overtaken by the masses, in which case the confrontation occurs anyway; or they succeed, in which case the fragmentation and stifling of workers' struggles against the mobilization of bourgeois forces weakens and demoralizes the proletariat and leads to its certain defeat at the hands of the bourgeois counteroffensive. In neither case can the Eurocommunist strategic project be realized.

Behind the entire Eurocommunist strategy, and behind Kautsky's 'attrition strategy' too, lies a manipulative and bureaucratic conception of the workers' movement and proletarian politics, indeed of politics in general. It is important to highlight this. The class struggle is reduced purely to its political aspect, or rather its politico-parliamentary aspect. Relations between classes are reduced to relations between political parties, or rather, between leaderships of political parties. A handful of 'chiefs' is supposed to represent and faithfully articulate the social interests of millions of people in all their complex interconnections, solely on the basis of election results. These social classes – made up of millions of people, tens of millions in the big countries – are supposed to stand at attention before their omniscient generals, marching forward or to the rear on command, acting like marionettes marshalled by a machine that controls their every move.[4]

---

[4] It must be acknowledged that in his time Kautsky included the spontaneity of the 'unorganized' masses in his strategic calculations: 'The broader is the

## Two Mystifications: 'Economism' and 'Corporatism'

Is it necessary to stress that this sort of machinery cannot function in a bourgeois society in which the organization, class consciousness, and combativity of the workers have gone beyond a certain threshold – unfortunately for the advocates of a conception of politics which ignores the laws of the elementary socio-economic class struggle, the spontaneous psychology of the masses and all the historical lessons of the cumulative effects of the victories or defeats of popular struggles? Although the toiling masses are not capable of spontaneously formulating and realizing a coherent project for the conquest of power or the organization of a socialist society, they are perfectly capable, in a pre-revolutionary situation in which class contradictions are exacerbated, of acting spontaneously, instinctively, or semi-consciously both to defend their immediate interests and to oppose the counter-revolutionary manoeuvres of the bourgeoisie. The whole history of revolutionary crises in the industrially advanced countries in the 20th century attests to this capacity. They are capable of acting independently of the instructions and orientations of their 'commanders', and even against them if need be. They are all the more capable of so doing if a vanguard critical of the reformist projects and the hesitations and vacillations of the bureaucratic apparatuses is present among the masses with growing numerical weight and influence, even if it is still a

---

organization, the more it includes hundreds of thousands of people throughout the country, the heavier becomes its machinery and the more difficult it becomes for it to act promptly when sudden and unexpected events sow great emotion among the total mass of the population and spur them to immediate action. In such situations, conditions for spontaneous mass actions arise again, which in some cases can sweep away whole systems of government. It is war that creates the most fertile ground in this regard. . . . But even a gigantic strike which paralyzes all social life can bring enormous surprises overnight. . . . The growth of proletarian organizations thus in no way eliminates the possibility, or even probability, of spontaneous mass actions forever; it only limits it in normal times. The same applies to universal suffrage' (Karl Kautsky: 'Die Aktion der Masse', p. 110, *Die Neue Zeit*, year 30, vol. 1, issue of 27 October 1911). The Kautsky of 1910–1911 was not yet a pure reformist. He was still a centrist. His thought oscillates, fluctuates, wavers ceaselessly between reformism and revolutionary Marxism, including on the question of the mass strike. On this subject he stands *in advance of* and not behind the Berlinguers, Marchaises, and Carrillos.

small minority. This vanguard must educate the masses and systematically prepare them for a revolutionary struggle through adequate political methods and language, avoiding all sectarianism and isolation and successfully taking credible and united initiatives.

Likewise, the exacerbation of contradictions and elementary and spontaneous class struggles in the factories, workshops, offices, neighbourhoods, and regions, and among oppressed sectors (women, youth, national minorities) and sectors sensitive to social problems (anti-capitalist ecologists), will also have cumulative effects, sweeping through society as a whole and contributing towards a head-on test of strength between the opposing classes, the proletariat and the bourgeoisie.

This *objective* tendency of the class struggle – which is largely independent both of the conciliatory and moderating will of the reformist leaderships and of the will of revolutionaries to drive ahead, although it obviously leads to very different results depending on the strength of the two forces – lends all periods in which strategic projects of the Eurocommunist variety arise the characteristics of pre-revolutionary periods. It is precisely this pre-revolutionary character of the period which renders the plan of averting the test of strength at all costs utopian.

When the class struggle reaches boiling point, the conciliators run out of devices and manoeuvres. They thus threaten to turn into the protagonists, even the organizers, of repression. The real choice is therefore this: either prepare the proletariat politically, organizationally, and psychologically for this confrontation, through successive experiences in struggle and self-organization, so that the working class enters the confrontation with the maximum chances of victory (an *absolute* guarantee of victory obviously being impossible), or else curb, weaken, and fragment the mobilization and combativity of the proletariat and undermine its confidence in its own strength and the ardour of its socialist and anti-capitalist convictions under the pretext of averting 'adventures'. The latter option condemns the proletariat to fight under conditions imposed by the enemy and to run greater risk of being defeated.

In the same context, it is crucial to pillory the demagogic and mystifying use of two concepts – 'economism' and 'corporatism' – by Eurocommunist defenders of a policy of class collaboration with the bourgeoisie. In classical Marxist terminology the concepts 'economism' and 'corporatism' have a precise content. 'Economism' refers to a tendency in the workers' movement which tries to *limit* workers' action to the defence of the material interests of the proletariat which arises from the class more or less spontaneously. 'Corporatism' is a tendency of the trade-union movement to limit the actions of the workers to the defence of the narrow material interests of each profession (or, in the best of cases, each branch of industry), if necessary in opposition to the interests of all the workers or of other sectors of the working class.

By inadmissible extrapolation, there have been attempts to identify rejection of 'economism' with condemnation of the defence of the material interests of the workers under the capitalist system, which supposedly must be subordinated to general political interests. One can seek in vain a single instance in which Marx or Lenin opposed workers' strikes for economic class demands under the pretext of some 'more important political project'. In a complete perversion of their meaning, the terms 'economism' or 'corporatism' have been used to refer to the defence of the economic conquests of the working class against aggression from the employers, under the pretext that this 'unreasonable' attitude 'would scuttle' the 'national economy', in other words, would undermine capitalist profits. Marx and Lenin would turn in their graves if they knew that such bourgeois ideas were being attributed to them. For what underlies this condemnation is the idea that the workers' movement and big capital have a 'common interest' . . . in defending the stability of the *capitalist* economy!

It should also be noted that the senseless charge of 'economism' or 'corporatism' levelled against the most combative layers of the proletariat goes back to the mechanistic separation of 'economic struggles' and 'political struggles' that was most characteristic of classical reformism. In a certain sense, it is merely the negative reproduction of this same idea. Marxism, however, proceeds in exactly the opposite manner. It bases itself on the spontaneous tendency of the proletariat to defend its immediate material interests and then seeks to make sure that this defence leads to an overall anti-capitalist political project.

## Is Eurocommunism the Executor of the Testament of Antonio Gramsci?

The Eurocommunist leaders, especially those of the Italian Communist Party, frequently refer to Antonio Gramsci, one of the major leaders of the PCI during the 1920s, as the real progenitor of the Eurocommunist strategy.[5] For people who still call themselves communists, it is obviously more comfortable to claim allegiance to Gramsci than to Kautsky.

Nevertheless, an analysis of the work of Gramsci as a whole demonstrates that it is fraudulent to invoke the heritage of this great Italian revolutionary in defending the neo-reformist orientation upheld by the Eurocommunist leaderships. Although it must be acknowledged that there was an evolution in Gramsci's thought between the foundation of *Ordine Nuovo* in 1919 and the drafting of his *Prison Notebooks*,[6] there is not the slightest evidence that Gramsci ever abandoned the conception that the socialist revolution implies the destruction of the bourgeois state apparatus and the replacement of bourgois-parliamentary democracy with socialist democracy based on democratically and freely elected workers' councils. This was the lesson Gramsci drew from the experience of the Russian revolution of 1917, the German revolution of 1918–19, and the Italian revolutionary crisis of 1919–20. It was above all a conclusion drawn from an analysis of the very character of the proletariat, the only really revolutionary class in bourgeois society, and of the organizational and psychological conditions required for the rise and triumph of the movement of the proletariat for self-emancipation.

Gramsci's famous concept of hegemony, developed in prison, is undeniably ambiguous. But even if this concept is interpreted in the manner most favourable to Eurocommunist doctrines, it still applies essentially to the *preparatory* period

---

[5] Santiago Carrillo: '*Eurocomunismo*' *y Estado*, p. 60; Jean Fabre, François Hincker, Lucien Sève: *Les Communistes et l'Etat*, Editions Sociales, Paris, 1977, pp. 69–73; Pietro Ingrao in: *Parti Communiste Italien: Aux Sources de l'Eurocommunisme*, interviews assembled by Henri Weber, Paris, 1977, pp. 165, 172.
[6] We are referring here essentially to the *Quaderni del Carcere* (Einaudi, 1964) and more especially to Volume 4: *Note sul Machiavelli*.

*prior to* the revolutionary crisis properly so called. It is in no way identified with the conquest of power by the proletariat. In no way does it dispense with the necessity for this conquest of power, nor does it imply that the revolutionary crisis can be averted in any way. Nothing in the concept of hegemony as it was discussed by Gramsci implies the idea of a 'gradual conquest of *some* powers', step by step, in an almost imperceptible manner, which is peculiar to the Eurocommunist strategy and to its Social Democratic predecessor.

Gramsci's positive contribution to the Marxist theory of the state lay in his stress on the fact that ideological hegemony and coercion complement one another in the exercise of class power, that no state can subsist solely on force or solely on the 'consent' of the exploited. Gramsci was, of course, developing ideas already incipient in Marx, who had emphasized in particular that the ultimate source of both the ideological and coercive power of the bourgeois state lies in the capital/wage-labour relationship itself.

This is not the occasion to deal at length with the real ambiguities inherent in the concept of hegemony.[7] What is valuable in it is its reminder that any rise of a revolutionary class within a mode of production that has already entered the stage of historical decadence is accompanied by a series of processes which progressively weaken the mechanisms of domination of the ruling class, before its political power is finally attacked frontally and overthrown. This was the case with the rise of the bourgeoisie within feudal and semi-feudal society. It is also the case with the proletariat in capitalist society.

Among these processes are: a challenging of the ideology of the ruling class by the theoretical and/or ideological elaboration of the revolutionary class; a progressive differentiation of ideologues, and more generally of 'intermediary layers of society', into defenders and opponents of the established order, between mercenaries and protagonists of the social revolution; a progressive emancipation of growing sectors of the revolutionary class and of the population from the preponderant influence of the ideology of the ruling class; a mounting or-

---

[7] See the analysis of Gramsci by Perry Anderson, 'The Antinomies of Antonio Gramsci', in *New Left Review*, No. 100.

ganization of the revolutionary class with a view towards attacking the established order; a progressive decline of the grip on society as a whole of the 'values' that contribute to the automatic reproduction of the predominant relations of production; divisions and progressive 'crises of consciousness' within the ruling class itself, especially among its youth. All these processes may best be summarized by the concept of a *general crisis of the social relations* which subtend and embody a given mode of production, a crisis which precedes the revolutionary crisis proper.

There is, however, a fundamental difference between the position occupied by the revolutionary bourgeoisie in semifeudal society and the position occupied by the revolutionary proletariat in capitalist society. The former is an owning class by its very nature, regardless of whether it is in power or not; the latter remains a dispossessed, exploited, and oppressed class until its own seizure of power. From this there follows a no less fundamental difference between the mechanisms of preparation for the unleashing of the bourgeois revolution and those of the proletarian revolution. The bourgeois revolution is prepared by those who are already the real masters of the economy, while the proletarian revolution must be prepared by those who remain economically dependent and exploited, at least until the bourgeoisie is expropriated.

Because of this, it is thoroughly unrealistic to expect the proletariat, before its seizure of power, to conquer the sort of 'hegemony' within capitalist society that the bourgeoisie conquered within semi-feudal society, as Gramsci incontestably believed.[8] For example, the bourgeoisie is able to lay hold of nearly all the means of communication before it commands political power, simply because of the weight of its capital. It is absurd to expect the proletariat to be able to conquer ideological hegemony over the press (let alone radio and television) before it has expropriated capital and conquered political power. The absolute monarchy was unable seriously to hinder the domination of bourgeois science and ideology in the educa-

---

[8] 'A social group can be, and even must be, the leading group before it conquers government power (this is one of the principal conditions for the conquest of power).' (A. Gramsci: *Quaderni del Carcere*, edited by V. Gerratana, Turin, 1975, p. 2010.)

tional system, particularly because of the very fact of their deep involvement in the rapid development of the natural sciences, technology, manufacturing, and big industry. To believe that an educational system in a bourgeois state can be dominated by Marxism is to credit fairy tales.

For the proletariat, the specific articulation of the mechanisms of economic, political, ideological, and cultural domination within capitalist society is such that its weight in this society cannot go beyond a certain threshold unless the two foundations of the class power of the bourgeoisie are directly attacked: private property in the means of production and exchange and the bourgeois state apparatus.

It must also always be remembered that the 'primitive accumulation' of forces and positions of the workers' movement within bourgeois society can produce its own negation. For it can transform the great workers' organizations, increasingly bureaucratized, from forces *contesting* this society into forces *integrated* into this society, precisely to the extent that this 'primitive accumulation' is not wholly aimed at theoretical and practical preparations for a global confrontation with the class enemy. This is what first occurred in the case of the Social Democracy on the eve of and just after the First World War. It is now occurring a second time with the mass Communist parties, since the Seventh Congress of the Comintern and especially since the evolution towards Eurocommunism.

This is a result not of a 'conspiracy' by traitorous leaders (although individual corruption may play a not altogether negligible role in this process), but of the very logic of bourgeois society. In this society, a little money is merely a means of exchange, an instrument with which to acquire the means of subsistence and consumption. A lot of money, on the other hand, inevitably becomes capital, which participates in one way or another in the distribution of social surplus-value. Now, the great workers' organizations necessarily possess a lot of money. The pressures, temptations, and attractions involved are immense. They become irresistible unless they are countered by constant education, theoretical and political training, insertion into a practice of mass anti-capitalist mobilization, and preparation of a revolutionary political project.

Large parliamentary caucuses and multitudes of mayors administering city councils composed of workers' parties have a direct interest in 'healthy public finances', that is, in the solvency of the bourgeois state, without which they threaten to be turned out of office or even to be deprived of their livelihoods. Powerful trade unions are led to invest the increasingly ample funds at their disposal, including their strike funds. (In the classical German workers' movement this was called 'the construction malady': *die Baukrankheit*.) Workers' cooperatives cannot survive without repeated recourse to bank credit. Workers' universities are condemned to demand more and more subsidies from the public authorities, to the very extent that they expand their facilities.

Now, under the capitalist system, 'healthy' public finances, real estate investments (not to mention stock investments), bank credit, and public subsidies, even those accorded by city councils administered by workers' parties or so-called left governments, forge increasingly inextricable links with capital, which controls the economy *as a whole*, until it is expropriated. Conservatism, followed by increasingly counter-revolutionary inclinations within the bureaucratic apparatuses, are the product of this implacable dialectic of 'partial conquests',[9] that is, the accumulation of forces of the workers' movement within bourgeois society. In the last analysis, theoretical revision of Marxism and political reformism are merely the ideological and strategic corollary of this dialectic, even though they in turn reinforce the 'integrationist' implications of the process.

The 'primitive accumulation of forces' of the workers' movement within bourgeois society can be effected with lessened risks of mounting integration only if these partial conquests are always conceived and presented as provisional rather than decisive gains, only if the proletariat is constantly educated in a spirit of intransigent opposition and hostility to and general dissent from bourgeois society as a whole, only if the daily practice of the workers' movement consolidates this education, above all by relying primarily on the extra-parliamentary struggle and mobilization of the masses.

But increasingly dissident daily *activity* by the broad masses

[9] See Ernest Mandel: *On Bureaucracy*, London 1974.

– indispensable for keeping anti-capitalist consciousness alive, since this consciousness cannot be nurtured solely by speeches, newspaper articles, or training schools (as important as these may be) – obviously accentuates the trend towards a frontal collision between the classes.[10]

The 'struggle for hegemony' thus leads either to reformist yielding, increasing integration of the bureaucratic apparatuses of the workers' movement into the bourgeois state, growing identification with it, and even commitment to this state at the moment of a revolutionary crisis, or to an accentuated orientation towards the extra-parliamentary mobilization and struggle of the masses, that is, towards the conscious and systematic preparation of this same revolutionary crisis. In neither case will the revolutionary crisis be averted. The former, however, objectively points to the defeat of the workers, the latter to the victory of the proletariat. The choice is between Ebert-Noske and Rosa Luxemburg, to take the German workers' movement as the model.[11] The Eurocommunist disciples of Kautsky, by contrast, will never realize their projects of 'hegemony'.

It is true that Gramsci himself, under the direct influence of the First World War and the polemic between Kautsky and Rosa Luxemburg, adopted the counterposition between mobile strategy (of manoeuvre) and trench strategy.[12] But although he considered 'trench strategy' inevitable in certain periods, it was not on the basis of the already acquired strength of the workers' movement – in the manner of Kautsky and Berlinguer – but on the contrary on the basis of a still unfavourable relationship of forces, because the question of the conquest of power

[10] Kautsky and Gramsci had a presentiment of this. But in the ardour of their excessive and unjustified polemic against Rosa Luxemburg, they constantly lost sight of this aspect of the problem.

[11] The great merit of Rosa Luxemburg is that she was the first to understand and explain that a working class must have had *systematic experience* in extra-parliamentary mass struggle in order to be capable of undertaking the struggle for power in a revolutionary manner. The conception that masses whose experience has been limited to electoral activity and wage struggles will 'rise up like one man' and fight by revolutionary methods 'the moment the enemy seeks to deprive us of universal suffrage (or freedom of association, or the right to strike)' is another illusion shared by the Eurocommunists of today and the left Social Democrats of yesteryear.

[12] Op. cit. pp. 65–68.

*was not yet posed.* The difference between Gramsci's position and that of the Eurocommunists is immediately visible. It is confirmed, moreover, by the formula used by Gramsci to define 'hegemony': The state is dictatorship plus hegemony.[13]

On the purely military plane, the experience of the Second World War disproved Gramsci's generalizations concerning the relation between these strategies and the very structure of bourgeois society. On the political plane, the idea that the class struggle of millions of wage-earners can be fought as 'trench warfare' for a long period is even less realistic than the idea of an 'attrition strategy'. It assumes that in the midst of a capitalist crisis, an extremely high level of discipline, spirit of sacrifice, and class consciousness can be maintained for a long period *even though* all these efforts fail to produce a rise in the living standards of the masses, which may, on the contrary, even decline seriously. This illusion completely ignores the conditions of the formation and elevation of class consciousness, reducing it to a purely politico-ideological norm.

We are not at all advocates of 'economism'. But to believe that *under the capitalist system* the proletarian army can suffer stinging and repeated setbacks in its living standards in the name of a strategy devised by the commanders, without suffering demoralizing effects, is to turn one's back on all the lessons of mass psychology and on all the lessons of class struggle under the bourgeois system.

In Gramsci's – and Kautsky's! – defence, it must be noted that they were to some extent conscious of this contradiction, as they were aware of the *inevitability* of spontaneous mass explosions under certain conditions.[14] They were also conscious of the fact that an inability of the 'commanders' to channel this spontaneity towards 'positive' aims – namely the seizure of power by the proletariat – would inevitably lead to a swing of the pendulum back towards reaction, even, at times, in its most extreme and violent form. History has only confirmed this presentiment. In this sense as well, the Eurocommunist leaders

---

[13] See Gramsci: *Selections From the Prison Notebooks*, Lawrence & Wishart, London, 1971, p. 239. See also this note of wisdom in the Prison Notebooks: 'One cannot choose the form of war one wants, unless one already commands overwhelming superiority over the enemy' (p. 66).

[14] Gramsci, op. cit. p. 199. See also the quotation from Kautsky in footnote 4.

remain well below the level of Kautsky, not to mention Gramsci.

## The Problem of Alliances

The question of the alliance between the proletariat and the petty-bourgeoisie – some would even blithely add, the petty and *middle* bourgeoisie – plays a predominant role in the justification of Eurocommunist strategy.[15] Without this alliance, any possibility of eliminating the rule of capital is considered utopian. Referring to the example of Chile, the leaders of the Italian Communist Party melodramatically affirm: The question is whether one can govern (better) with 37%, 50%, or 65% of the vote![16]

Let us leave aside the question of who will actually govern within this 'historic compromise', with its 65% of the vote. The experience of the Popular Front governments and the de Gaulle–Thorez and de Gasperi–Togliatti coalition governments have decidedly not taught our learned strategists anything. After imposing a wage freeze and proclaiming that 'the strike is the weapon of the trusts', after calling upon the workers 'to produce first' so as 'to reconstruct the national economy', which was an economy (even then!) of 'anti-fascist democratic order', Thorez and Togliatti found themselves ousted from these coalition governments overnight, once they had served their useful purpose in the eyes of the bourgeoisie. The system they had helped restore proved to be precisely that of the trusts, and not that of a mythical 'anti-fascist democratic order'. Nor will we linger on the fact that rhetorical references to a semi-colonial country – an incomplete and partially false reference anyway[17] – in the analysis of the relationship of socio-political forces in the highly industrialized capitalist countries are surprising coming from a current which insists so strongly on the 'national specificity' of political situations.

[15] See, in particular, G. Amendola: 'Above all, there are broad petty-bourgeois layers, whose existence cannot be ignored, because *their behaviour depends on the outcome of the political struggle between the right and the left*' (*PCI: Aux Sources de l'Eurocommunisme*, p. 92, emphasis added).

[16] Enrico Berlinguer: 'Reflections on Italy After the Events in Chile', articles published in *Rinascità*, 28 September and 5 and 9 October 1973.

[17] In fact, Unidad Popular won an absolute majority of the vote in the municipal elections of 1972.

The entire attempt of the theoreticians of Eurocommunism to reduce the weight of the Western proletariat to that of a minority within society is founded on a simple revision of the definition of the proletariat as the class of wage labourers to be found in Marx and in all the classics of Marxism.[18]

If we keep to this definition, the proletariat appears as the totality of all those *compelled* to sell their labour-power in a continuous manner because they have neither access to the means of production nor access to the means of subsistence (which implies that they do not command sufficient reserves of money – of means of exchange – to gain access to the means of subsistence without selling their labour-power). Thus, the proletariat cannot be reduced to 'productive workers' or 'manual workers' and still less to 'workers in big industry'.

As admirably formulated by Lenin, the industrial workers constitute the vanguard of the proletariat but not at all the entirety of its forces. The proletariat also includes the agricultural wage-earners, salaried employees (including commercial and bank employees), all smaller functionaries whose mediocre salaries prevent them from constituting capital and who thus have no protection against a decision by the administration to remove them, and in general all white-collar employees with the exception of the highest ranks,[19] as well as technicians and all the 'new layers' of wage-earners.

This is not a purely theoretical definition on which discussion can proceed without reference to the reality of the class struggle. In all the imperialist countries, *the progressive pro-*

[18] In the draft programmes of the Russian Social Democratic Labour Party, written by Plekhanov and Lenin and scrupulously revised by Lenin himself, we read the following formulas: 'proletarians who possess only their labour-power and can subsist only by selling it' (first draft, by Plekhanov); 'in ever greater numbers, the labourers are compelled to sell their labour-power, to become wage workers' (second draft, by Lenin); 'persons possessing no means of production (the proletarians)' (draft of the commission; the commission had added 'and of circulation' after the words 'of production', which Lenin proposed to delete). Lenin formulated no objection whatever to any of these three formulas, which he manifestly considered correct and adequate. (Lenin: *Works*, Vol.   , pp.   –   .)

[19] The highest ranks are not *compelled* to sell their labour-power once their remuneration is high enough to enable them to accumulate enough capital to be able to live on the interest. Moreover, in general even if they continue to receive a salary, such personnel usually own capital and thus have an interest in the protection of private property in the means of production.

letarianization of the 'new middle classes', provided they are wage-earners, is manifested in practice by their growing unionization, the rising integration of their unions into the great trade-union federations in which the unions of the industrial workers are predominant, the growing adoption by these unions of classical trade-union practices (mobilizations for demands, strikes, strike pickets, strikes with occupations, etc.), the progressive adoption of clearly anti-capitalist programmes demanding the collective appropriation of the means of production (that is, opposition to private property), and even their evolution towards the most radical wing of the union movement in their respective countries.

But once one heeds the evidence and maintains the classical Marxist definition of the proletariat, the whole Eurocommunist argument about the 'decisive' and 'vital' character of 'class alliances' in West Europe collapses. For far from being a minority, the proletariat as we have defined it is a social class that represents 70–90% of the active population of the Western imperialist countries. In this case, the problem of alliances – which obviously remains important, especially the alliance with the small, toiling peasantry in countries like Spain, Italy, Portugal, France, and with the modest layers of the urban petty-bourgeoisie in other countries – becomes secondary compared to the really burning problem of the unity in action of the wage-earners themselves. In reality, this is the key problem for a genuine, neither imaginary nor demagogic, strategy for the socialist revolution in the industrialized countries.

We may be answered: this is only a semantic quarrel. If you include the 'proletarianized new middle classes' in the working class, you simply shift the problem of alliances from outside to inside the proletariat itself. But since this extension of the concept of the proletariat manifestly implies a much greater diversity of particular interests, political sensibilities, and levels of consciousness than that which was previously manifested within the industrial working-class properly so called, a problem of alliances is still clearly posed.

Let us leave aside the assumption that the proletariat was allegedly more homogeneous in the past than it is today. There is no empirical evidence to support it. On the contrary, many facts indicate that the range of remuneration, level of organization, and level of consciousness within the total mass of wage-earners have tended to narrow rather than widen over time. But this is not the real problem. What the advocates of Eurocommunism must demonstrate is that some sector of this mass has a genuine interest in the maintenance of private property in the means of production.[20] There has been no such demonstration. Moreover, any attempt at it would be contradicted by the already mentioned fact that more and more unions of public employees, office workers (including bank employees), and technicians in West Europe have unambiguously pronounced themselves in favour of the collective appropriation of the means of production.

The sleight of hand continues when the advocates of the Eurocommunist strategy identify a policy of alliance with middle strata with a policy of alliance with bourgeois parties that systematically stifle and trample on the interests of these strata. The practical consequences of such an alliance can only be counter-productive. The bourgeois parties in the service of big capital generally impose an economic policy that is ruinous for middle strata, who are then typically driven to the right or the far right. The political significance of this unnatural alliance is even more pernicious. Instead of seeking to win the toiling middle strata to the political project of the proletariat – that is, fighting for the political hegemony of the proletariat over all the toiling layers of the nation – the Popular Front type policy consolidates the political hegemony of the bourgeoisie over the middle strata, simultaneously sowing divisions among the working class.

To identify the success of a 'policy of alliances' with respect for private property and the bourgeois order inevitably implies rejection of the unity in action of the workers. It is unthinkable that the entire class will accept systematic subordination of its class and group interests, both immediate and historic, to those of the bourgeoisie, represented in the 'left blocs' by one or another of its political fractions. (In the case of the Italian

---

[20] Giorgio Amendola, resolutely taking the field against the demagogy of Berlinguer, boldly affirms: 'The major obstacle in Italy is not only these external conditions; it is that the majority of the Italian people are not convinced that the transition to socialism is necessary' (*PCI: Aux Sources de l'Eurocommunisme*, p. 202). Obviously, he offers no evidence to support this assertion.

historic compromise this contradiction assumes grotesque forms; there the Eurocommunists propose an alliance, under the pretext of an 'anti-monopoly alliance', with Christian Democracy, which is the major party of the bourgeoisie and precisely the party of the great monopolies.) The policy of 'alliances' thus implies an inevitable break between the most conscious and combative wing of the proletariat, progressively won to the theory and practice of autonomy and class independence, and the most retrograde wing, still wholly under the sway of reformist strategy.

The situation is no better if we approach the problem from the angle of the famous 'consensus', the other magical concept of the Eurocommunists, besides that of 'hegemony'. In a society divided into antagonistic classes, and *a fortiori* in a phase of class contradictions exacerbated by the entire economic and political context, no 'consensus' between the bourgeoisie and proletariat is possible. There is not, and there cannot be, any 'consensus' for the transition to socialism on the part of the bourgeoisie, no more than there is or can be any 'consensus' among the proletariat for the defence of capitalist profit, the austerity policy, and the maintenance of permanent structural unemployment, that is, for the defence of the system of private property. The Eurocommunists are deluding themselves and deceiving the working class if they hope to gain the 'consensus' of the bourgeoisie for a socialist project, provided democratic rights are guaranteed. They will have an unpleasant surprise if they believe they can gain the 'consensus' of the proletariat for the defence of profit under the pretext of defending the 'national economy' and the 'democratic order'.

Thus, the vain search for 'consensus' between the antagonistic social classes is transformed in reality into an enterprise intended to maintain the social *status quo* (under the pretext that one cannot resort to minority violence, that old battle cry of classical Social Democracy). In practice this becomes ideological, and increasingly even physical, repression against that section of the working class which refuses to sacrifice its class interests on the altar of the 'democratic order'.[21] The conse-

---

[21] Lucio Magri, a leader of the Manifesto group who has nevertheless moved quite close to the Communist Party, lucidly acknowledges: 'The spontaneous workers' response to the Andreotti plan in October 1976, in spite of the passivity

quence is scarcely any 'consensus', and still less any 'détente' in social relations. The only result is a change of allies. Instead of an alliance of the entire working class, there occurs an alliance with the bourgeoisie against the most combative section of the working class. Ebert-Noske did this in 1918–19. The results are well known.

The only rational kernel in the entire rigmarole about the 'policy of alliances' and 'consensus' is that the impressive numerical growth of the proletariat, of the mass of wage-earners, and the growing inclusion within it of layers of increasingly diverse social and political origin is indeed inevitably accompanied by a political differentiation of the organized workers' movement before, during, and after the victory of the socialist revolution. Without a minimum of 'consensus' *within the mass of wage-earners*, no socialist project can be realized in the West today.[22] Such a project demands real unity in action and a united front of the workers' movement, and a zealous defence of socialist democracy both within workers' organizations today and the future workers' state tomorrow. In this sense, the defence of the principle of a plurality of political parties and of the genuine extension of democratic rights under the dictatorship of the proletariat must be an integral part of any realistic and effective strategy for socialist revolution in the highly industrialized countries.

But the defence of these pluralist principles must be based *on a foundation of class politics*. It must be integrated into a project of social revolution. It must assimilate all the lessons of the socialist revolutions of the past and of their subsequent ups and downs. It must be based on the profound anti-bureaucratic sentiment that – fortunately – is now rooted among the western working class. It is incompatible with a strategy of class collaboration which, under the pretext of a 'policy of alliances'

---

and even hostility of the PCI, and the political maturity of this resistance, show that it will not be possible to obtain capitalist stabilization without an overtly repressive policy' (*PCI: Aux Sources de l'Eurocommunisme*, p. 202).

[22] During the revolutionary process in Portugal in 1975 the bank employees, in spite of the hegemony of the Socialist Party among them, were perfectly capable of being drawn into the dynamic of self-organization, direct anti-capitalist action, and coordination of this action with that of the industrial working class proper.

and a 'search for consensus', fragments and stifles a growing portion of workers' struggles and therefore leans strongly towards the suppression of political pluralism (right of tendency) in the workers' movement and above all in the great trade unions.

It is not by accident that revolutionary Marxists have recently been the most systematic, consistent, and impassioned defenders of the unity in action of the workers, both during the course of the Portuguese revolution and during the upsurge of mass struggles in Spain and elsewhere. The modification of the relationship of class forces which results from genuine workers' unity in action precisely lends maximum credibility to the revolutionary project as opposed to the reformist project of the 'gradual transformation' of society. For without a resolute policy of unity, there is no way to convince little by little the majority of toilers still under reformist influence that the revolutionary project is both possible and preferable.

To augment the cohesion, consciousness, and anti-capitalist dynamism of the proletariat, the great majority of the nation – such is the major objective of any communist strategy worthy of the name in the industrialized capitalist societies. To sacrifice it in the name of an alliance with the bourgeoisie under the pretext of an alliance with middle strata is suicidal.

## The International Context

We have saved for last the major argument the Eurocommunists hold in reserve to justify their neo-reformist strategy: the international context. The Cold War, they claim, made any overthrow of capitalism in West Europe impossible without risking the immediate unleashing of nuclear war by American imperialism. The situation has improved with the 'détente', but not to the point of rendering possible any change at all. At a pinch, a gradual change in the socio-economic situation could be accepted by imperialism without risk of catastrophe, but a socialist revolution proper still implies a terribly increased threat of war. Under these conditions, the Eurocommunist strategy is the only realistic strategy for socialism in West Europe, for it takes account of the weight of the two 'superpowers' on the chessboard of world politics and of the international context as a whole, without risking adventures of a criminal irresponsibility.[23] The argumentation here actually unfolds on two planes which are often arbitrarily mixed, and even confounded.[24] Sometimes the 'international context' refers essentially to the economic context, that is, the impossibility of France, Italy, Spain, or even West Europe achieving 'economic autarky', or seceding from the world market, without risking a catastrophic deterioration of the living standard of the masses. Sometimes the 'international context' is, more crudely, the presence of NATO forces on the European continent and the risks of a direct U.S. military intervention.

Let us take the economic argument first. It is singularly superficial and characterized by a lack of any rigour in reasoning. One may suppose – correctly – that imperialism will react strongly to any loss of its economic power in a European country, especially if it is an important country. In that case, however, the reaction would occur whether the transformation is 'gradual' or 'sudden'. The reaction would be against the transformation itself, and not against its forms or the pace at which it occurs. Who can seriously argue that a person in relatively good health would passively accept the amputation of his left arm simply because he is assured that an anaesthetic will be used?

Historical experience, moreover, confirms that international capital's economic reactions to previous attempts at 'gradual transformation' have been violent (the Chile of the Unidad Popular and France under the 1936 Popular Front being two striking examples). In such cases, 'gradualism' does not prevent, or even retard, the reaction of the enemy, but merely allows him time to prepare his riposte and revenge in full tranquillity. This is an advantage for capital, and not at all for the proletariat.

Does the economic reaction of international capital condemn

---

[23] Santiago Carrillo: '*Eurocomunismo*' y *Estado*, pp. 83, 138–9; Amendola, op. cit. p. 74. Fabre, Hincker, and Sève (op. cit. p. 200), on the contrary, write: 'In the world today and particularly in the specific case of France, an *overt foreign* intervention – military, political, or even economic – is increasingly perilous for imperialism'.

[24] For example, Santiago Carrillo, op. cit. pp. 134–38.

a socialist revolution in West Europe to certain failure or to a rending choice between a demoralizing and thankless withdrawal to autarky or capitulation? This has not at all been demonstrated. West Europe is not Cuba or Cambodia. It has a formidable industrial, economic, and technological potential, with the most advanced working class and technical intelligentsia in the world. It is also, from the capitalist standpoint, the second-largest market in the world, after the United States. For West German capital, to cite just one example, any 'blockade' of a socialist zone composed of France, Italy, Spain, and Portugal would mean a loss of 25% of its exports. Where, in today's world, could German capital compensate for such a loss overnight? Does anyone seriously believe that it would automatically and immediately engage in such a suicidal operation?

The assumption that the victorious socialist revolution in one or several countries of West Europe would be condemned from birth to isolation and therefore to suffocation by international capital cannot be demonstrated. The world today is no longer that of 1919. The imperialist bourgeoisie is now not the only force commanding decisive economic weapons. There are the bureaucratized workers' states. There are the nationalist bourgeoisies and petty bourgeoisies in power in the semicolonial countries, always on the watch for an opportunity to increase their share of the pie. There is the working class and the workers' movement in the other capitalist countries, beginning with the other nations of West Europe, where the Common Market has necessarily already determined a certain internationalization of class struggle, albeit at a very insufficient pace given the much more rapid internationalization of capital.

Even after the October Revolution, the imperialist bourgeoisie was unable to continue a policy of overt (but limited) military intervention beyond a short lapse of time, two or three years. It was compelled to acknowledge the revolutionary *fait accompli*. International solidarity played an important role in this.[25] How is it possible not to see that the international

---

[25] On this subject, see in particular *La Révolution d'Octobre et le Mouvement Ouvrier Européen*, a collection presented by Victor Fay, EDI, Paris, 1967. Unfortunately, this collection lacks a report on the solidarity movements in Britain, which were especially important from the strategic standpoint.

relationship of forces is much more favourable today than it was at the end of the First World War? There is no reason to suppose that international solidarity with a genuine socialist revolution could not paralyze imperialism politically.

The workers' movement of South-West Europe must certainly prepare itself for Brest–Litovsk style economic and financial negotiations. This time, our major trump card could probably be television, which Lenin and Trotsky lacked in 1918. The most profitable investment – the first, in fact – that should be made by a workers' government in France, Spain, Italy, and Portugal is the installation of the world's most powerful television broadcasting system, with all the relay stations needed to reach, every night, into German, British, Dutch, Swedish, Austrian, and Danish homes. It should constantly hammer away at the millions of trade-unionists of these countries, asking these questions: will you let us go hungry because we are in the process of applying *your* programme, the programme of *your* organizations? Do you agree to risk your jobs and living standards for the greater glory of private property? Do you agree that we should be denied the right democratically to choose the road to a self-managed and free socialist society? Or would you prefer us to pool our resources to build together a world without unemployment and hunger, a world in which the workers will finally be masters of their own fate, in liberty?

But such a policy must be prepared immediately, by forging links among the workers of the subsidiaries of the multi-nationals, by stepping up the meetings of trade-union delegates of particular industrial branches in various countries, by consolidating the initial agreements for trade-union unity in action on a European and international scale. In the preparation of this future, the only realistic prospect to assure the survival of the socialist revolution in West Europe, any policy of 'produce French', encouragement of protectionism, and lethargy in the defence of immigrant workers, is suicidal in the strictest sense.

There is no reason to suppose that a victorious socialist revolution under these conditions will not command a broad field of manoeuvre that would be able to avert any short- or medium-term strangulation, provided its leadership evinces the political audacity, resolution, and capacity to take the offensive into the enemy camp, to make the question of the possible sabotage and blockade of a genuine socialist experiment, clearly supported by the majority of the nation and the workers, the major subject of discussion and political struggle within the other countries of Europe. *For the Socialist United States of Europe! For a socialist development plan for Europe and the Third World!* Those are the secret weapons any victorious socialist revolution in West Europe would command. They would not be simply formidable weapons of political propaganda and agitation. They could also be highly effective economic weapons.

In this regard we may cite the diagnosis of one of the most moderate French Social Democrats, which furnishes a convincing response to the economic panic the Eurocommunists are trying to sow in regard to the possibility of a socialist revolution: 'The France of the united left will have to loosen these constraints. Its economic weight, capacity for innovation in basic and applied research, its developed agriculture, and its place in the European market equip it with strong assets for negotiation with its partners. Whereas the present government places the desires of international capitalism above all else, a different industrial policy could increase our autonomy of decision-making and therefore our freedom to determine our own behaviour and our own weight in international affairs. Thus, we must audaciously conceive of an offensive strategy counterposed to the temptation of withdrawal. The offensive cannot and must not be limited to international economic relations, but must extend to ideological combat. . . . Such an offensive policy tallies with the permanent aspiration for socialism. If internationalism has known disappointments in the past, the idea behind it remains applicable today. The solidarity of the workers beyond borders flows from a general spirit, but also from necessity. Otherwise, how can the challenge of the multinationals be met? How can we envisage resolving the problems posed by the international division of labour?' (Jean-Pierre Cot in *Le Monde Diplomatique*, September 1977). If this is true for the 'France of the Vision of the Left' wouldn't it be a thousand times more true for the France of the victorious socialist revolution?

There remains the military aspect of the question. Here again the good faith, if not the coherence, of the Eurocommunist argumentation may be doubted. Imperialism, the Eurocommunists say, will not tolerate a 'sudden change in the relationship of forces'. Is it not rather the case that imperialism will react to *any* change in the relationship of forces, whether sudden or 'gradual'? Where has it ever been demonstrated that the victory of the socialist revolution in France would represent a harsher blow to imperialism than a parity in multiple nuclear warheads attained by the Soviet army or a decisive progress in electronics in the USSR? But we have never heard our severe critics, who reproach us for 'irresponsible adventurism', propose a halt to Soviet rearmament or to the qualitative development of the technology of Soviet industry.

The problem is thus reduced to its proper proportions. Political and military reactions by imperialism are inevitable in face of any advance of the revolution anywhere in the world, and certainly in Europe – just as these reactions are inevitable in face of any serious increase in the strength of the USSR or the 'socialist camp'. That is incontestable. But it remains to be seen *what forms* these reactions will take, whether the most probable reaction is to unleash a massive military intervention (500,000 troops and 5,000 planes, as in Vietnam) or even to unleash a nuclear war.

Now, this does not depend solely on the desires and military strength of imperialism. It also depends on the relationship of forces on a world scale and on the domestic political and social conditions in the United States. Few observers would deny that because of the situation created by the political defeat inflicted on imperialism by the Vietnamese revolution, the short- or medium-term repetition of a Vietnam-style adventure in West Europe or Africa is *politically impossible* for the United States. It would threaten to create such grave socio-political tension in the United States itself that the risks for the survival of imperialism would be even greater. The same remark would apply still more to the unleashing of a nuclear war against a victorious socialist revolution in Europe.

Granted, this situation is only temporary. It can change if there is a change in the socio-political climate in the United States. Such a modification could occur. It could even be systematically prepared once the spectre of communism re-emerges in West Europe. But it would take time to complete such an enterprise of remobilization of the American 'silent majority'. Who is to say that the 'silent majority' would remain silent at the folly of such an undertaking? Who is to say that socialism with a human face in Western Europe would not provoke a formidable development of consciousness among the American proletariat itself?

Time is of the essence and it must be used. That is not the least of the arguments for a revolutionary strategy in Western Europe: it enjoys an international context that is temporarily extremely favourable. For the first time since 1917, there is a chance of escaping an immediate military intervention on the part of its international enemies.

# Index